Biblical Spirituality

Also by David L. Larsen

The Anatomy of Preaching
Identifying the Issues in Preaching Today

The Company of the Creative
*A Christian Reader's Guide to Great Literature
and Its Themes*

The Company of the Preachers
*A History of Biblical Preaching from
the Old Testament to the Modern Era*

Telling the Old, Old Story
The Art of Narrative Preaching

Biblical Spirituality

Discovering the Real Connection
Between the Bible and Life

DAVID L. LARSEN

kregel
PUBLICATIONS

Grand Rapids, MI 49501

Biblical Spirituality: Discovering the Real Connection Between the Bible and Life

Published by Kregel Publications, a division of Kregel, Inc., P.O. Box 2607, Grand Rapids, MI 49501. Kregel Publications provides trusted, biblical publications for Christian growth and service. For more information about Kregel Publications, visit our web site: www.kregel.com.

Cover design: John M. Lucas

Library of Congress Cataloging-in-Publication Data
Larsen, David L.
   Biblical spirituality: discovering the real connection between the Bible and life / David L. Larsen.
     p.   cm.
   Includes bibliographical references and index.
   1. Spirituality—Biblical teaching. 2. Bible—Theology.
I. Title.
BS680.S7 L37   2001   230—dc21   2001029020
                                          CIP

ISBN 0-8254-3099-2

Printed in the United States of America

1 2 3 4 5 / 05 04 03 02 01

Dedicated to the intercessors who have
prayed for us—
especially Marguerite, who has prayed for our
family every week since 1963.
"You help us by your prayers."
—2 Corinthians 1:11

CONTENTS

Introduction | 9

The New Life in God | 11

1. The Bible: Conduit of Truth | 13

2. The Holy Trinity: Absolute Perfection | 25

3. The Metaphysical Attributes of God: Ultimate Being | 38

4. The Moral Attributes of God: Absolute Goodness | 51

5. The Human Family: Made in His Image—but Marred | 65

6. Jesus the God-Man: The Only Savior | 81

7. The Healing Cross: Our Bleeding God | 98

8. The Vacant Tomb: The Groundbreaking | 115

9. The Ascension: The Neglected Doctrine | 131

10. The Life-Giving Spirit: The Divine Barrister | 149

11. Justification by Faith Alone: The Final Acceptance | 166

12. Sanctification by Grace: Crisis and Growth | 184

13. Beloved Community: The Divine Commonwealth | 204

14. The Strategy of Providence: The Passionate Mover | 222

15. The Eschatological Wedge: The Presence of the Future | 241

Notes | 261

Scripture Index | 291

Subject Index | 297

INTRODUCTION

. . . the form of teaching to which you were entrusted.
—Romans 6:17

What you heard from me, keep as the pattern of sound teaching, with faith and love in Christ Jesus.
—2 Timothy 1:13

For the time will come when men will not put up with sound doctrine. Instead, to suit their own desires, they will gather around them a great number of teachers to say what their itching ears want to hear.
—2 Timothy 4:3

Our day and age is awash with spirituality. But what kinds? Many postmoderns long to "connect the dots" and yet oppose any idea that there is a "big picture" to reality. Others pursue the vague, New Age spirituality. The Dalai Lama offers spirituality without deity. Even some evangelicals have created a spirituality of discipline and rigor, yet one that lacks normative theology. Indeed, our times display a bias against normative theology or, for that matter, any theological construct.

A commentator on the syncretism of spirituality recently asked, "Does spirituality have any real meaning outside historical beliefs and institutions? Can one be spiritual without the meaning of that being shaped and filled by creed, doctrine, dogma? Can one be spiritual apart from the Holy Spirit?"[1]

Biblical Spirituality is based on the conviction that authentic spirituality is to be found only in Scripture, in that which "is in accord with sound doctrine" (Titus 2:1). Herein considered are fifteen basic doctrines, each explored in ways that apply sound theology to the quest for the authentic spiritual experience that is found in Christianity. Suggestions for further reading are in the notes at the end of the book, and practical stimulus for in-depth study is provided at the end of each chapter.

Practical and ethical principles for Christian behavior must be rooted in the Word of God, and are necessarily grounded in our experience of God—who God is, what he has done, and what he will do. We must begin with the person and the acts of God, manifested and performed in and through Jesus Christ by the Holy Spirit. We must then seek to understand that Person and those acts as interpreted by Scripture and analyzed in our doctrines. T. W. Manson said,

> Historic Christianity is first and foremost a Gospel, the proclamation to the world of Jesus Christ and Him crucified. For the primitive church, the central thing is the Cross on the Hill rather than the Sermon on the Mount, and the characteristic Church act is the Communion rather than the conference.[2]

For many years I have taught basic and advanced courses in Christian spirituality and spiritual formation at Trinity Evangelical Divinity School. I have also lectured and shared my development of these themes with ministers and laypersons in this country and abroad. I give thanks to God for my students, who have taught me so much, and for the wife of my youth, who for these many years has lived the truths of these themes before me and our family. *Ad gloriam dei.*

THE NEW LIFE IN GOD

God, who created us and all things, loves us. And although the Bible discloses both the love and goodness of God, it also demonstrates the severity of God. All are culpable before him and under his wrath because of our sin and rebellion. But Scripture offers us much more than God's holiness and wrath. The focus of both testaments of the Bible is God's solution for sin and his provision for deliverance, which he promised in the Old Testament and fulfilled in the New through the person and work of Jesus Christ.

Jesus Christ, Son of God, is the God-man. Having lived a life of perfect obedience; having died a sacrificial death for our sins; and having been raised victorious over sin, death, and the Devil, he has redeemed us from sin. In the very moment of repentance and faith, the sinner is forgiven of sin, adopted into God's family, and is indwelt by the Holy Spirit. In Christ, the powers and life of the age to come break into this evil age, thus transforming believers into the people of the future.

To combat sin in the believer, the Holy Spirit fosters a process of crisis and growth through prayer and the Word in the context of the community of faith. Communion with God and lives of ministry and service are possible through union with Christ and through the empowerment of the Holy Spirit, who guides both the inner and the outer journey.

Maturing in faith, imbued with love and hope, the believer faces life with confidence—a confidence founded upon the doctrines that empower the believer's faith in God. To our God be all of the glory!

1

THE BIBLE

Conduit of Truth

Before everything else I must set before you the truth as it is contained in the Scriptures, in its naked and clear simplicity, unspoiled by rouge or make-up, unadorned by curls and unobscured by the false glitter of borrowed colours.

—Episcopius, d. 1643

Thy word is very pure, therefore Thy servant loves it.
—Psalm 119:140 NASB

The Bible is the textbook for those who quest for God. It is the source from which we draw strength and the spring from which we drink. The product of forty different human writers who, over a span of fifteen hundred years, labored under the tutelage of the Holy Spirit, the canonical Scriptures are the revealed truth. "Your word is truth" (John 17:17b).

Although divine in source, Scripture is, nonetheless, conveyed in human language that can be translated into concrete meaning. And notwithstanding its antiquity, the message—"in, with and under the Holy Spirit"—has impact today for believers at all levels of spiritual maturity. Augustine observed, "Scripture is like a river in which elephants can swim and little children can wade. We can only stand in awe before the mystery of divine speech."

Although God's first and foremost Word is, of course, the incarnate and living Word, the Father teaches us through the written word. G. Campbell Morgan was right: "[Christians] have always been a Bible people." Yet in a time when theology is often reduced to human experience, and Christian spirituality "dumbs down" to "total experientialism," the critical issue remains biblical truth and authority. And Holy Scripture remains the authoritative conduit of truth for those who desire to live godly lives.

The Flow of Divine Communication

When you have read the Bible, you will know it is the Word of God, because you will have found it the key to your own heart, your own happiness, your own duty. I am sorry for the men who do not read the Bible every day. I wonder why they deprive themselves of the strength and of the pleasure.
—President Woodrow Wilson (1856–1924),
28th President of the United States

Some urge us to choose the personal over the propositional, relationship over revelation. But these choices are unnecessary and create false dichotomies. After all, we do not choose love in marriage over legality in marriage—we choose both. In fact, a marriage without legal sanction places love in jeopardy, because the long-term rights and interests of both parties would not be safeguarded.

Likewise in theology, relationship without revelation would be like a love affair with an unknown and unknowable God. We sing, "Beyond the sacred page, I seek thee, Lord." But apart from what the New Testament tells us of who he is, what he has done, and what he will do, how can we know that the Lord is in fact the Lord Jesus Christ? What do we know about Jesus that the New Testament does not tell us? Scripture as the Word of God not only sustains the inner life by which we live (Matt. 4:4), but it reveals propositionally the parameters of spiritual truth.

That our God reveals truth about himself through words is clear from the first page of Genesis. If the narratives in Scripture do not embody truthful propositions, then there is no basis for discussion. Although it is true that he and his words provide information that our intellects only faintly comprehend, his inspiration nonetheless addresses our rebellious wills (Ezek. 2:2) and quickens our spirits and bodies (Rom. 8:11). Joseph the patriarch, for instance, maintained a fruitful and righteous life even before the giving of canonical Scripture or the Ten Commandments, no doubt because of the transmission of oral tradition. Certainly something of the divine intention of monogamous marriage (Gen. 2:22–24) stands behind Joseph's chasteness in Egypt (Gen. 39:9). His grasp of God's nature—based on God's disclosure of his five names and bequeathed to Joseph through his ancestors—formed the wellspring that made possible his bearing of fruit (Gen. 49:22f.).

Joshua was later directed to the inscriptured word of God (Josh. 1:7–8). Thereby he is the prototype of the person who, through meditating on the divine law day and night, becomes like a tree "planted by streams of water" (Ps. 1:2–3; Jer. 17:8). Sincere piety and vital ministry are related to a life grounded in the Word of God. Job said that the words of God's mouth meant more to him "than my necessary food" (Job 23:12 KJV). He meant not bibliolatry but the appropriate treasuring of God's Word. Psalm 119 is an exquisite meditation on the wonders and glories of the Word of God. We are to seek it (119: 45) and choose it, amid many options (119: 30, 173). We are to long for it, love it, and delight in it (119: 40, 97, 113, 143). We are to hide it in our hearts and remember it (119:11, 52). The Word of God that was fire in Jeremiah's bones (Jer. 20:9) and the seed of Isaiah's proclamation (Isa. 55:10–11) becomes inexhaustible treasure for the child of God, wealth beyond any portfolio of stocks and securities. His "testimonies are wonderful!" (Ps. 119:129).

Thus God conveyed his truth in spoken and written words. Then in a climactic revelation of God, he who is called "faithful and true," whose name is the Word of God (Rev. 19:11, 13) comes into time and space as the living incarnation of divine communication (Heb. 1:1–3). Jesus knew the Word, trusted the Word, loved the Word, and used the Word. "That it might be fulfilled" was his watchword. "The Scripture cannot be broken" was the confidence of him for whom an argument hinged on one word of Scripture (John 10:35).

Standing in this succession of those who looked to the Word of God as true revelation are the disciples of our Lord (2 Tim. 3:16–17)—such church fathers as Augustine, who descried the notion of anything false in the Bible; the reformers, like Luther, who was "captive to the Word," and who, like Calvin and Zwingli, called the people of God back to the centrality and sufficiency of Scripture; and a great company of saints down to the present who relished *lectio divina* (the divine reading), which nourished and nurtured their inner lives.[1] John Knox strode into St. Giles' Cathedral in Edinburgh and moved the pulpit from the side to the center, symbolizing the Reformation conviction about the place of the Bible.

Neither has the Word of God been peripheral in our culture. Our history and our literature evince Scripture,[2] and even a cursory dip into the font of Western culture makes clear our debt to the Bible.[3] And notwithstanding the impact of the Bible through time, "God still speaks through what He has spoken."

THE FUNCTION OF SCRIPTURE IN SPIRITUAL FORMATION

> The Word of God is perfect: it is precious and pure: it is truth itself. There is no falsehood in it. . . .
>
> Christians receive Christ, the Son of God, as the central content of Holy Scripture. Having learned to know him, the remainder becomes meaningful to them and all scripture becomes transparent.
>
> —Martin Luther

Like the Savior of whom they speak, the Scriptures come to us in a humble and lowly form (cf. Is. 53:2ff.). Written in the vocabulary of ancient and obscure cultures, the Bible has been denigrated as nothing more than a collection of contradictions and fables. But just as our Lord's humble mantle could not conceal his wonder from those who trusted him, so the wonder of the Word never ceases to enthrall believers (1 Peter 2:6–7). In our Lord are "hidden all the treasures of wisdom and knowledge" (Col. 2:3) and so, too, Scripture is the repository of immeasurable wealth. But the Bible's value is not apparent to the unbelieving mind. "The Bible will no more speak to some minds than Christ would speak to Herod when delivered to him by Pilate."[4]

Down through the centuries, in both personal and corporate experience, the people of God have been renewed when they recovered or rediscovered the Word of God (2 Chron. 34:14ff.). As Casper Wistar Hodge said in his history of old Princeton Seminary,

> The majestic testimony of the Church in all time is that its advances in spiritual life have always been toward and not away from the Bible, and in proportion to the reverence for, and power of realizing in practical life, the revealed Word.[5]

Consider how Scripture functions in relation to the spiritual life.

1. The Word Is the Midwife at the New Birth.

The Holy Spirit (John 3:5) and the Word converge to bring alive that which is dead. "He chose to give us birth through the word of truth" (James 1:18). So we are enjoined, "Accept the word planted in you, which can save you" (v. 21b). The apostle Peter underscores the same truth in asserting that "you have been born again, not of perishable seed, but of imperishable, through the living and enduring word of God" (1 Peter 1:23). The role of Scripture in fostering faith makes the Bible irreplaceable as the agency of regeneration (Rom. 10:17).

Savonarola characterized his conversion by saying, "A word did it!" Later, John Wesley credits the Word for engendering rebirth when he clearly dissociated regeneration from baptism. He "would not allow that infants could be regenerated . . . regeneration for him must be a conscious experience."[6] The emphasis by Wesley and the Pietists on the conscious experience of conversion, however, may rely too heavily on totally subjective factors. Yet without evangelistic "revivalism" and personal experience with assurance the result is a dead orthodoxy and lifeless liturgies. The inception of spiritual life by the Spirit and the Word not only launches the Christian life but provides to our spirits the assurance of salvation *(certitudo salutis):* We are, indeed, the children of God (Rom. 8:16).

2. The Word Is Mother's Milk for Spiritual Growth.

"Like newborn babes, crave pure spiritual milk, so that by it you may grow up in your salvation, now that you have tasted that the Lord is good" (1 Peter 2:2–3). The Word is analogous to milk—nature's most perfect food—and is calculated to foster what Peter elsewhere terms "grow[ing] in grace and knowledge of our Lord and Savior, Jesus Christ" (2 Peter 3:18). We are what we eat, nutritionists tell us, and living in an X-rated culture affords a bewildering array of sensory options that can, at minimum, jade the believer's appetite for the Word.

The Scripture is "living and active. . . . Sharper than any double-edged sword" (Heb. 4:12). It announces pardon for the guilty, wealth for the impoverished, and is a love missive from the lover of our souls. The believer ingesting Scripture is always in the presence of its divine author. How can food such as this be dull and unappetizing?

In contrast to the pedantic educational ideals in the ancient Greek and

Roman world, the Jews' technique surrounded the learning experience for their sons with positive associations. In Barclay's description of the first day of school for the young Jewish boy, note the references to sweet food:

> The boy was wakened early, before dawn, and when it was still dark. He was bathed, and then dressed in a gown "with fringes." As soon as dawn came, he was taken to the Synagogue, by his father, or by a wise friend of the family, if his father was not available. He was put on the reading desk with the roll open in front of him at Exodus 20:2–26, the passage which tells of God's revelation of the Law to Moses. That passage was then read aloud as the passage for the day. He was then taken to the house of the teacher, who welcomed him by enfolding him in his arms. He was shown a slate, with the alphabet written on in it various combinations. These things the teacher read to the lad, and the lad repeated them after the teacher. The slate was then smeared with honey, and the lad was bidden to lick it off. Then he was given sweet cakes to eat, with passages from the Law in praise of the Law written on them. Finally there was a prayer to the angels to open the boy's heart and to strengthen his memory and school had begun for another Jewish boy.[7]

How concerned and careful we must be about the ambiance within which new believers experience their early feedings.

3. The Word Is Nutritious Food for the Journey to Spiritual Maturity.

The passing of time should see steady progress in the climb toward spiritual maturity, but some believers stall out, stymied and stunted. At those times teachers of the Word need to feed their students not milk but solid food (Heb. 5:12). Milk is a marvelous food, but it has first passed through the digestive system of someone else. Some believers continue to live on milk and are "not acquainted with the teaching about righteousness" (vv. 13–14). "Constant use" of spiritual teeth makes it possible to masticate the solid meat of the Word, the "deep things of God" (1 Cor. 2:10). Being skillful in the Word and dexterous in applying it are made possible through the ministry of the Holy Spirit (1 Cor. 2:9–16). "Comparing spiritual things with spiritual" (2:13b KJV) describes what laypersons as well as ministers and academics should aspire to.

Will Houghton pointed the way when he urged us to "lay hold on the Bible until the Bible lays hold on you." Are we reading the Word in this way? In *Books We Think We Have Read,* Roger Nicole asked, Is our attention with intention? The great missionary bishop Charles Brent lived a life of purposeful prayer, but in the context of his life in the Word. Speaking of the many complex demands made upon Bishop Brent, Robert Handy says of him, "To keep from being overwhelmed he developed an intense devotional life."[8] He intentionally carved out his time with God and so must we, whether we use the One-Year Bible, or McCheyne's *Calendar for Daily Readings,* or some other discipline.[9] We cannot achieve or maintain spiritual growth without well-planned, nourishing meals of the Word. J. A. Bengel, the venerable exegete and divine, counseled,

> Eat simply the bread of the Scriptures as it presents itself to thee; and so do not distress thyself at finding here and there a small particle of sand which the millstone may have left in it. Thou mayest, then, dismiss all those doubts which at one time so horribly tormented myself. If the Holy Scriptures—which have been so often copied and which have passed so often through the faulty hand of ever fallible men—were absolutely without variations, the miracle would be so great, that faith in them would no longer be faith. I am astonished, on the contrary, that the result of all those transcriptions has not been a much greater number of different readings.
>
> —J. A. Bengel to his student Reus, 1721[10]

4. The Word Is Medicine for Every Malaise.

Over the entrance to the monastery library in St. Gall in Switzerland are the words, "Enter here the Pharmacy of the Soul." The versatility and practical application of the Scriptures, as well as the prowess of the divine Apothecary, never cease to amaze us. Jesus said to his apostles, "You are already clean because of the word I have spoken to you" (John 15:3). The Word is not only able "to make us wise for salvation" (2 Tim. 3:15) but as the "God-breathed" book "it is useful for teaching, rebuking, correcting and training in righteousness, so that the man of God may be thoroughly equipped for every good work" (vv. 16–17). If we are to feed others, we must be fed. I have often said to my students who were preparing for Christian ministry, "If you take care of the depth of your ministry [and this through the Word], God will take care of the breadth."

No movement within the history of Christian spirituality has been as dedicated to the practical application of Scripture as has Puritanism. In the Puritan sermon, the final section—"uses"—built on the exegesis and doctrine of the passage. Application was made to every aspect of personal and societal life. For John Owen, then, "rightly dividing the word of truth" (2 Tim. 2:15) meant properly applying the exegesis and doctrine.[11] Deft and careful application of Scripture is not patronizing, as some "without authority" have argued, but it is not easy. More heresy has likely occurred in making application than at any other juncture of Christian communication.

But the supreme heresy is to not apply Scripture at all. As Zuck observes, "Neglecting to apply the Scriptures to [our] lives makes [our] study of God's Word incomplete and deficient."[12] But thank God there is a balm in Gilead. There is a physician for what ails us (Jeremiah 8:22). In the Word, we have both a mirror in which to scrutinize our malady and the solvent to apply to our defilement (John 17:17).[13]

ATTACKS ON BIBLICAL AUTHORITY

Whoever takes another meaning out of Scripture than the writer intended, goes astray, but not through any falsehood in Scripture. . .
    Now faith will totter if the authority of Scripture begin to shake. And then, if faith totter, love itself will grow cold. For if a man has fallen from faith, he must necessarily also fall from love; for he cannot love what he does not believe to exist.
                    —Augustine, *On Christian Doctrine*

I cannot pretend to be indifferent about the veracity of the records which profess to reveal him whom I believe to be not only the very Truth but the very Life.
                    —Bishop J. B. Lightfoot, scholar

Challenge to the integrity of scriptural authority was virtually nonexistent for 1500 years. No article affirming the truthfulness of the Bible is to be found in any of the early creeds (such as the Apostles', Nicene, or

Chalcedonian symbols), nor in the Reformation creeds, until the Westminster Confession of 1643. Then in 1546 the juxtaposition of Scripture and tradition by the Council of Trent resulted in a tragic demotion of Scripture. Subsequently, Renaissance Humanism and the Enlightenment advanced the supremacy of human reason over divine revelation and gave rise to the ravages of higher criticism. In effect Scripture has been lost from large quarters of Christendom and the western world, indeed a regrettable circumstance.

Leading the charge to empty Christianity of its intellectual content was the German philosopher Immanuel Kant (1724–1804), whose ghost hovered over religious liberalism's initial rejection of biblical authority and then its claim that truth was totally subjective.[14] Kant's anti-intellectual agnosticism spawned both Schleiermacher's romantic mysticism (which made Christianity the proclamation of one's own experience) and neo-orthodoxy's denigration of cognition, which is encapsulated in Brunner's assertion that "nothing is truly accomplished by regarding all that is said in the Bible as true," and Karl Barth's notion of the Word of God as true myth.

Carl F. H. Henry is correct: "The overriding issue in the twentieth century has been the crisis of authority."[15] One poll indicates that only 28 percent of Americans strongly believe in absolute truth. The outcome of modernity's infatuation with the higher criticism of the Bible is seen in the triumph of secularism and the dissolution of the very idea of truth. The modernist's approach to the Bible is one of doubt and denial *(dubito ergo sum)*, and the fallout often includes a failure by conservatives to sustain engagement with Scripture. What James Smart called *The Strange Silence of the Bible in the Church* (Philadelphia: Westminster, 1970), with respect to mainline denominations now applies to evangelicals. When some authors call for *Reclaiming the Bible for the Church* (Carl E. Braaten, Robert W. Jenson, eds. [Memphis: Fortress, 1998]), they are in fact speaking of a need that exists all across North American Christendom.

More recently, with the rise of postmodernism and deconstructionism in academic approach to faith and reason, there has occurred a widespread flight from hermeneutical realism, which further reinforces Kant's scepticism. It is now widely alleged in the new irrationalism that we have come to the end of text and fixed meaning altogether. In modernism there was argument over which interpretation of the truth was correct, but in postmodernism it is held that there is no such thing as truth. The author is dead and the text is dead; of significance is the reader only, who makes of the text what he or she chooses. The reader, in effect, becomes the writer and biblical text, then, has no authority whatsoever.[16]

In Western culture, a consequence of this battering of biblical authority is a massive increase in biblical illiteracy both outside and within the church. Some time ago, Sir Charles Marston lamented the "almost incredible disappearance of the Bible in Britain and America." More recently, Wolfhart Pannenberg agrees:

> In a secular milieu, even an elementary knowledge of Christianity— its history, teachings, sacred texts, and formative figures dwindles. It is no longer a matter of rejecting Christian teachings; large numbers of people have not the vaguest knowledge of what those teachings are. This is a remarkable development when one considers how foundational Christianity is to the entire story of Western culture. The more widespread the ignorance of Christianity, the greater the prejudice against Christianity.[17]

The wholesale abandonment of text-driven preaching in favor of market-driven or audience-centered preaching is but another symptom of the waning confidence in the Bible as truth. Theology is becoming an amalgam of psychology and sociology, Emersonian "selfism" thrives as the American religion, and practical solutions to the meaning of life are sought apart from theology.[18] As postmodernism in architecture is characterized by a lack of order and coherency, so too is the collapse of the logic of Christian discourse and the genesis of moral disorder, its disintegration and desensitization in our times.[19]

But the Enlightenment and postmodernism have overreached themselves. We must remember that "all men are like grass, and all their glory is like the flowers of the field; the grass withers and the flowers fall, *but the word of the Lord stands forever*" (1 Peter 1:24–25). Despite its reported demise, the Word of God is having a mighty effect in changing lives and the course of history in Central and South America, on the rim of the Pacific, in sub-Sahara Africa, in the former Soviet Union and other eastern bloc countries. The gospel of Christ is still God's power to save (Rom. 1:16–17).

Our posture as believers must still be daily reading of the Word and obedience to its precepts. At a university that emphasized science and technology, one ecumenical campus minister was quoted recently as being amazed "by the significant amount of biblical literalism" abounding on her campus. What she had dismissed as outdated "authoritarian and dogmatic" theology—which our parents, grandparents, and great-grandparents accepted as truth because "they knew no better"—had somehow survived in the face of it all. An astounded American professor of religion records in the very ecumenical publication *Christian Century* that in England—of all places!—and in Cambridge—can you believe it?—about a dozen "flourishing and charismatic churches" exist for which "the Bible has great authority" and the growing numbers of adherents of which wait upon "expository biblical preaching." Appeals to the young and to evangelism are taking place, with thousands of students worshiping, particularly at Eden Baptist, St. Andrew's Street Baptist, Round Church, and Holy Trinity (Anglican).[20]

Bishop Jewel (1522–1571) was right in saying, "Show me something in the Bible I don't teach and I will start teaching it; and something I do teach which is not in the Bible, and I will cease." The words of martyred Archbishop Oscar Romero are eloquent: "The Word remains. This is the great comfort of one who preaches. My voice will disappear, but my Word, which is Christ, will remain!" Hallelujah.

As always, life in God flourishes not in meanderings about the sacred text, but in *lectio divina,* bringing one's whole self into the text.[21] But of what value is strong argument for the authority of Scripture if we do not obey its teachings? And of what significance is an authoritative Scripture if we do not recognize and live within the sufficiency of Scripture?[22]

In her gripping tale, *Babette's Feast,* Isak Dinesen describes two dour sisters who are members of a rigid religious sect and who live on the windswept flatlands of Jutland in Denmark. Their spiritual life is constricted. Babette, who had been a chef in a fancy restaurant in Paris, takes refuge as a servant in their household and winces under their joylessness. When Babette wins the lottery in Paris, she prepares a sumptuous dinner for the sisters and their compatriots. It is delicious beyond description. No one at the feast says much and they eye each other with suspicion to see if anyone is enjoying it too much. Finally at dessert, they loosen up and even sing. Scripture is just such a sumptuous repast. Is it not time we bear witness to the richness and texture of our gourmet feast? "Taste and see that the Lord is good. . . ."

For Personal Blessing

Study Psalm 119, "the song of the Word." List various names given to the Word and the uses of the Word as suggested in the psalm. Meditate on such metaphors for the Word as light, fire, hammer, treasure, milk, meat, sword, honey, water for washing, etc. From your own experience or reading, note an example when the Word fulfilled the role of each.

2

THE HOLY TRINITY

Absolute Perfection

Every wise man must acknowledge *that* to be the true religion which ascribes the greatest perfection to the Supreme Being, and not only conveys the worthiest conception of all His attributes, but demonstrates the harmony and equality existing between them. Now their religion [i.e., Islam] was defective in acknowledging only two active principles in the Deity, His will and His wisdom, while it left His goodness and greatness inoperative, as though they were indolent qualities and not called forth into active exercise. But the Christian religion could not be charged with this defect. In its doctrine of the Trinity, it conveys the highest conception of the Deity as the Father, the Son and the Holy Spirit in one simple essence. In the Incarnation of the Son it evinces the harmony that exists between God's goodness and His greatness; and in the person of Christ displays the true union of the Creator and the creature; while in His Passion it sets forth the divine harmony of infinite goodness and condescension.

—Raymond Lull (1315), evangelist to Muslims

"In the beginning God . . ." (Gen. 1:1). From its first sentence, the Bible assumes and does not argue for the existence of God. Although the historic proofs for the existence of God have come under fire in the wake of Hume and Kant, taken cumulatively the evidence for God's existence is of value—for the believer more than the skeptic. The Bible asserts that "the fool says in his heart, 'There is no God'" (Ps. 14:1), and it advances evidence of God's existence from creation and design (Ps. 19:1ff.; Rom. 1:20ff.). And while these proofs testify as to the infinite power and wisdom of God, they reveal a fearsome God. As has been observed, "The God of nature does not extend loving arms."

The book of Genesis, however, reveals to us a God who speaks, sees, divides, calls, makes, sets, creates and blesses (1:1–25). It is clear, therefore, that God is personal.[1] This personal God is an obsession with human beings, and the ways in which we seek to know God is called religion. John Baillie said, "Neither history nor geography can show us any tribe or people which is devoid of all religious awareness." Yet, apart from biblical revelation, we would not know that this great God is knowable. Douglas Clyde MacIntosh was right: "To know God to be knowable makes more difference than to know [that] men and things are knowable." God is both transcendent and immanent, that is, both far away and near, both hidden and made known.

In his infinite being God is, of course, incomprehensible; we shall continue to learn about him throughout eternity. But that we can't know everything doesn't mean we can't know anything. The unique biblical affirmation about God that is disclosed to us in special revelation is his triune nature as Father, Son, and Holy Spirit. In his remarkable little book, *The Secret of the Universe,* Nathan Wood, longtime president of Gordon College of Theology and Missions in Boston (now Gordon-Conwell Theological Seminary), set forth his thesis that the whole universe is absolute oneness and absolute threeness. If Wood is correct, we are only confirmed in what Scripture makes clear: God is triune and every aspect of spirituality hinges on the Holy Trinity.[2]

In approaching a theme as awesome and infinite as the Holy Trinity, one feels like the little boy whose newborn brother had just come home from the hospital. His mother saw the boy creep up to the crib and heard him say, "Hey, little Danny, tell me about God before you forget."

THE HOLY TRINITY AS THEOLOGY

Therefore, let everyone who reads these pages proceed further with me, where he is as equally certain as I am; let him make inquiries with me where he is as equally hesitant as I am; wherever he recognizes the error as his, let him return to me; wherever it is mine, let him call me back. Thus let us enter together on the path of charity in search of Him of whom it is said: "Seek his face evermore." This is the sacred and safe compact into which I, in the presence of the Lord our God, shall enter with those who read what I am writing, in all my writings, and especially in the present one where we are investigating the unity of the Trinity, of the Father, the Son and the Holy Spirit. For nowhere else is the error more dangerous, the search more laborious, and the results more rewarding.

—Aurelius Augustine, *De Trinitate,* 1.3.5

In the interest of learning more about the Trinity, of growing in love for the Triune God as well as the personal distinctions that constitute his essence, and of living indeed in the Triune nature of God, I recommend reading with care and prayer some of the great theological formulations. They include Augustine's classic work, *De Trinitate* (On the Holy Trinity), which he began as a young man and finished as an old man.[3] Read especially from books 4–7. Another example of "beautiful theology" is Calvin on the Trinity in *The Institutes.*[4]

The Bible is our only source of knowledge about the Holy Trinity. Although the word *trinity* is nowhere found in Scripture, the doctrine is everywhere found. That three eternal, personal distinctions exist in one, unified, divine essence is clearly implied. In a polytheistic world, for instance, the people of Israel affirmed monotheism in the famous *Shema* of Deuteronomy 6:4: "The Lord our God is one." The word "one" *(echad)* denotes not a mathematical unity, but a complex unity, as in "one flesh" (Gen. 2:24) or "a single cluster of grapes" (Num. 13:23).[5] In the Old Testament, there is frequent use of the name *Elohim*—meaning "the God of all power"—which is a plural noun, but used with a singular verb.

Such references in the Old Testament make sense within a Trinitarian framework. Herman Bavinck, the classical Dutch theologian, is cautious but correct in asserting that "the Old Testament gives a vague idea of God's trinitarian existence," and he cites passages in which the Word or Wisdom of God is personified, or the Spirit of God is referred to as a distinct person.[6] The Angel of the Lord, for example, seems to be a divine person (Gen. 16:6–13; 18; 19; 22; 28:13–18). Of note, too, are the instances of the plural *we*. Such may well be the plural of majesty, but the complex nature of this unity, as in Genesis 1:26; 3:22; 11:7 is nonetheless striking. The threefold "Holy, holy, holy" of Isaiah 6:8 is noteworthy, as is the threefold Aaronic Benediction in Numbers 6:24–26. Psalm 2 is triadic, and Psalm 45:6–7 mentions *God and God,* just as Psalm 110 mentions *Lord and the Lord.*

Proverbs 30:4 supports the idea that God has a son. Isaiah 48:16, along with other similar passages, appears to presume the complex unity of a triune God.

The earliest followers of Jesus were monotheistic Jews, but when they came into contact with Jesus Christ, they realized he was the fulfillment of messianic prophecy, that he did the work of God and was, in fact, God. At this juncture, they could be described as "binatarian." They further sensed that the Holy Spirit's healing, empowering, and enabling presence was, in fact, the Spirit of Christ sent by the Father. Thus they were now trinitarian; that is, they were trinitarian first in experience and then drew the inference as reflected in their communication and doctrine. They subsequently used a baptismal formula, as recorded in Matthew 28:19–20, that uses *name* in the singular along with the three persons of the Godhead. To place the three persons on the same level of power and glory would have been unthinkable apart from the very clear trinitarian evidence. The same is true of the Apostolic Benediction in 2 Corinthians 13:14. Christ was worshiped as God (John 20:28) and the Holy Spirit regarded as deity (Acts 5:3–4). Every passage buttressing the deity of Christ (such as Col. 2:9) or the deity of the Holy Spirit is prima facie evidence of the ontic reality of the Holy Trinity.

The implications of the being of God are immense; the formula is not $3x=x$ but rather $3x=y$. We worship God in three persons and can appreciate each member of the Godhead, pondering the attributes of God and acknowledging them in prayer. While we ordinarily pray to the Father in the name of the Son in the power of the Holy Spirit, it is not improper to pray on occasion to each member of the Godhead. Direct address to the Lord Jesus is, of course, common in the Gospels and Acts, and prayer also is made to the Holy Spirit on occasion (Ezek. 37:9). All praise be to the Father, the Son, and the Holy Spirit.

THE HOLY TRINITY AS PLAYGROUND FOR CULTS

We believe in one God the Father All-sovereign, maker of heaven and earth. . .

And in one Lord Jesus Christ, the only-begotten Son of God, Begotten of the Father before all the ages, Light of Light, true God of true God, begotten not made, of one substance with the Father. . .

And in the Holy Spirit, the Lord and the Life-giver, that

proceedeth from the Father and the Son who is worshipped together
and glorified together, who spoke through the prophets.

—from the Nicene Creed

The early Christians faced the necessity of defining further the mysterious doctrine of the Holy Trinity without sacrificing either threeness or oneness. Analogies—whether St. Patrick and his shamrock, or a three-legged stool—are not particularly convincing. Since there is nothing like a triune being in our experience, we are left to form reasoned judgments from scriptural revelation and then to respond in faith.

It is not surprising that the doctrine of the Holy Trinity has been the object of assault through the centuries, inasmuch as both the deity of Christ and the personality of the Holy Spirit are indissolubly linked with the trinitarian formulation, and are at the very core of what Christianity is. In the fourth century, the view of Arius that Christ is a created being was challenged by the orthodoxy and bravery of Athanasius and was definitively faced down in the Nicene Creed in A.D. 325. (Yet Arianism flourishes today in Unitarianism and in the Jehovah's Witnesses and other nontrinitarian groups.) Episodically, like a recurring fever, the denial of Christ as "the eternally begotten Son of the Father" has harassed and hounded the church over the centuries. Such notables as John Milton and Isaac Newton apparently succumbed. Like a vicious wasp, Socinianism (or Unitarianism) has plagued the church throughout its history.[7]

In speaking of the economic trinity, it is generally agreed that there is a division of labor in God, as in creation, redemption, and in the application of salvation. But Christians face a difficult task in navigating between tritheism (overstressing the threeness) and modal monarchianism or Sabellianism (overstressing the oneness). Each of us likely ventures more closely to one or the other of these hazards. Karl Barth spoke of "modes of being," but placed the doctrine of the trinity as the starting point in his doctrine of God.[8] But it could be argued that the apostle Paul stressed oneness; although God the Son made the atoning sacrifice, Paul spoke of "the church of God which he bought with his own blood" (Acts 20:28). Early liberals, including Schleiermacher and Ritschl, were Sabellian (denial of the threeness). Neither did Emil Brunner believe that the trinity was "a biblical doctrine." One large segment of American Pentecostalism ("Jesus only") is nontrinitarian and are really unitarians of the second person. The fastest growing religious group in America, the Mormons, are zealously

antitrinitarian in their polytheistic notion that believing human beings are
on their way to becoming gods. Even more recently, a concerted attack on
orthodox trinitarian theology by radical feministic critics has called for alternative names to "Father, Son and Holy Spirit." Advocating the use of
"Mother God" is clearly part of an effort "to dismantle the received lin-
guistic structure of Scripture" and can no more be countenanced than a
denial that the Lord Jesus was of the male sex. This is part of what Scripture
has revealed about God.[9]

Thus the specter of two thousand years of church history continues to
challenge the people of God about their trinitarian faith. Nevertheless, the
biblical foundations remain a solid bedrock. We stand with the fathers of
the church, who with great heroism and courage took their stands. Credible expositions of the orthodox doctrine have strengthened the saints of
God across the centuries.[10] On the Lord's Day, we gather to express our
faith:

> Holy, Holy, Holy! Lord God Almighty!
> Early in the morning our song shall rise to Thee;
> Holy, Holy, Holy! Merciful and Mighty!
> God in Three Persons, blessed Trinity!
> —Reginald Heber

THE HOLY TRINITY AS PARADIGM FOR COMMUNICATION

> The economy of harmony is led back to one; for God is One. It is
> the Father who commands, and the Son who obeys, and the Holy
> Spirit who gives understanding: the Father who is above all, the
> Son who is through all, and the Holy Spirit who is in all. And we
> cannot otherwise think of one God, but by believing in truth in
> Father and Son and Holy Spirit. . . . For it is through this Trinity
> that the Father is glorified. . . . The whole Scriptures, then, proclaim
> this truth.
>
> —Hippolytus (c. 235),
> *Against the Heresy of Noetus* 14

The Holy Trinity is a way of life for the Christian. Our great God is
triune and we are made in his image (Gen. 1:26–27). The image of God in
us is obviously not physical or material (as the Mormons maintain, thereby

denying the spirituality of God, that "God is spirit") but rather spiritual, rational, and relational. As spiritual beings we, like God, are self-conscious beings. Unlike the lower creation, we can turn our minds to reflection on who we are. As rational beings we are capable of abstraction, generalization, and universalization in thinking. God's thoughts are higher than our thoughts (Isa. 55:8–9), but we can think God's thoughts after him. In humankind's relationship with God, there has always existed communication, because God, as the omnipotent creator, deigns to give to us the opportunity to converse with him. Although across the millennia the vocabulary has been in the context of history and culture, still in prayer we communicate with God (remember the great words of Chrysostom: "God rules the world through the prayers of his saints").

The three centers of consciousness that constitute the triune God—God the Father as creator, God the Son as redeemer, and God the Holy Spirit as sanctifier—perform activities that are complementary and creative. In all of this, communication is essential for communion and is, as we can see in the Holy Trinity, the paradigm for communication itself.

In recent years, deconstructionism in literary criticism has led to "the new irrationalism" in discourse regarding Scripture. In using texts as we please, text has become an endless labyrinth. Because author and authority are absent the reader becomes the author. Professor Kevin Vanhoozer, my colleague, offers an alternative to our modern "rejection of hermeneutical realism." He follows Augustine's argument that the Holy Trinity is the ultimate guarantor of that meaning of text that is necessary for communication to take place. As Vanhoozer argues, "God communicates with others ['In the beginning was the Word']" and we are, as created in his image, "likewise communicative agents."[11] In Christ, the Word has taken human form, and as "the Logos indwelt the flesh of Jesus, so meaning indwells the body of the text."[12] Maintaining the viability of language is crucial for upholding human responsibility. Communication requires "the covenant of discourse," yet this covenant can be broken and ruptured by willfulness and waywardness on our part.

Nevertheless, the possibility of authentic communication is upheld by the very nature of our covenant-keeping God. He guarantees meaningfulness in a world of nonsense. Islands of meaning and truth exist because he exists and speaks. He speaks so that we can speak. He genuinely listens, and we must genuinely listen. Truth and meaning, two-way speaking and listening, constitute the portal of prayer, divine-human communication par excellence. Examples of this paradigm are in clear evidence from very early on in Scripture:

> *When Moses entered the Tent of Meeting to speak with the Lord, he heard the voice speaking to him from between the two cherubim above the atonement cover on the ark of the Testimony. And he spoke with him.*
> —Numbers 7:89

The experience of Samuel's early life is arresting:

> *In those days the word of the LORD was rare. . . . The word of the LORD had not yet been revealed to him. . . . "Speak, LORD, for your servant is listening. . . ." The LORD continued to appear at Shiloh, and there he revealed himself to Samuel through his word.*
> —1 Samuel 3:1b, 7b, 9b, 21

THE HOLY TRINITY AS A PATTERN OF COMMUNITY

> If you ask for change, someone philosophizes to you on the Begotten and the Unbegotten. If you ask the price of bread, you are told, "The Father is Greater, and the Son is inferior." If you ask, "Is the bath ready?" someone answers, "The Son was created from nothing."
> —Gregory of Nyssa,
> *On the Deity of the Son
> and the Holy Spirit*

Widespread discussion of trinitarian theology may have been common in the days of the Cappadocian fathers, but in more recent times it has not been widely so in our circles. They spoke of *perichoresis,* or "the mutual interpenetration and embracement of the Three Persons through the possession by each, in his own proper way, of the totality of the one, divine essence."[13] *Perichoresis* is an enrichment within an orthodox understanding of the trinity.

In the most recent years, however, we have seen an increase in discussion of the nature of the Trinity. Among us, Baptist theologian Millard Erickson has taken the lead. Jurgen Moltmann, of "the theology of hope," has written several significant books on what he calls "the trinity of crucifixion."[14] Although his language is quite orthodox on the whole and his focus on the cross of Christ appealing, Moltmann denies the two natures of

Christ and rejects "objectivistic orthodoxy."[15] Whereas the Roman Catholic Karl Rahner saw no practical relevance in the doctrine of the trinity, the Notre Dame systematician Catherine Mowry LaCugna has emphasized that because God saves through Jesus Christ by the power of the Holy Spirit, the Holy Trinity is at the heart of the enterprise of salvation. Although her approach to Christology is from below, that is, doing theology without an avowed dependence on Scripture, her insistence on trinitarian theology as that of relationship, both vertical and horizontal, is nonetheless suggestive and sound. The communion within the Godhead is without "any kind of subordination, inequality, or hierarchy."[16] That type of egalitarian communion is the true pattern for *koinonia* within the Body of Christ, although for purposes of ministry and mission, a working pattern of complementary submission is indicated when in the incarnation Christ practiced voluntary economic subordination to his Father.

What is sometimes described as "a social life in the Godhead" is illustrative of love before creation—love involving only two is imperfect, but with three achieves perfection. The illustration holds importance for our society and culture. Robert Bellah and his associates from the University of California have long been insisting that the healthy, pristine individualism that made this country great has become an exaggerated and selfish individualism, a relentless self-interest that inhibits commitment.[17] Bellah sees the decline of voluntary associations in our culture (the increase in "Bowling Alone," for example) and the erosion in civic membership as ominous. In 1985 Bella found that political participation was on the wane and that union membership had declined. His ten-year follow-up only demonstrated a further reduction in social capital.[18] We see evidence of Bellah's findings in the weakening fabric of community in our churches. Christian life and Christian piety are not meant to be like Kipling's famous cat—"out on its wild lone." Instead, we are "members one of another."

Multiple metaphors in the New Testament reinforce the necessity for a church community, as does the triune nature of God. In a recent study, Miroslav Volf emphasized the need for perceiving the church in the image of "the social trinity."[19] Every believer is ecclesiologically "indispensable" and, indeed, the nature of our common life and our mission in the world are defined in terms of the trinity. Volf argues that "a congregation simply misunderstands God if it becomes exclusive or self-absorbed or ethnically enclosed or hierarchically structured." Christian spirituality can never be nurtured in isolation. The church is our context and incubator.

In his call for combating spiritual "cocooning" and spiritual amnesia, Volf also strikes some of the chords of his mentor, Jurgen Moltmann. But Volf also echoes Leonard Hodgson's emphasis on the Christian's being adopted into trinitarian life through the post-Pentecostal experience of participation in the life of God through the Holy Spirit.[20] Thereby, the currents of family love flow into our beings through the Holy Spirit and as friends of Jesus we bear fruit because we now know the Master's desire (John 15:15).

THE HOLY TRINITY AS THE CORNERSTONE OF CHRISTIAN WORSHIP

Whatever attributes you [Marcion] require as worthy of God, must be found in the Father, who is invisible and unapproachable, and placid and [so to say] the God of the philosophers; whereas those qualities which you censure as unworthy must be supposed to be in the Son, who has been seen, and heard, and encountered, the Witness and Servant of the Father, uniting in Himself man and God, God in mighty deeds, in weak ones man, in order that He may give to man as much as He takes from God. What in your esteem is the entire disgrace of my God, is in fact the pledge of man's salvation.

—Tertullian,
Adversus Marcionem 2:27

In affirming with the church the threefold being of God, one more facet of "the glory of the Eternal Trinity" must be explored. Cyril Richardson, though not a reliable guide on all matters trinitarian, spoke thoughtfully about what he called "the trinity of mediation"; that is, in the Son's eternal being we find the seeds of his mediatorial role from all eternity; and further, in the Spirit's proceeding we have the basis for his mediatorial role with reference to the Son (cf. John 14:26; 16:14–15).[21]

Since there is no activity higher or more significant than the worship of the true and living God, it is crucial that we celebrate the mediatorial functions of the Son and Spirit in relation to the Father. The Son has always been revealing (exegeting) the Father (John 1:18), and the Spirit of truth testifies about the Son (15:26). Christ as the mediator bridges the approach of sinful human beings to a holy God (1 Tim. 2:5–6). Hence, triadic patterns in worship are not surprising to us, such as the lyrical doxology of Ephesians 1, in which praise is lifted to the Father (vv. 3–6), the Son (vv. 7–12), and the Spirit (vv. 13–14). Because orthodoxy means "right praise," we note how each joyous outburst concludes: "to the praise of his glorious grace" (v. 6), "for the praise of his glory" (v. 12), and "to the praise of his glory" (v. 14).

Not only are the apostle Paul's praises triadic, but his prayers follow the same pattern seen in Ephesians 3:14–21, where Paul's intercession is that we be strengthened "with power through his Spirit in your inner being" (v. 16); that "Christ dwell[s] down deep in our hearts" (v. 17); and that we are "being filled to the measure of all the fullness of God" (v. 19).

In an age of revolution in worship, the doctrine of the Holy Trinity keeps the balance between transcendence ("a throne high and exalted," Isa. 6:1) and immanence ("the word is near you," Rom. 10:8). Reinhold Niebuhr related his visit to Yorkminster Cathedral in England and how he was gripped by the numinous—the sense of "the Holy Other"—and was moved to reverence before *das heilige* (the Holy One, as per Rudolph Otto, the great German thinker). Yet he longed for the ministry of the Word, which was so painfully lacking. He said,

> Without an adequate sermon, no clue is given to the moral purpose at the heart of the mystery, and reverence remains without ethical content. But a religion which never goes beyond a sense of awe is no more complete [though perhaps less serviceable] than one which has reduced life's ultimate and ineffable truth to a pat little formula which a proud little man expounds before a comfortable and complacent congregation. I am sorry that there is no more ethically vital preaching in the cathedral. . .but I am equally sorry that the sense of awe and reverence has departed from so many of our churches.[22]

God is unimaginably awesome, but he is eminently approachable; and both traits are set forth in and guarded by the doctrine of the Holy Trinity. And thus we sing:

> Holy Father, Holy Son, Holy Spirit,
> Three we name thee, though in essence only one;
> Undivided God we claim thee, and adoring
> Bend the knee, while we own the mystery.
> —based on a fourth century Te Deum

In sum, then, we must insist that the doctrine of the Holy Trinity is not some dry-as-dust formulation by and for scholastic stuffed-shirts in the ivory towers of the academy. Rather it is the center of Christian experience, inasmuch as we know the living God through his son, Jesus Christ, by the Holy Spirit. Irenaeus stated long ago,

> This, then, is the order of the rule of our faith. . . . God the Father, not made, not material, invisible; one God, the creator of all things: this is the first point of our faith. The second point is this: the Word of God, Son of God, Christ Jesus our Lord, Who was manifested to the prophets according to the form of their prophesying and according to the method of the Father's dispensation; through Whom [i.e., the Word] all things were made; Who also, at the end of the age, to complete and gather up all things, was made man among men, visible and tangible, in order to abolish death and show forth life and produce perfect reconciliation between God and man. And the third point is: the Holy Spirit, through Whom the prophets prophesied, and the fathers learned the things of God, and the righteous were led into the way of righteousness; Who at the end of the age was poured out in a new way upon mankind in all the earth, renewing man to God.
>
> —Irenaeus (b. 130–135), *Dem. 6*

In a mammoth downtown cathedral; on a sprawling suburban church campus; in a humble clapboard building at a country crossroads; in an evangelistic tabernacle with sawdust on the floor; in a cross-cultural setting where we might not even understand the language being used—in all of these settings, we can and do worship the triune God. His triune nature transcends all barriers of generation and ethnicity. And even if in worship we retain individual tastes and preferences, let us by all means worship the living God.

To Ponder

The general pattern for prayer is to pray to the Father, in the Name of the Son, in the power of the Holy Spirit. Under what circumstances might we address our prayer to Jesus or to the Spirit? (cf. Ezek. 37:9). Write several pages in which you relate biblical instances as well as your own experience wherein the "oneness" of God is emphasized and important. Complete the same exercise for passages where the "threeness" of God is emphasized in terms of the Father, the Son, or the Holy Spirit. Examine collections of worship hymns or songs in terms of trinitarian patterns.

3

THE METAPHYSICAL ATTRIBUTES OF GOD

Ultimate Being

God has no origin.

—Novatian (c. 251), *On the Trinity*

Therefore, O Lord, thou art not only that than which a greater cannot be conceived, but thou art a being greater than can be conceived. For, since it can be conceived that there is such a being, if thou art not this very being, a greater than thou can be conceived. But this is impossible.

—Anselm of Canterbury (1033–1109),
Proslogium XV

A mother watched her little daughter, who was drawing frantically.
"Susan" she asked. "What are you drawing?"
"Mother, can't you tell? I am drawing a picture of God."
"But Susan," said her mother. "No one really knows what God looks like."
"Well," Susan replied with confidence, "they will when I get through."
We continue to meditate on who God is. Our level of confidence in knowing God correlates to the seriousness with which we take what the Bible tells us about God. If we accept Tozer's definition of an attribute as "whatever God has in any way revealed as true of himself," the God of Scripture has innumerable attributes. [1] Throughout the history of theology, God's attributes have been discussed as being of two kinds: the incommunicable (those without any analogy to our experience) and the

communicable (those with analogy to our experience). Millard Erickson calls the two kinds "attributes of greatness" and the "attributes of goodness." In this and the next chapter, the terms for the two categories of God's attributes will be *metaphysical* and *moral*.

Examining several typical attributes should encourage meditation on God by reflecting upon his nature. Within the historic and medieval world view, Anselm of Canterbury defined God as one who is "greater than which nothing can be conceived." But in modern theology, the idea of God has shriveled into the finite god of personal idealism, the captive god of process theology, or the impersonal pantheistic god of the New Age. In *Your God Is Too Small*, J. B. Phillips captured this disease.[2] Such ideas, however, are not solely modern. Calvin argued that the human mind is an idol factory; we glibly state that God made us in his image, but then we return the compliment. Hosea, the prophet of old, characterized the process: "They. . .have made. . .idols according to their own understanding" (Hos. 13:2 KJV). In speaking of the futility and folly of idol-making, the psalmist argues, "Those who make them will be like them, and so will all who trust in them" (Ps. 115:8).[3]

Ours is now the privilege and task of reversing the slide into idolatry (Rom. 1:18ff.): Knowing God in order to glorify and honor him.

GOD IS SELF-EXISTENT

We have been trying for several centuries to uphold a particular standard of ethical values which derives from Christian dogma, while gradually dispensing with the very dogma which is the sole foundation for those values. . . . If we want Christian behavior then we must realize that Christian behavior is rooted in Christian belief.

—Dorothy Sayers

Theology. Dogma. Doctrine. Can't we move beyond these anachronisms and get to human experience and practical matters for living? Such seems to be the modern mood (cf. 2 Tim. 4:3–4). Yet, in doctrine and theology reside the essential foundations for experience and applications. Johannes Semler of the University of Halle (d. 1791), the radical rationalist, surrendered the supernatural authority of Scripture, but continued to pray and have family devotions. His descendants had neither the doctrine nor the personal piety.[4]

A critical caisson of our faith is the biblical depiction of our great God as the personal and living God. In sharp contrast to the world of idols and false gods, our God is alive. Following Nietzsche, gravediggers in our culture proclaimed that God is dead. It appears that the God-is-dead movement has itself expired, but to many in western culture, God is in effect dead.[5]

C. S. Lewis, however, claiming that God is active in our lives, calls God "the Transcendental Interferer."[6] In the Old Testament alone, the Lord says, "As I live" twenty-three times; "as the Lord lives" is used forty-three times. Daniel was called "the servant of the living God" (Dan. 6:20); young David saw Goliath as challenging "the armies of the living God" (1 Sam. 17:26, 36); we serve "the living and true God" (1 Thess. 1:9–10); we are "temples of the living God" (2 Cor. 6:16); ours is a "hope set on the living God" (1 Tim. 4:10). That God is alive is the fulcrum upon which he acts in our lives! Is that not the lesson of the book of Job?

And this living God whom we worship and serve has always been the uncreated One, the self-existent One. His great Old Testament name, the covenant-keeping God, Yahweh, derives from the verb "to be" and could be translated, "I'll be around," "I am who I am" (Ex. 3:13–14).

God, as self-sufficient love, is not dependent on anyone or anything. His relationship to his creation and his creatures is not based on any necessity on his part or on his need of us. Preachers sometimes imply—even state—that God needs us. Nothing could be further from the truth. He creates not out of any inherent necessity but (to use a Platonic notion that may be helpful) because of the principle of plenitude; that is, because he loves to do it and finds delight in doing it.[7] But God requires nothing for his fulfillment and completion.

Although he does not need us, it is inescapable that we need him; he is the author of our being. Our chief problem has arisen because we want to be like God—independent and sovereign, just as Satan before us aspired to be (cf. Isaiah 14:13–15).

John Calvin begins *The Institutes* with a discussion of the interrelationship between our knowledge of God and our knowledge of ourselves. Arguing that "our very being is nothing else than subsistence in God alone," he asserts that "man never attains to a true self-knowledge until he has previously contemplated the face of God, and come down after such contemplation to look into himself."[8] We are frail and dependent creatures who rely on God for every breath we draw. Edward John Carnell counsels that until a person acknowledges that he or she did not create him- or herself, nothing can be done for that person other than adding him or her to one's prayer list.

Will we let God be God? Is our walk *coram deo* (before God)? Or is our real affinity with Nietzsche, who lamented that if there were a God, Nietzsche could not stand not to be God, and therefore Nietzsche concluded that there is no God.

Total self-surrender and yieldedness to God are but proper responses to reality. "It is He who has made us, and not we ourselves" (Ps. 100:3 NASB). We shall not know God apart from living in this reality. Can we honestly say to God, "O LORD, our God, other lords besides you have ruled over us, but your name alone do we honor" (Isa. 26:13)? He is the uncompelled One; we are those who are justly compelled (2 Cor. 5:14).

> Dear Christ, I hear Thy pleading call:
> To spurn I cannot move;
> My heart is conquered; take my all,
> For less insults Thy love.

GOD IS IMMUTABLE

I the LORD do not change.
>   —Malachi 3:6

But you remain the same, and your years will never end.
>   —Hebrews 1:12

. . . the Father of the heavenly lights, who does not change like shifting shadows.
>   —James 1:17

> Change and decay in all around I see:
> O Thou who changest not, abide with me!
>   —Henry F. Lyte

Linked closely with God's self-existence is his immutability. In the catechism, we confess his immutability, which is "that divine perfection whereby God is changeless in His being, attributes, purposes, and promises." How profitable in this world of flux and ferment to meditate on him who is the believer's rock and refuge, who in the stability of his essential being saves us from incoherence and chaos. Hereupon we rest and rely—"Jesus Christ is the same yesterday, today and forever" (Heb. 13:8).

We may be overly influenced, however, by Greek philosophical ideas of a deity who is immobile, impersonal, and impassive, "the unmoved mover" of Aristotle or "the One" of Parmenides. The God of the Bible, in his transcendence, is always self-consistent, without contradiction or inner conflict. Yet, in his immanence, he is compassionate, interactive, and responsive in relation to his creatures. So Samuel acclaims him as "the Glory of Israel [who] does not lie or change his mind; for he is not a man that he should change his mind" (1 Sam. 15:29).

Yet God appeared to change his mind about the destruction of Nineveh (Jonah 3:10). Regardless of appearances, however, God's purpose was steady. The change effected through the warning of the prophet was the behavior of the Ninevites. God's purpose did not change; the Ninevites changed and thus became the objects of God's compassion.[9]

Consider, however, a curious theory that questions the immutability of God. Under the influence of Alfred North Whitehead of Harvard and Charles Hartshorne of the University of Chicago, there has arisen in this century a school of thought called Process Philosophy and Theology. This school claims that everything ultimately changes, even God. God is seen as inseparable from his creation and caught up in *becoming* (rather than being). The process view denies both *creation ex nihilo* (creation out of nothing in the beginning) and the fall of man as well as predictive prophecy.[10] The resulting deity is not unlike de Chardin's evolutionary God.

Although process theology has in general disappeared (because of its many problems), some younger evangelical scholars are still being influenced and ensnared by it.[11] Process theology is really the rejection of structure in the universe and is itself to be rejected.[12] Because God is already perfection itself, he does not grow or have potential. Our God is a suffering God, as Luther pointed out and as we see in many biblical passages. He feels and knows absolutely and God's suffering is focused above all in and through the incarnation of the Son of God. That our supernatural God is timeless and immutable, that he is compassionate and responsive to our cries under no necessity external to himself, is the ground of our hope and salvation.

Hartshorne himself was a pantheist, and his process theory is surely a quagmire to be avoided. Demarest quotes Royce Gruenler, a former process theologian who came back to orthodoxy: "The Limitation of God to time and space has to be considered a modern idolatry."[13] If God himself is caught in the same quandary in which we find ourselves, how can he help us? His immutability guarantees both his being and character. God is not subject to fluctuation or emotional cycle. What he has been he will be, and therein lies the bedrock of his faithfulness. We shall not ever cajole him into our schemes. Our hope is alignment with him and his will. *Our God can be counted on!* Tozer quotes Charles Wesley's beautiful meditation on the immutability of God:

> And all things as they change proclaim
> The Lord eternally the same.[14]

GOD IS OMNISCIENT

Do not hang back then, but labour in it until you experience the desire. For when you first begin to undertake it, all that you find is a darkness, a sort of cloud of unknowing; you cannot tell what it is, except that you experience in your will a simple reaching out to God. This darkness and cloud is always between you and your God, no matter what you do, and it prevents you from seeing him clearly by the light of understanding in your reason. . . .

To you, O God, every heart stands open and every will speaks; no secret is hidden from you. I implore you to purify the intention of my heart with the gift of your grace that I may love you perfectly and praise you worthily. . . . Amen.

—from *The Cloud of Unknowing*

In seeking to know God, we confess that "we know in part and prophesy in part" (1 Cor. 13:9). We thus live on the margins of mystery in "the cloud of unknowing." Our finitude cannot fully grasp infinitude, but our great God has no such limitations in his knowledge of us and all things. Although he deals with us in time and space, as the timeless One he speaks out of eternity. Scripture presents him as knowing absolutely all things (Ps. 139:1–6; Matt. 24:36; Acts 15:18; Heb. 4:13; 1 John 3:20). And because reality—consisting of all things—is an eternal *now* for God, we assert that he lives in an indivisible present and thus has knowledge of all things at all times.

Time, however, is one of the most vexing topics in theology and philosophy. In his *Confessions* Augustine said of the conundrum of time and eternity, "When nobody asks me, *I know*. When somebody asks me, *I do not know.*" We are temporal creatures, and God is supratemporal. Yet time is a creation of God and is real. Thus Oscar Cullmann, in his classic study on Christ and time, warns against yielding to Greek influence in totally detaching God from time. From our standpoint, eternity is the eternal succession of the ages, time stretching endlessly forward and backward.[15] For Plato and the Greeks in general there is no real place wherein God can contribute to the development of history, and thus there is no framework for eschatology or the doctrine of the last things. Scripture sees time and history as linear (and probably multilinear), and God's plan and purposes take shape and form within real history. For example, "When the time had fully come, God sent his Son, born of a woman, born under the law, to redeem those under the law" (Gal. 4:4).

Some have argued that for God to derive any foreknowledge from anything or anyone he has created would be to deny that he is God and make him a slave to what he has created. But to make God's foreknowledge a function of his decree is to make God responsible for all evil, indeed every vile act and profanity and obscenity of humankind. Yet the Bible speaks of predestination as based on God's foreknowledge (Rom. 8:29, notice the *kai* as precluding the identity of foreknowing and predestining; see also 1 Peter 1:2). William Lane Craig, in arguing against both philosophic or theological fatalism, shows how divine foreknowledge enables God to know in advance about our prayers and to include them in the mix of his gracious interventions (cf. Isa. 65:24; Matt. 6:8).[16]

But doesn't foreknowledge of events mean predetermination? Demarest and Lewis—in demonstrating that "God's precognition of evil choices by his creatures is not equivalent to God's predetermination of evil"—refer to Augustine—who wanted to maintain the doctrines of both foreknowledge and free will—likening God's foreknowledge to his recognition of a psalm perfectly memorized: upon hearing someone recite it, God knows perfectly well when it is half done or imperfectly recited.[17] David Hocking uses the analogy of seeing an NFL game and then subsequently watching a rerun. To know what is coming does not predetermine what is coming.[18]

Some young evangelicals ensnared in process theology deny that God knows the future, because the future is unknowable. Others, who are less philosophically sophisticated and followers of the Moral Government Movement, likewise deny that God knows the future.[19] But such denial is to fly in the face of the massive body of predictive prophecy found in both Testaments. The Lord has spoken on this matter through the prophet Isaiah:

This is what the LORD says—Israel's King and Redeemer, the LORD Almighty: I am the first and I am the last; apart from me there is no God. Who then is like me? Let him proclaim it. Let him declare and lay out before me what has happened since I established my ancient people, and what is yet to come—yes, let him foretell what is to come. Do not tremble, do not be afraid. Did I not proclaim this and foretell it long ago? You are my witnesses. Is there any God besides me? No, there is no other Rock; I know not one.

—Isaiah 44:6–8

Life is lived *oram deo*—that is, before God—"in the sight of the Lord" (repeated one hundred times in the Old Testament), in the full knowledge of God with nothing hidden or unnoticed by God. God's total knowing of each of us is humbling and heartening and horrifying. Humbling in that Almighty God takes such notice of us (numbering even the hairs of our heads); heartening in that "he knows the way" that we take (Job 23:10) and "he knows our frame and remembers we are but dust" (Ps. 103:14); horrifying in that none of our pettiness and petulance escapes him. And here in the very nature of our God is that which calls us to prayer, moves us to seek pardon, and offers us the solace and comfort of a totally understanding and empathetic friend.

GOD IS OMNIPRESENT

Surely the LORD is in this place, and I was not aware of it.
—Genesis 28:16

Where can I go from your Spirit? Where can I flee from your presence?
—Psalm 139:7

The heavens, even the highest heaven, cannot contain you. How much less this temple I have built!
—1 Kings 8:27

A pitfall in our times has been the exaggerated divine transcendence promulgated by dialectical theologians (such as Karl Barth and Rudolf Bultmann) who claim that "the infinite qualitative distinction between God and man" precludes any doctrinal or propositional information about God being transmitted to us.[20] Similarly, extreme involvement in eastern mysticism can make knowledge of God inaccessible except to a small cadre of initiated individuals. Or, yet again, some are so skittish as the result of the epistemological wars that they shrink back from any notion of objective truth. For them, "Jesus did not arrive among us enunciating a set of propositions that we are to affirm," nor did he "call for cognitive assent."[21] It's true, of course, that Jesus did not come solely to preach and teach. But surely we can use reason and the mind to discern the truth of what he said. Otherwise we would be left in a knowledgeless vacuum and epistemological limbo. But our position in God is, indeed, both personal and propositional, both relational and revelational. Cognition is part of what we are as made in the image of God. We cannot know as God knows, but within our limitations we can think God's thoughts after him. To assert that we cannot know everything about God is not to say that we cannot know something.

An astute observer has referred to "the dangerous illusion of a manageable deity." We mortals often would prefer a well-domesticated deity who fulfills our purposes and is at our beck and call. To dispel such notions, however, one need only consider our vast and infinite God. The early astronomer Johannes Kepler loved to scan the skies because it "greatly enlarged" his conception of God. Thus, nature and conscience reveal the proper magnitude of God (Ps. 19; Job 38–41).[22]

Although we are temporal and God deals with us in time, God himself is supratemporal. And although we are spatial and God deals with us in space (his beloved son taking to himself spatiality in the incarnation), God is nonspatial. "God is spirit" (John 4:24) and, contrary to Mormon theology, does not have a corporeal body (Deut. 4:15ff.). Idolatry is sin against the spirituality of God. An idol is any person or thing from which we seek to derive the essential satisfaction of our being; it is a tangible substitute for the true and living God. Any representation of the invisible God is therefore false.

Although God is everywhere present, we must be careful to not incline toward New Age pantheism (a problem also for some mystics who do not carefully maintain the Creator/creature distinction). God is not to be equated or identified with any part of his creation. God is not present in the same way and in the same degree in every place; God's presence and glory are manifested extraordinarily in the place called heaven (Matt. 6:9; John 14:2; Heb. 1:3; Rev. 4:1). Similarly, God has shown himself in special ways in the Holy of Holies in both the tabernacle and temple in the Old Testament. A temple is a point in time and space where the glory and greatness of God are particularly manifested. This is what the disciples experienced in the being of Jesus (John 1:14; 2 Peter 1:16). As believers, our bodies are temples of the Holy Spirit (1 Cor. 6:19–20), the portability of the manifestations of the glory and greatness of God being imperative. The absence of a temple in the City of God (Rev. 21:22) is noteworthy, bespeaking the end of a localized expression of the Lord's presence in God's new order.

While certain "death-of-God" theologians bemoaned the absence of God,[23] it is possible that we too occasionally convey the possibility of the Lord's absence. In an effort to quiet the chaos in a classroom, for example, a desperate Sunday school teacher might plead, "Boys and girls. Please be quiet. This is God's house. God is here"—as though he were not everywhere present. Certainly, reverence for special places and special times and special relationships is appropriate, for if everything is sacred, then nothing will be sacred. In our times, however, we face an agenda that is striving to eliminate any notion of the sacred. The word "profane" literally means "in front of the fane or church," which implies that anything outside of the church is not sacred or holy. While it's true that God is present in a special way in his church, God is also present in the world; when Jesus promises, "I am with you always," he guarantees that his presence is real in all circumstances, even in the "valley of the shadow of death" (Ps. 23:4).

Because the distance between God and humankind is spiritual (so that everlasting hell is, among other things, everlasting and final separation from God), we draw near to God through Jesus the mediator (Eph. 2:13ff.; Heb. 10:19–22). Nearness to God, or the enlarging awareness of his presence, becomes the function of spiritual sensitization and yieldedness. The believer in Christ is ever more aware of how awesome is creation and thereby exults in God:

> Heaven above is brighter blue,
> Earth beneath is softer green;
> Something shines in every hue
> That Christless eyes have never seen.

Brother Lawrence, who was converted at age eighteen, learned to practice the presence of God through conscious, constant communion with the Father. Even in picking up the straw, he conversed with God. He did little things for the love of God, always expecting "the pardon of our sins from the blood of Jesus Christ."[24] Indeed, so saturated was he with the sense of God's presence, that Brother Lawrence testified,

> The time of business does not with me differ from the time of prayer, and in the noise and clatter of my kitchen, while several persons are at the same time calling for different things, I possess God in as great a tranquility as if I were upon my knees at the blessed sacrament.[25]

So let us not petition God to be with us in the services or to go with us on the journey. All this is already vouchsafed to the believer. But what we should ardently seek is our awareness and consciousness of him who has promised never to fail us or forsake us.

> The fellowship of being near unto God must become reality, in the full and vigorous prosecution of our life. It must permeate and give color to our feeling, our perceptions, our sensations, our thinking, our imagining, our willing, our acting, our speaking. It must not stand as a foreign factor in our life, but it must be the passion that breathes throughout our whole existence. . . . Stress on creedal confession, without drinking of these waters, runs dry in barren orthodoxy, just as truly as spiritual emotion, without clearness in confessional standards, makes one sink in the bog of sickly mysticism.
>
> —Abraham Kuyper,
> theologian and prime minister
> of the Netherlands (1837–1920)

God Is Omnipotent

You, O God, are strong.

—Psalm 62:11b

Our God is "the mighty God." Amid the turbulence and tumult of the book of Revelation, twelve times we find reference to the rule of God in relation to his throne. And those before the throne intone "Hallelujah! For our Lord God Almighty reigns" (Rev. 19:6). And yet, of this transcendent and all-powerful God, the Scriptures tell us,

> *For this is what the high and lofty One says—he who lives forever, whose name is holy: I live in a high and holy place, but also with him who is contrite and lowly in spirit, to revive the spirit of the lowly and to revive the heart of the contrite.*
>
> —Isaiah 57:15

The Lord said to Abraham and Sarah, "Is anything too hard for the Lord?" (Gen. 18:14). The angel assured Mary that "nothing is impossible with God" (Luke 1:37). God alone determines all possibilities. When we say that God cannot lie or cannot deny himself, we are not limiting his omnipotence. God can do anything consistent with his holy character. He cannot square a circle or make a rock so big he cannot lift it. God's nature defines what good is, and God is the eminently and incomparably capable and competent One. When refracted through the prism of his being, God's power yields three resplendent rays:

1. Creative Power

The immensities of our infinitely expanding universe (if we assume Hubble's Law) leave our finite minds spinning. God made all that exists out of nothing *(ex nihilo)*. Unlike human craftsmen, God was not dependent on preexisting materials. "By the word of the Lord were the heavens made, their starry host by the breath of his mouth" (Ps. 33:6). Whether considering the wonders of the macrocosm or the marvels of the microcosm, how can we but praise and worship him: "How great thou art!"

2. Redemptive Power

The "he is able" texts of Scripture canvass something of the sweep and scope of what God can do. That "he is able to save completely those who come to God through him" (Heb. 7:25) is to reverse the apparently irreversible, to do the impossible, to salvage the unsalvageable. The conversion of sinners is the new creation (2 Cor. 5:17). Prefigured in the deliverance of the Israelite slaves from Egyptian bondage by blood and power, is the power that is in the blood of Jesus Christ that more than adequately addresses the appalling predicament of humankind. And with the passing of the centuries we can be as confident as was the apostle Paul that God's saving power is undiminished (Rom. 1:16–17). The editors of the *New York Times* are obviously puzzled that, ten years after the Tiananmen Square uprising, three of its key leaders have turned to Christ and "found a new agent for change—Christianity." These dissidents have concluded that "only the word of Christ can save China."[26] This is the saving power of God at work.

3. Affective Power

In a total inversion of values, the paradox is that God's weakness is in fact the supreme demonstration of his strength. Christ "was crucified in weakness" (2 Cor. 13:4). But we human beings, caught up in a game of power and control, exhaust our concept of power at brute force, repression, and the wonders of this atomic age. "The weakness of God is stronger than man's strength" (1 Cor. 1:25). What some adjudge to be weakness in God is his love, but this love is a constraining and compelling love (2 Cor. 5:14). Christ's miracles showed his power over all the hosts of darkness. Calvary love is the capstone of his omnipotence. A. W. Tozer tells the moving story of A. B. Simpson, the Presbyterian pastor who founded the Christian and Missionary Alliance. Simpson was broken and depressed and ready to quit the ministry when he chanced to hear a simple Negro spiritual:

> Nothing is too hard for Jesus,
> No man can work like Him.

Simpson's soul was restored and he was enabled to serve God "prodigiously" for many years.[27] And so may we as we exult in Ephesians 3:20–21.

APPLYING THE ATTRIBUTES

List the five attributes of God discussed in this chapter and supply three Old Testament instances in which each attribute is critical. Then also find three references in the New Testament. To see how the attributes translate into real life, trace the outworking of each attribute, the first being the self-existence of God or the living God.

4

THE MORAL ATTRIBUTES OF GOD

Absolute Goodness

The world is charged with the grandeur of God.
—Gerard Manley Hopkins

It is no exaggeration to say that with the vanishing of belief in the
personality of God there must vanish the whole round of spiritual
life of which faith, love and prayer are functions, except in some
verbal sense which would obviously be far-fetched and unnatural.
—H. R. Mackintosh

God is light; in him there is no darkness at all.
—1 John 1:5

You are good, and what you do is good.
—Psalm 119:68

"God is good and God is great." Everything in Christian experience and
worship hinges on the nature and being of the God who is revealed in
Scripture. What in our time is called "the domestication of transcendence,"
or the loss of the sense of the overwhelming greatness and grandeur of
God, robs us of ultimate authority and leaves us with only plastic values.
Pluralism and relativism run rampant in New Age religion, which is often
a pantheistic hodgepodge of worshiping Mother Earth, plotting ancient
Kabbalistic mysteries, living in the vapors of gnosticism, and seeing Jesus
Christ only as one of many prophets. The New Age is really a revival of
ancient paganism with its pantheon of deities in which there is always room
for one more.

In his "solemn and blessed contemplation of some of the wondrous and lovely perfections of the divine character," Arthur Pink reminds us that "the original meaning of our English word *God* is "the good."[1] We have seen that even the metaphysical attributes of God are inseparably interwoven with his moral character and nature. In examining the divine omnipotence, it was seen that God cannot do evil, but that this is no limitation of his power, since God, by definition, can do anything consistent with his character. In contrast, the gods of the Greeks and Romans presented a troubling spectacle of deities who lied, stole, and committed fornication. One cannot help but see the similarity to contemporary idols in pop culture. Addressing our contemporary "values deficit," in fact, are books like *The Loss of Virtue: Moral Confusion and Social Disorder in Britain and America,* edited by Digby Anderson, or William Bennett's *The Death of Outrage,* which set forth "the spiritual depletion of the West and the marginalization of the moral."[2]

Regardless of modern and empty quests for "spirituality," ours is a moral universe created and sustained by a God whose nature and character define the good. If, then, we persist in rubbing our fingers against the moral grain of the universe, we shall get severe slivers. It is imperative that we firmly ground ourselves in the moral character of God lest we fall, as is so common in our time, into overfamiliarity with the Lord God of the cosmos. Leander Keck warns against replacing God-centered praise with man-centered utilitarianism, "which tames and domesticates the Lord of Scripture by ridding him of his jealousy and wrath and reduces God to the great Enabler who has little to do except to warrant our causes and help us fulfill our aspirations." Too often, today, Keck insists, we see that the chief end of God is to glorify us and to be useful to us indefinitely.[3]

Instead of asking, then, *"What would Jesus do?"* we should ask, "What does Jesus Christ, because of his life and death and resurrection, enable his disciples to do?"[4]

HOLINESS: GOD IS FAITHFUL AND TRUE

Who among the gods is like you, O LORD? Who is like you—majestic in holiness, awesome in glory, working wonders?

—Exodus 15:11

God hath spoken in his holiness.

—Psalm 60:6 KJV

Your eyes are too pure to look on evil; you cannot tolerate wrong.
                                                 —Habakkuk 1:13

At the apex of Plato's hierarchy of values and ideas is the idea of the good. The idea of the good for Plato has a creative function and even Plato's deity is subservient to it. Undercutting this notion, however, is what is called the Socratic fallacy: If we truly know the good, we will infallibly choose it. In contrast is the God of the Bible, whose commands are "holy, righteous and good" (Rom. 7:12) and whose nature and being define what is holy and righteous and good. God is goodness itself, personified and embodied. What God wills is the good.

The Old Testament describes the learning process that God initiated to instruct Israel of not only his goodness but also his severity (see Rom. 11:22). J. I. Packer speaks memorably of "Santa Claus theology," in which sin is no problem and atonement superfluous.[5] That our God is a jealous God (Ex. 20:5), who "reveals his wrath from heaven against all the godlessness and wickedness of men who suppress the truth by their wickedness" (Rom. 1:18) quickly dispatches the notion of God as "celestial Santa Claus." For even his love is a holy love, and this lesson was indelibly etched on the minds of God's ancient people at Mt. Sinai in the giving of the law, "when the people saw the thunder and lightning and heard the trumpet and saw the mountain in smoke," and they "trembled with fear" and "stayed at a distance" (Ex. 20:18).

The fabricated god of modernity, however, frightens no one and is as common as an old shoe. The sacrificial system of the Old Testament reinforced the truth that a holy God can only be approached through a mediator; only priests could go into the Holy Place and only the high priest could enter the Holy of Holies, and that only once each year on the Day of Atonement, and this by virtue of blood sacrifice.

The word *holy* in both Testaments means "set apart" or "cut off from." Thus, "holiness is fundamentally separation from that which is profane, common, ordinary, ungodly, unholy."[6] Holiness is the essential being and a distinguishing characteristic of God, which he shares with no other. (It is interesting that in the Koran Mohammed does not use the Arabic word for *holiness* even one time.)[7] Thus in the book of Revelation we hear the "song of Moses the servant of God and the song of the Lamb":

> *Great and marvelous are your deeds,*
>   *Lord God Almighty.*
> *Just and true are your ways,*
>   *King of the ages.*
> *Who will not fear you, O Lord,*
>   *and bring glory to your name?*
> *For you alone are holy.*
>   —Revelation 15:3–4

Even as I write, I feel convicted of my own carelessness and heedlessness. I have become comfortable and casual in my attitudes toward and approach to God. What we need in our times above all else is a fresh and powerful new baptism, an outpouring of a sense of the holiness and majesty of our God, attended by appropriate fear and awe. The flabbiness of our repentance and the superficiality of our worship stem in large part from a deficient sense of him with whom we have to do. Let us take more seriously that "the fear of the Lord is the beginning of wisdom: and the knowledge of the holy is understanding" (Prov. 9:10 KJV). We are "to be thankful and so worship God acceptably with reverence and awe, for our God is a consuming fire" (Heb. 12:28–29). "It is a dreadful thing to fall into the hands of the living God" (10:31).

How often God has demonstrated the tragedy of trifling with holy things. Consider Nadab and Abihu, the sons of Aaron (Lev. 10:1ff), who apparently were inebriated and offered strange fire on God's altar; or Uzzah, who reached out and tried to steady the ark (2 Sam. 6:6ff.); or Ananias and Sapphira, who lied to the Holy Spirit (Acts 5:1–11), and how consequently "great fear seized the whole church" (v. 11). The paradigm for worship is seen in Isaiah's coming before the Lord "in the year that King Uzziah died" (Isa. 6:1ff.). He "saw the Lord seated on a throne, high and exalted" and heard the seraphim:

> *Holy, holy, holy is the Lord Almighty;*
> *the whole earth is full of his glory.*
>   —v. 3

A right understanding of the holiness of God—along with conviction of and cleansing from sin, and commitment for service and ministry—is true worship of the living God. How have we strayed so far from solemnity in our sense of "the Holy One"?

A. W. Tozer points out that the English word *holy* comes from the Anglo-Saxon *halig.* The root word, *hal,* means "well, hale, or whole." Tozer asserts, "God's first concern for the universe is its moral health" and that is why he hates sin.[8] And so it is that he calls his own to holiness (1 Thess. 4:3, 7). The clarion could not be clearer: "But just as he who called you is holy, so be holy in all you do; for it is written: 'Be holy, because I am holy'" (1 Peter 1:15–16). The collapse of character and Christian constancy in our age is due, in large part, to our grievous loss of the awareness of who God is and what he is like.[9]

Few have seen how vital is the vision of the holiness of God as have the Puritans. They saw "the beauty of holiness" (Ps. 110:3), which explains much about the century-and-a-half of their spiritual ascendancy. Arthur Pink quotes John Howe to the effect that holiness is indeed "a transcendental attribute. . . . It is an attribute of attributes."[10] As Stephen Charnock put it, "Power is God's hand or arm, omniscience his eye, mercy his heart, eternity his duration, but holiness is his beauty."[11]

JUSTICE: GOD IS FAIR AND TRUSTWORTHY

Will not the Judge of all the earth do right?
—Genesis 18:25

But let justice roll on like a river, righteousness like a never-failing stream!
—Amos 5:24

If we confess our sins, he is faithful and just and will forgive us our sins.
—1 John 1:9

Justice and power must be brought together, so that whatever is just may be powerful, and whatever is powerful may be just.
—Blaise Pascal

Since God is the embodiment of all goodness, we can consider his veracity, his righteousness, and his justice to be "modes of his holiness" (William Shedd). God's strict adherence to rectitude is both unchanging and unalterable. The Methodist W. B. Pope sees God's judicial righteousness as the attribute that assures and guarantees perfect justice.[12] Berkhof understands God's justice as the expression of his moral government, which is the sanction of reward and punishment.[13] God's moral excellence is inseparably linked with his judgment. God is ethical and "justice is what he wills, because such is his nature."[14] Yet, thank God, his justice is tempered with mercy.

Throughout Scripture, God is seen as fair, even though that fairness may not always be apparent. Although "his judgments" are "unsearchable" and "his paths beyond tracing out" (Rom. 11:33), God is nonetheless champion of the oppressed and the downtrodden: "The Lord looked and was displeased that there was no justice" (Isa. 59:15b); "For I, the Lord, love justice; I hate robbery and iniquity" (61:8); God's King is endowed with his justice and "will judge your people in righteousness, your afflicted ones with justice" (Ps. 72:1–2); widows and orphans are God's special concern (James 1:27) for indeed "he will deliver the needy who cry out, the afflicted who have no one to help. He will take pity on the weak and the needy and save the needy from death. He will rescue them from oppression and violence, for precious is their blood in his sight" (Ps. 72:12–14). God detests false weights and measures. He is impartial and without favoritism. He is fair.

Demarest and Lewis argue that, from the nature of God himself, the people of God are to present to the watching world "an authentic exhibit of justice tempered with mercy."[15] It cannot be denied that a desire for justice resides in human nature: "He has showed you, O man, what is good. And what does the Lord require of you? To act justly and to love mercy and to walk humbly with your God" (Mic. 6:8). Unfairness in our fallen world offends even the unconverted (as when some driver swerves in ahead of him or her in traffic, or parks in his or her parking place).[16]

God's people, then, can be a witness to the world in expressing offense at, drawing attention to, and working to address inequities: the widening gap between the "haves" and the "have-nots"; miscarriages of justice; a salary scale that pays women less than men for doing the same task; farmers who feed the world, but can't make subsistence returns and therefore lose their farms; masses of the unborn murdered in the "abortuaries" of the world; racial prejudice and ethnic stereotyping.

Our God moves from a base of absolute justice and fairness, and he is intent on remunerative justice (for the good) and punitive justice (for the evil). Scripture is clear: "God will bring every deed into judgment, including every hidden thing, whether it is good or evil" (Eccl. 12:14). His judgments upon the disobedient uphold his faithful character, and if he delays in rendering judgment, let it not undercut our confidence in him. Recall the preacher of old:

> *When the sentence for a crime is not quickly carried out, the hearts of the people are filled with schemes to do wrong. Although a wicked man commits a hundred crimes and still lives a long time, I know that it will go better with God-fearing men, who are reverent before God. Yet because the wicked do not fear God, it will not go well with them, and their days will not lengthen like a shadow.*
> —Ecclesiastes 8:11–13

While in our time it may seem that the antibodies combating evil in our culture are largely dormant, we may rest well-assured that everywhere in Scripture God is presented as reliable and trustworthy, faithful to his promises (Pss. 145:13; 146:6). The unchanging God (James 1:17) establishes a "fixedness, stability and realization of the Truth," which is everywhere "contrasted with that which is transient, uncertain and illusory."[17]

To the earliest Christian preachers, Jesus Christ was the "Holy and Righteous One" (Acts 3:14; 4:27, 30) to whom all judgments have been committed and—as Paul proclaimed in Athens—the one appointed "to judge the world with justice" (17:31). The Fall has twisted and convoluted the image of God in humankind, but has not totally effaced or obliterated it (cf. Rom. 2:14–15). In his offer of salvation through Christ, God has presented the climactic demonstration of his justice "so as to be just and the one who justifies" (Rom. 3:26). In the consummation of all things, the ultimate testimony will be

> *Yes, Lord God Almighty, true and just are your judgments.*
> —Revelation 16:7

> *Hallelujah!*
> *Salvation and glory and power belong to our God,*
> *for true and just are his judgments.*
> —Revelation 19:1–2

> *But let him who boasts boast about this: that he understands and knows me, that I am the* LORD, *who exercises kindness, justice and righteousness on earth, for in these I delight.*
> —Jeremiah 9:24

Love: God Is the Tender Father

God is love.
—1 John 4:16

And I pray that you, being rooted and established in love, may have power, together with all the saints, to grasp how wide and long and high and deep is the love of Christ, and to know this love that surpasses knowledge.
—Ephesians 3:17–19

God loves each of us as if there were only one of us to love.
—Aurelius Augustine

In denying revelation and authoritative tradition, Peter Berger, in *A Rumor of Angels,* seeks what he calls "signals of transcendence." But he does not recognize even a glimmer of the greatest fact in the universe—that the everlasting God loves us (Jer. 31:3). No other religion outside of the Bible presents a God who is "a gracious and compassionate God, slow to anger and abounding in love, a God who relents from sending calamity" (Jonah 4:2). Scripture throbs with God's great and infinite love. The Hebrew word *hesed,* which refers to God's unfailing covenant love, occurs 245 times in the Old Testament. God's love is shown in his loyalty to his covenant promises (Ex. 20:6), and love is, in fact, the agent of the covenant and its promises, many of which are unconditional (Deut. 7:7–9). The prophet Hosea married a woman who became a prostitute. He loved her and brought her back, and, as James Moffatt puts it, "Hosea's interpretation of the character of God is reached through the tender, chivalrous love of an injured husband for his wife, a love which magnanimously survives the offence, though it by no means condones it" (Hos. 11:8f.).[18]

Love as a word in English is today so degraded and diluted that it is used without thought. But the rich vocabulary of the New Testament points to the highest kind of self-giving love—agape—which is a spontaneous and unconditional love, neither kindled nor quenched by the level of attractiveness of its object.[19] Agape has been manifested and became incarnate in the person and work of the Lord Jesus Christ, above all in his healing cross. As Paul says, "God demonstrates his own love for us in this: While we were still sinners, Christ died for us" (Rom. 5:8). Thus God—not by definition only but in demonstration—is love, as he is—by demonstration—"light"

(1 John 1:5) and "a consuming fire" (Heb. 12:29). God's love possesses a feeling like that of a father pitying his children (Ps. 103:13) or a mother comforting her child (Isa. 66:13; Matt. 23:37). Jesus did not weep crocodile tears. His is the love of God.

GOD'S LOVE IS INCLUSIVE

For God so loved the world that he gave his one and only Son, that whoever believes in him shall not perish but have eternal life.

—John 3:16

Can we be certain that God loves us despite our sin? Can we say to anyone we meet: "God loves you!"? What is the range and scope of God's love? Some have argued that God's love for the world does not include each and every person in the world, but "the world of God's elect."[20] Thus John 1:29 is understood as a limited atonement in which the Lamb of God taking away "the sins of the world" refers only to the sins of the elect.

Certainly, God has a special love for his beloved son (Matt. 3:17; 17:5) and he has a special love for those who comprise his church (Eph. 5:25). But God loves every human being in the world—the *world* being inclusive. Berkhof argues that what God loves in human beings is himself and his work in human beings.[21] True, God loves the sinner but not the sin (as he expects us also to do), but does he not love each person as a "unique, unrepeatable personal event"? Only those whom the Father draws come to him (John 6:44), but John makes it clear that the crucified Christ draws all men to himself (12:32). The word *world* in John's gospel seems comprehensive, referring to all who are part of Satan's system in opposition to God (cf. 1:9–10; 3:17, 19; 4:42; 6:33, 51; 7:4, 7; 8:12, 23; 12:47; 14:19; 15:19; 16:8, 11; 17:6, 9, 14, 21, 23; 18:36–37). God wants every person to be saved (1 Tim. 2:5–6; 2 Peter 3:9), and this on the basis that "Christ is the atoning sacrifice for our sins—and not for ours only, but also for the sins of the whole world" (1 John 2:2). Even those who are eternally lost are those for whom "the sovereign Lord" died (2 Peter 2:1). So while nuances exist regarding who is called and who responds, we yet can proclaim to every human being, "God loves you." The wonder is that he loves me! (Gal. 2:20). Basic to everything Christian is God's initiative: "We love because he first loved us" (1 John 4:19).

GOD'S LOVE IS CREATIVE

He loved us very much when he made us in his likeness, but he loved us more when he bought us with his precious blood, suffering death for us of his own will in order that we might be saved from the devil's power and the pains of hell. And yet he loves us most intimately when he gives us the gift of the Holy Spirit, who is love, by which we are able to know him and love him, and are comforted, assured that we are his children and chosen unto salvation. On account of this love we are even more indebted to him than we are for our physical creation and for our human life. For though he had made us and purchased us, unless he had also extended himself to us in salvation, what ultimate profit would we have of our created existence or our life? None at all.

—Walter Hilton,
Toward a Perfect Love
(14th century)

Humanistic and secular notions of love run amok in Western culture. The modern mood is mirrored even by so-called evangelical pulpiteers who proclaim, "If it's going to be, it's up to me," or "Make your thinking big enough for God to fit in," or "I can choose any dream I want and go for it." But Scripture calls us back to holy love[22]: "God has poured out his love into our hearts by the Holy Spirit, whom he has given us" (Rom. 5:5). And thereby God shows us that "Just at the right time, when we were still powerless, Christ died for the ungodly" (v. 6). The genius of God's creative love is that "love found a way" to satisfy justice, and yet provides a way of salvation for lost sinners.

The grand theme of salvation will receive sharper focus in chapter 6, but here it is appropriate to marvel that God, in his infinite wisdom, has expressed his immeasurable love in a way that is fully consistent with his holiness and purity. His love is not insipid; it is not wilted in an accommodation that destroys the moral foundations of the universe. God's moral standards have not collapsed. His love is strong and fuses two diametrically opposed considerations—righteousness and peace—and this supremely at the cross of Christ. Thus in dealing with us God can achieve his goal: a "harvest of righteousness and peace" (Heb. 12:11), each fully expressed without sacrifice to the other.

In thus lifting Adam's progeny to heights of which our first parents never dreamed, God gave some of the early church fathers occasion to speak of *beata culpa,* or the happy fall. This lavish expenditure of "the unsearchable riches of Christ" is "to make plain to everyone the administration of this mystery. . . . That now, through the church, the manifold wisdom of God should be made known to the rulers and authorities in the heavenly realms, according to his eternal purpose which he accomplished in Christ Jesus our Lord" (Eph. 3:8b–11). Thus, in his unrivaled resourcefulness and ingenuity, "[God's] divine power has given us everything we need for life and godliness" (2 Peter 1:3). And so we praise Him.

God's Love Is Illustrative

This is how we know what love is: Jesus Christ laid down his life for us. And we ought to lay down our lives for our brothers.
—1 John 3:16

How different our personal histories and church history would be if we knew 1 John 3:16 as well as our treasured John 3:16. Christ's great love compels us (2 Cor. 5:14) in shaping our lives. He has modeled the Christian pilgrimage for us: "Greater love has no one than this, that one lay down his life for his friends" (John 15:13). Self-emptying love is our model (Phil. 2:5ff.). The love of Calvary is to be our standard, as our Lord made clear: "As I have loved you, so you must love one another. All men will know that you are my disciples if you love one another" (John 13:34–35). It is easy to imagine the definitions of love in 1 Corinthians 13:4–7 and the fruit of the Spirit in Galatians 5:22–23 as a portrait of the Lord Jesus. The gospel accounts are replete with illustrations in which Jesus exhibited these traits.

> Loved with everlasting love, Led by grace that love to know;
> Spirit, breathing from above, Thou hast taught me it is so!
> Oh, this full and perfect peace! Oh, this transport all divine!
> In a love which cannot cease, I am His and He is mine.
> —George W. Robinson

God's Mercy: Far-Reaching and Free

You do not stay angry forever but delight to show mercy.
—Micah 7:18b

Depth of mercy! can there be
Mercy still reserved for me?
Can my God His wrath forebear,
Me, the chief of sinners, spare?
              —Charles Wesley

The vocabulary setting forth the goodness of God bespeaks, too, the depths of his goodness. Mercy and grace are, in a sense, functions of God's love and benevolence. Mercy, sometimes translated "lovingkindness," is God's patience and forbearance, out of which he holds back our deserved judgment and punishment: God "is rich in mercy" (Eph. 2:4) and is "merciful and gracious, slow to anger, and plenteous in mercy" (Ps. 103:8 KJV).

The New Testament word *grace* is the propensity of God to bestow his favor and forgiveness upon those who deserve the very opposite. "Grace and truth came through Jesus Christ" (John 1:17), in whom we can experience "the fullness of [God's] grace" (v. 16). Grace from God is, of course, the basis of our salvation (Eph. 2:8–9; Titus 2:14ff.). When George Whitefield preached, in almost every sermon he would come to the point of God's free gift in Christ and literally gasp, "Oh, the grace of God, the wonderful grace of God!" This "amazing grace" is indeed far-reaching, beyond our comprehension, in that "where sin abounds, there does grace much more super-abound" (Rom. 5:20, author's translation). How profitable and encouraging just to ponder the generosity of our great God, who "gives us more grace" (James 4:6; Gk., "a greater grace").

Considering God's attributes makes our minds swim. God does care, is concerned, and shows compassion. Truly "he does not treat us as our sins deserve or repay us according to our iniquities" (Ps. 103:10). If we will face the enormity of our sin and guilt, we can obtain salvation. "At one time we too were foolish, disobedient, deceived and enslaved by all kinds of passions and pleasures. We lived in malice and envy, being hated and hating one another. But when the kindness and love of God our Savior appeared, he saved us, not because of righteous things we had done, but because of his mercy. He saved us through the washing of rebirth and renewal by the Holy Spirit, whom he poured out on us generously through Jesus Christ our Savior, so that, having been justified by his grace, we might become heirs having the hope of eternal life" (Titus 3:3–7).

How well I remember a young rascal in our home. One summer afternoon, he spied an implement in a kitchen drawer, and he asked his mother,

"What is this?" She replied, "That is a cabbage chopper, and I want you to put it back into the drawer and go out to play." Instead, the boy slipped it into his pocket and, once outside, looked at the white wooden cornice blocks on the house and wondered if they might be chopped with a cabbage chopper.

Chop! Chop! Chop! So nicely did the implement do its work that the child remained blissfully engaged until he sensed a presence: His father had come home early from work. Suffice it to say that the two had a "little session." Even after he was spanked, the boy couldn't help but go "Huh, huh, huh" in spasms of sobs.

"Huh, huh, huh," he continued long after he wanted to stop.

Later, he saw his father working the garden way down at the end of the lot. He slowly walked down and stood near his dad. "Huh, huh, huh" he gasped. "Hey, Dad, I'm so lonesome." The boy would never forget what happened next. His father put down his spade and picked up his son, squeezing him so tightly that the boy thought he might be crushed. Then he saw something he had never before seen—tears coming down his father's cheeks. Then my dad said, "I'm lonesome too, Dave," and he hugged and kissed me again. That is something like our God's great feeling for us wayward creatures.

Our Appropriate Response

Learn then, O Christian, from Christ the manner in which you ought to love Christ. Learn to love Him tenderly, to love Him wisely, to love Him with a mighty love. Tenderly, that you may not be enticed away from Him. Wisely, that you may not be deceived and so drawn away. Strongly, that you may not be separated from Him by any force. Delight yourself in Christ who is Wisdom, beyond all else, in order that worldly glory or fleshly pleasures may not withdraw you from Him. Let Christ, who is the truth, enlighten you, so that you may not be led away by the spirit of falsehood and error. So that you may not be overcome by adversities, let Christ who is the Power of God strengthen you. Let charity render your zeal ardent; let wisdom rule and direct it. Let constancy make it enduring. Let it be free from lukewarmness, not timid, nor lacking discretion. Are not these three things prescribed to you in the Law, when God said: "You shall love the Lord your

God with all your heart, with all your soul, and with all your strength"? (Deuteronomy 6:5).[23]

—Bernard of Clairvaux,
The Love of God

TAKING IT TO HEART

List the four moral attributes discussed in this chapter. Write a paragraph citing your own or someone else's experience that verifies these qualities in God, outlining what was at stake and what were the results of each incident.

5

THE HUMAN FAMILY

Made in His Image——but Marred

All who deny this, call it "original sin," or by any other title, are but Heathens still, in the fundamental point which differences Heathenism from Christianity.

—John Wesley

What then is it that, when we would go in one direction, drags us in the other?

—Seneca

Whatever else is true, it is certain that man is not what he was meant to be.

—G. K. Chesterton

As for you, you were dead in your transgressions and sins, in which you used to live when you followed the ways of this world and of the ruler of the kingdom of the air, the spirit who is now at work in those who are disobedient. All of us also lived among them at one time, gratifying the cravings of our sinful nature and following its desires and thoughts. Like the rest, we were by nature objects of wrath.

—Ephesians 2:1–2

Topsy said to Miss Eva, in *Uncle Tom's Cabin,* "Oh Miss Eva—I tries so hard to be good but it don't appear I was made to it, nohow."

A young boy told his mother, "Mom, there's something in me that loves to be naughty."

Samuel Johnson observed, "We all have knowledge of ourselves that we would not tell our nearest friend."

Goethe admitted, "There is no sin ever committed that I am not capable of committing."

The apostle Paul confessed, "I know that nothing good lives in me, that is, in my sinful nature" (Rom. 7:18).

Having bathed in the goodness and mercy and majesty of God, it is imperative to face the misery of humanity and what hinders our quest for the godly life. The glory that is the good news of Christ will never grip us until we have come to terms with the bad news of human sinfulness and alienation from God. Scripture and our experience bear more than ample testimony that we are all damaged goods. At a juncture in history when the depths of human depravity and inner darkness are clearly in evidence (battered children; ethnic cleansing; addictions to drugs, alcohol, and sexual depravity; instances of "man's inhumanity to man"), it is regrettable that some today call for the church to be more "user-friendly," more "upbeat," and to soft-pedal any serious teaching about sin.

We can warble day and night about the good table the Lord has set for us, but we must also confront our chronic disinclination to recognize that sin is a spiritual reality. Even the more worldly among us have serious concerns about the evil which threatens to engulf us.[1]

Yet this is the hour when many evangelicals are becoming soft on sin, and they advise us to form new strategies that take into account that "people don't want to hear that they are sinners and are lost." Others propose new paradigms that bypass the need for right teaching on this subject and thereby bypass not only Paul's Romans Road but repentance and the cross as well. In dissociating himself from the apostle Paul on the subject of sin and repentance, Robert Schuller espouses a "new theology," which is, in fact, "another gospel" (Gal. 1:9).[2] Long ago, I heard the late Bernard Ramm say that every heresy begins with a tampering with and trivializing of the doctrine of sin. If the cross of Christ is the moral epicenter of the universe, we eviscerate its power and wisdom by mincing words or minimizing sin. Genesis 3, the story of the fall of our first parents, is the one chapter in the Bible without which all the rest of Bible history would be meaningless. So rather than succumbing to "thus says the latest feel-good theology," let's hold with "Thus saith the Lord."

INVESTED WITH SACRED VALUE

Christianity is strange. It bids man recognize that he is vile, even abominable; and bids him desire to be like God. Without such a counterpoise, this dignity would make him horribly vain, or this humiliation would make him terribly abject.

—Blaise Pascal

I am made of sin.

—Bishop Lancelot Andrewes

I defy the devil himself to equal me.

—John Bunyan, *Grace Abounding*

So God created man in his own image, in the image of God he created him; male and female he created them.

—Genesis 1:27

"What is man that you are mindful of him, the son of man that you care for him?" (Ps. 8:4). An old Waldensian catechism, written long before the Reformation, inquires of mankind, "What art thou?" and replies, "A created being, both moral and mortal." Indeed, a humbling and accurate admission must be made: "Know that the Lord is God. It is he who made us and not we ourselves" (Ps. 100:3). Evolutionary theory would deny that God made us and would further insist that humankind has an animal ancestry. Clearly, when the Bible says we are made by God from "the dust of the ground," it is not saying that we derive from lower forms (Gen. 2:7), for indeed we are later told that thorns and thistles also come from the ground and that we shall return to the dust (3:17–19). In a moment of time God created man and then created woman as described (2:18–23).

Our uniqueness as human beings and our value to God stem from our being God's creative masterpiece. A pause before the creative act, a silence, a counsel within the Godhead emphasize the discontinuity between humankind and animal life (Gen. 1:26). A human being is tripartite, consisting of a body (capacity for consciousness of the external world); a soul, that is, will, emotion and intellect (capacity for consciousness of the self); and a spirit (capacity for consciousness of God) (note 1 Thess. 5:23; Heb. 4:12). Above all, what distinguishes human beings from animals is that God created us in his own image (Gen. 1:27). God is personal—he thinks and loves and wills—and we resemble him. This makes every human being a unique, unrepeatable, personal event, imbued with innate dignity. We are self-conscious beings who speak of ourselves as "I." We have rationality and think God's thoughts after him, making communication possible with both one another and with God. We are free moral beings with conscience; animals don't stay awake at night worrying about their sins. We are spiritual beings with a created capacity for experiencing God; the highest forms of animal life do not display a religious awareness. Although our likeness to God is not physical (cf. Deut. 4:14ff.), even "man's erect posture, intelligent countenance and quick-glancing eye" reflect his relational and structural likeness to God. In creating us as man and woman, God created us by love and for love, in his image.

God placed our first parents in a perfect habitat on earth for the noble purpose of ruling the earth and restoring the planet to divine hegemony, which Satan had usurped.[3] Infinitesimal as the earth is in the universe, it is uniquely the locale of moral confrontation between the eternal God and the rebellious Lucifer and all of his cohorts (Rev. 12:4). Our first parents in Eden represent God's challenge to Satan's primal revolt and fall. The cultural mandate to "fill the earth and subdue it" (Gen. 1:28) suggests that we are progressively to exclude satanic influence and to expand the beachhead of the kingdom of God upon planet Earth.

The divinely revealed fact that God created all things and pronounced them good (Gen. 1:31) pits the biblical account of origins against all naturalistic accounts, which turn on an evolutionary axis. Modern human beings have a strong disinclination to belief in creation because we want to be autonomous.[4] The virtual collapse of Darwinian theory in our time has not changed our desire to declare independence from God. The work of creation science, for instance, has appealed to many with its entirely different theory to fit the empirical facts. The insights of Hugh Ross; affirmations of the existence of God by such philosophers as Richard Swinburne; the efforts of Philip Johnson to expose the inadequacy of evolutionary presuppositions have been of immense encouragement to biblical theists. Michael Behe's biochemical challenge to Richard Dawkins's reluctance to embrace intelligent design in the universe is refreshing.[5]

Scripture plainly asserts that in the beginning God made all things from nothing: "By faith we understand that the universe was formed at God's command, so that what is seen was not made out of what was visible" (Heb.

11:3). The first step, then, toward the life in God is to acknowledge that we are not the authors of our own beings, for "without faith it is impossible to please God, because anyone who comes to him must believe that he exists and that he rewards those who earnestly seek him" (v. 6).

But this good earth that God created experienced a debacle and a disaster. Dysfunction exists at every level of human relationship. What went wrong? What transpired? These questions plague the spirit of every reasoning person.

INVADED BY SATAN

Doubtless there is nothing more shocking to our reason than to say that the sin of the first man has rendered guilty those who, being so removed from its source, seem incapable of participating in it. Certainly nothing offends us more rudely than this doctrine, and yet without this mystery, the most incomprehensible of all, we are incomprehensible to ourselves.

—Blaise Pascal

Therefore, just as sin entered the world through one man, and death through sin, and in this way death came to all men, because all sinned.
—Romans 5:12

Man's nature, so to speak, is a perpetual factory of idols.
—John Calvin

God placed our first parents in a pleasureland of loveliness, allowing them freedom within the limits of divine sovereignty (Gen. 2:15). Total and unfettered autonomy would not have been compatible with being made in God's image.[6] Adam and Eve were created able to sin and able not to sin. Had they not sinned, they apparently would have been confirmed in righteousness and then been not able to sin. But the possibility of sinning exists in a free universe, as indeed does the possibility of pain, as C. S. Lewis so well argued.[7]

Totally foreseen by God was Satan's clever ploy to frustrate and thwart God's purpose for humankind as his vicegerents here on earth. That something terribly wrong happened is clear, and this "wrongness" is what we call the Fall. Even with innumerable evidences of God's creative and sustaining genius in his world, there is obviously still much that has gone awry. Satan the deceiver has become "the god of this world" (2 Cor. 4:4); "The whole world is under the control of the evil one" (1 John 5:19b). This world-system is in revolt against God, and humankind is in full complicity with Satan and his minions in their lawlessness.

The noble image of God in humankind has been fractured and flawed through deliberate rebellion. While defaced and marred, the image has not been effaced or obliterated. Sin distorts human reason, for instance, and subjects us to error of a high magnitude, yet the law of God remains written on our hearts (Rom. 2:15). Such remains our struggle, but without that contradiction, communication with God would be impossible. The temptation of our first parents centered on their response to the word that God had spoken to them:

1. They doubted the Word of God: "Did God really say 'You must not eat from any tree in the garden'?" (Gen. 3:1). Satan succeeded in getting Eve to entertain doubts about God's Word.
2. They denied the Word of God: "You will not surely die" (Gen. 3:4). Lying is always Satan's strategy.
3. They disobeyed the Word of God: "She took some and ate it. She also gave some to her husband, who was with her" (Gen. 3:6). Here we see the trinity of temptation for the first time: "the lust of the flesh, and the lust of the eyes, and the pride of life" (1 John 2:16 KJV).

Luther described the sin of Adam as *incurvatus en se* or "turning in on oneself," that is, making self rather than God and his will the center. Newbigin argues that sin begins with distrust of God and then progresses to embracing a substitute for the living and true God—idol worship with its attendant and inevitable corruption. The result for Adam and Eve was immediate and paralyzing self-consciousness, cascading guilt, debilitating disharmony with God and with one another, and a raft of heavy losses, including expulsion from the garden.

Although the Fall is what Scripture teaches, theistic evolution has no place for such a fall. The doctrine of original sin is, after all, "a hard doctrine," exceedingly repulsive to modern thinkers, and the trend in this last century has run strongly against it.[8] Reinhold Niebuhr construed original sin to be simply the fact that every person sins, but this theory does not explain death. Niebuhr's theory, in fact, flies in the face of the apostle Paul's explanation that the transmission of the guilt of original sin to all subsequently born is reason for the universality of death (Rom. 5:12–21). Further, if such a historical fall by our historical parents were but myth without historical substance, how can it be argued in light of Romans 5:12–21 that redemption requires a historical Savior and a historical Cross? Rather, the interconnectedness of the race with Adam as our federal head is foundational to much that we believe. Although making many significant concessions to modernity in a recent disputation on original sin, the Roman Catholic theologian Edward T. Oakes stands virtually alone—even against his beloved Hans Urs von Balthasar—in opposition to the prevailing notions of universal reconciliation, which "hop[es] for an empty hell."[9] Oakes adduces history (especially from Rousseau to Stalin) as evidence "that we are stuck, like it or not, with the doctrine, nay the reality, of original sin."[10] He argues that the doctrine fits the reality we experience in the world and in ourselves better than the arguments of any of his competitors.

Sin is more than the Augustinian lack of something. It is transgression of the moral law; it is falling short of God's glory; it is an inborn tilt toward the self rather than toward God. A deeper and more drastic problem resides in us than simply the ripple effect of one generation's decisions on another generation (Ex. 20:5). What one generation does cannot absolve the next and succeeding generation from responsibility for their own decisions (Ezek. 18:1–32). Sin has ruined us, but it has not robbed us of our responsibility to obey the law. The very existence of judges and courts underscores the fact that "infidelity" is not "in the genes" as psychobiology would argue. Samuel Johnson remarked to a rigid determinist, "We are free, Sir. We are free. And we know it in our hearts."

The precise mechanism for the transmission of what ails us spiritually is not explicitly stated in Scripture. Yet King David's lament in Psalm 51:5 is consistent with what we infer from elsewhere in the Bible: "Surely I have been a sinner since birth, sinful from the time my mother conceived me." Early thinkers posited the existence of the "golden bridle" to hold us in balance, but we slipped out of that bridle and have run spiritually amok as a consequence. We are in a tilt toward sin and selfishness from which we are unable to extricate or right ourselves. We are ravaged and devastated as the result of the Fall and our own deliberate choices.

Infected with Sin

The heart is deceitful above all things and beyond cure. Who can understand it?
—Jeremiah 17:9

I was more loathsome in my own eyes than a toad, and I thought I was so in God's eyes too. Sin and corruption, I said, would as naturally bubble out of my heart, as water would bubble out of a fountain. I thought now that every one had a better heart than I had. I could have changed heart with any body.
—John Bunyan, *Grace Abounding*

All of us have become like one who is unclean, and all our righteous acts are like filthy rags.
—Isaiah 64:6

We are sick. How serious is our sickness? The writers of Scripture are dire in their analysis of the human predicament. In both Testaments, the anguish and agonies of humankind are seen as the consequences of sin in the race generally ("The wages of sin is death," Rom. 6:23), as well as more personally and individually ("the soul who sins is the soul who will die," Ezek. 18:4b). Pelagius, the Welsh heretic in the early church, was just plain wrong in his notion that we can pull ourselves up by our own bootstraps. Both St. Augustine and St. Jerome saw how wrong he was and were unflinching in their opposition to him.

Spiritually, we are inert and impervious to the stimuli of the Holy Spirit (1 Cor. 2:14). The Bible insists that we are in fact "dead in our transgressions and sins" (Eph. 2:1), essentially unresponsive and unable to rectify our situation. The death metaphor must not be stretched to suggest that the unconverted hear nothing and can grasp nothing of the truth in the Bible. Language does have meaning, and truth is communicable, as every preacher's weekly experience testifies. The Holy Spirit in prevenient grace is always at work.[11]

All efforts to soften the biblical verdict of "guilty before God" (Rom. 3:9–20) have been disastrous for the church in its mission and in its spirituality. Thomas Aquinas in the Middle Ages taught that the Fall did not touch man's "rational essence"—that is, the Fall did not affect man in the whole but only in the part—a teaching that admitted a significant and serious element of "humanism," which will have unfortunate ramifications.[12] The failure to come to terms with the noetic effects of sin—and the impairment of the intellect because of sin—weakens the biblical doctrine of depravity. Both Charles G. Finney and A. W. Tozer made a serious and dangerous concession as they insisted on man's moral ability; that is, if God tells us to do something, this means we are able to do it.[13] The logic has appeal in the interest of the fairness of God, but man's total moral ability has been the cornerstone of Pelagianism. Kant argued, "If I ought, then I can." The Bible says that we ought, but we cannot. The children of Israel boasted that they could keep the Law (Ex. 19:8), but they did not keep the Law. If it were possible to keep the Law, why has not some human being ever done so? Reinhold Niebuhr showed great perception in his argument for the necessity of an impossible ethical ideal,[14] which is like a mirror to show us our sin (Rom. 7:7; Gal. 3:23–25). The glorious gospel announces God's way of enabling us to fully meet "the righteous requirements of the law. . .not. . .according to the sinful nature but according to the Spirit" (Rom. 8:4).

Many in Christendom have been happy to throw overboard the biblical understanding of a sinful race, under the aegis of an evolutionary notion of origins in which the brute in human beings would yield to the cultivation and refinement of education and to inevitable progress. Theologically thin and vapid ideas of the universal fatherhood of God and the universal brotherhood of man prevailed as the golden age of human achievement seemed to be within reach. Then came the two world wars of this century and the Holocaust, with educated and refined people calculating evil designs without precedent. Neo-orthodoxy, such as informed Karl Barth, turned to the Scriptures, particularly Romans, and while not abandoning liberal convictions with regard to Scripture, did rediscover the truths about human beings as sinners and what it means to be estranged from God. The prominent British philosopher C. E. M. Joad disdained Christianity and found unacceptable the Prayer Book's claim that man is born in sin and that the human heart is desperately wicked. But experience led him to making a moving confession:

My eyes were gradually opened to the extent of my own sinfulness in thought, word and deed; so that, finding that it was only with great difficulty and effort that I could constrain myself to even the most modest degree of virtue.[15]

Now with the end of the Cold War and periods of the most remarkable prosperity and materialistic well-being the West has ever known, we are seeing again the loss of a serious view of sin among evangelicals, and wholesale accommodation to the ethos of our times. And one more conservative spokesman, from a mainline denomination that has lost one-third of its members in the last twenty years, calls on the church as a whole to understand and adjust to a culture in which "people don't want to hear they are sinners and are lost." New paradigms are pressed upon us that urge us to seek experience of God, after which right teaching can be given. Proponents of the "experience of God" movement claim that, after all, the Crucifixion, the Resurrection, and Pentecost predated their propositional declaration. This is, of course, not the case. The entire Old Testament and the Gospels present propositional declaration on the meaning of these events in regard to salvation.

How can we jettison the doctrine of sin? If there is no facing of sin there can be no call to repentance. If we do not come to terms with the matter of sin, where does that leave the cross of Christ? As one man said to another, looking at a painting of Christ on the cross, "If I'm OK and you're OK, what is he doing up there?" After conversion, and in the course of our Christian lives, we shall realize more fully how profoundly sick we have been, but we will not listen to the good news until we have heard the bad news. Luther was right: first law, then gospel; or preferably, some gospel, then law, and then gospel (as in Romans).

Infested with Selfish Vice

That sin by the commandment might become exceedingly sinful.
—Romans 7:13 KJV

Jesus replied, "I tell you the truth, everyone who sins is a slave to sin."
—John 8:34

Everything that does not come from faith is sin.
—Romans 14:23b

Anyone, then, who knows the good he ought to do and doesn't do it, sins.
—James 4:17

All unrighteousness is sin.
—1 John 5:17 KJV

In talking about our national moral dilemma, one well-known television personality spoke of "atoning for one's transgression," but quickly added, "whatever that means." He obviously knew as much about this subject as an owl knows about astronomy. The biblical view of sin and its resultant alienation from God suffuses all of Scripture, as indeed it must, considering the very active ministry of the Holy Spirit in convicting us of sin (John 16:8–11). The action of the Holy Spirit is seen often in the book of Acts, piercing men's hearts (the same verb used to describe what the Roman centurion did to the body of Jesus on the cross) and bringing them to the brink of repentance and contrition (Acts 2:36–37). The late Professor Emile Cailliet of Princeton pointed out that the biblical view of sin is quite different from the classical Greek notion of man's inevitable and inescapable fatal flaw.[16] The Greek view, however, like Reinhold Niebuhr's contention that man as created finite must inevitably sin, makes God responsible for human sin.[17] But the biblical view demonstrates that "sin is essentially alienation from an all-loving God who truly grieves over an estrangement amounting to betrayal." This grief is expressed in the words of Jeremiah—"They have forsaken me" (2:13)—and portrayed by the father who waits for the return of his child in Jesus' parable of the prodigal son (Luke 15:11–32).

How sad, then, to hear a theologian talk about sin as "a relic in the theological jungle." Or to hear disparagement of core biblical doctrine telling us that "sin is too much appetite and too little digestion" or "the backward pull of an outworn good." Psychology is not helpful when it tells us that the human problem is "obsessive-compulsive neurosis" or "the psychopathic aspect of an adolescent mentality." Sin is more than "error of the mortal mind" or "the trace of the brute" in humankind. Our problem with sin cannot be cured by "culling the defect"; nor can it be minimized by seeking merely to develop the "embryonic goodness"; or glossed over by labeling our sin condition "righteousness in process of formation," or the struggle upward or "the desire for something better." Our rebellion consists of more than "the misorientation of freedom."

The truth is, "there is no health in us." A spiritual virus plagues our souls. Paul, in Romans 5, characterizes us as weak, and as sinners, as godless and, indeed, enemies of God. John Henry Jowett gave us a classic definition of sin: "a voluntary breaking away from the Divine order, a conscious and deliberate violation of the Divine will. Sin results in a certain distortion, a certain twist in our relationship to the Highest, which evidences itself in the disturbing and maiming sense of guilt." To confront sin properly and thereby begin to excise it, we need to probe and plumb a little deeper and to pray with the psalmist, "Search me, O God, and know my heart; test me and know my anxious thoughts. See if there is any offensive way in me, and lead me in the way everlasting" (Ps. 139:23–24).

1. Sin Is Disobedience

"Everyone who sins breaks the law; in fact, sin is lawlessness" (1 John 3:4). God's nature, as we have seen, defines *good,* and the Law is a reflection of his perfect will. It is indeed "holy, righteous and good" (Rom. 7:12b). To break any one of the commandments is to be guilty of an infraction of the whole (James 2:10); that is, one need fall out of only one window to be outside the house. We are lawbreakers and indeed guilty. Comparisons with one another are odious because, whatever differences between us, we all fall far short of the goal. Romans 1–3 is the darkest section in all of literature tracing human perfidy, and "we have all sinned and come short of the glory of God" (Rom. 3:23 AV).

2. Sin Is Self-Centeredness

Sin is the assertion of self to the exclusion of God. It is making self the center, even as did Satan in his revolt (Isa. 14:13–15). The difference between heaven and hell is the difference between saying, "Thine is the kingdom, the power and the glory" and insisting, "Mine is the kingdom, the power and the glory." The apostle Paul foresaw increasing narcissism in the "terrible times of the last days" (2 Tim. 3:1ff.). "People will be lovers of themselves," he indicates. Instead of denying self, the modern cult of self-esteem trumpets rights and opportunities with few responsibilities, "duties, denials, inhibitions, restraints."[18] How easily we are caught in self-preoccupation, giving to ourselves in worship and adulation what rightly belongs only to the Creator. We want to be in the driver's seat, we want to be the boss. This steady and persistent tradition in American thought probably emanated from Ralph Waldo Emerson's "transcendental gnosticism," as epitomized in his famous essay on "Self-Reliance." Humanism has become what Harold Bloom calls "the American religion," and it is captured in Walt Whitman's celebration of the self, "I sing of myself," in *Leaves of Grass*. Yet Erich Fromm conceded that humanistic ethics would be untenable if "the dogma of man's innate natural evilness were true." Still, self-centeredness has been coupled with American "manifest destiny" and Jamesian "pragmatism," resulting in a lethal selfism, which has dominated many American preachers, including Horace Bushnell, Henry Ward Beecher, Phillips Brooks, Norman Vincent Peale, and Robert Schuller.

3. Sin Is Hardness of Heart

Professor E. La B. Charbonnier disappoints us in some respects but is on target in characterizing sin as "misplaced allegiance," that is, resistance to God that leads to unbelief.[19] The writer to the Hebrews quotes the psalmist in pleading, "Today, if you hear his voice, do not harden your hearts" (4:7). The hallmark of the idolater is hardness of heart. Jesus said, "You refuse to come to me to have life" (John 5:40).

Sin is therefore from every vantage point a serious and a seismic predicament. Sin can become corporate indifference to felt human needs and, moreover, sin can reap a harvest of tragedy for innocents beyond our own lives, for "none of us lives to himself alone and none of us dies to himself alone" (Rom. 14:8). If we are not willing to face the enormity of our predicament in sin, our understanding and experience of salvation will be diminished and life in God irreparably short-changed and short-circuited. "If we claim to be without sin, we deceive ourselves and the truth is not in us. If we confess our sins, he is faithful and just and will forgive us our sins and purify us from all unrighteousness" (1 John 1:9).

AN INSIDIOUS VOICE

Things are getting worse very quickly now. The list of what we are required to approve is growing ever longer. Consider just the domain of sexual practice. First we were to approve sex before marriage, then without marriage, now against marriage.

First with one, then with a series, now with a crowd. First with the other sex, then with the same. First between adults, then between children, then between adults and children. The last item has not yet been added, but will be soon: you can tell from the change in language, just as you can tell the approach of winter from the change in the color of leaves. As any sin passes through its stages from temptation, to toleration, to approval, its name is first euphemized, then avoided, then forgotten. A colleague tells me that some of his fellow legal scholars call child molestation "intergenerational intimacy": that's euphemism. A good-hearted editor tried to talk me out of using the term "sodomy": that's avoidance. My students don't know the word "fornication" at all: that's forgetfulness.

—J. Budziszewski,
"The Revenge of Conscience,"
First Things

He who has slight thoughts of sin has never had great thoughts of God.

—John Owen

Pronounce *sin* and you hear the hiss of the serpent; look at *sin* and at the center is the proud perpendicular "I," unbent and unbowed, that is our real problem. "I know that nothing good lives in me, that is, in my sinful nature" (Rom. 7:17). Sin is our nemesis, our scourge, our bondage, and our sarcophagus—were it not for redemption. To love what is right and good means that we must hate what is evil (Ps. 97:10). The great preacher Chrysostom exasperated the wicked empress because he so vehemently hated what was wrong, and he would not compromise. Yet sin so easily draws us and entangles us (Heb. 12:1). Sin is so alluring, and the blandishments of the Enemy are hard to detect and to resist. Satan comes like an angel of light (2 Cor. 11:14), and we are so quickly snared. Both Wesley and Whitefield became literally sick because of ensnarement in sin. Are we really facing the problem of sin in our lives and in our world?

Whether we consider sin as the root of all problems or sin as the fruit of indwelling sin, it is nonetheless sin that makes us guilty before a holy God. We are riddled with guilt and guilt is still the greatest source of human suffering. Thus at times I've found myself saying to my hearers, "Now, I don't want to put you on a guilt trip," when this may be just what the Holy Spirit is proposing to do. Without the disruption and devastation brought by guilt, no human would be moved to repentance.

Consider the theme of guilt in literature: It haunts Roskolnikov in Dostoevsky's *Crime and Punishment;* in Nathaniel Hawthorne's *Scarlet Let-*

ter Hester and her lover, the Reverend Arthur Dimmesdale, are caught in the calamity of infidelity; in Tolstoy's *Anna Karenina,* all the main characters at some point are plagued by guilt (sometimes neurotic guilt, which is not real guilt); William Golding's *Lord of the Flies* opens a terrifying vista of what depraved humans do to each other, as does Langdon Gilkey's *Shantung Compound,* a true story of experience in a Japanese prison camp.

As sin pervades Western literature, it pervades human experience. There's no denying it, rationalizing it, suppressing it, or repressing it. In order to receive redemption, we need to face it. Scripture is clear: "He who conceals his sin does not prosper, but whoever confesses and renounces them finds mercy" (Prov. 28:13). It was said of the old Scottish divines that they confessed their sins more and more and practiced them less and less.

1. Sin Is Deceptive

Satan is a liar and the original spinmeister. The Bible speaks of "sin's deceitfulness" (Heb. 3:13). Archbishop Temple alleged that some mischiefmaker had gotten into the modern store window and put all of the expensive labels on the cheap goods and the cheap labels on the expensive goods. And we have allowed ourselves to be taken in by the trick! How many today are hoodwinked by "the deceitfulness of riches," for instance, and have been deluded in thinking that wealth is a worthwhile and safe objective? How many in Scripture were deceived, beginning with Lot, Esau, Achan in the Old Testament, down to Judas Iscariot, Ananias and Sapphira, and Demas in the New Testament? But the pleasures of sin last but "a short time" (Heb. 11:25). All human idols are in process of decay. "They promise freedom, while they themselves are slaves of depravity" (2 Peter 2:19).

2. Sin Is Progressive

Sin begins as a microbe in the soul, a thought incubated in the mind, and then an act, then a habit, then a character, and then a destiny (James 1:13–15). Sin begins unobtrusively like the camel's nose in the tent door. We countenance a little lie, take just one drink, indulge our appetite "just this one time" and soon the threads of sensual pleasure weave a stronger and stronger web around us. So there is no such thing as a "little" sin. Satan is stronger than any of us, but we have the promise of God in the face of temptation (1 Cor. 10:13). We need not succumb to sin's allure.

3. Sin Is Destructive

The Bible assures us that "the way of the transgressor is hard" (Prov. 13:15 AV). Satan's motive is to harm and to destroy, as is seen in the impulse of the demon-seized pigs that ran over the cliff to their deaths. Sin is like a frenzied wild beast that will track us: "Be sure that your sin will find you out" (Num. 32:23b). Sin, then, is stupid, so insane, so utterly irrational. Sin is futile.[20]

A FULFILLING EXERCISE

Take some quiet time to read sections of Proverbs and the New Testament—particularly Romans—asking the Lord, as R. A. Torrey suggested, "First Lord, show me myself. Then Lord, please show me Thyself." Gregory the Great listed what he felt were the seven deadly sins, those deviant ways to which we are the most vulnerable. He listed pride, envy, anger, sloth or idleness, avarice, gluttony, and lust. Human nature hasn't changed much over the centuries. Try reading one of the helpful and searching studies of these sins. My favorite is Henry Fairlie's *The Seven Deadly Sins Today*. Another splendid study is Anthony Campolo's *Seven Deadly Sins*.[21] Campolo makes us squirm, but do we not need to be resensitized to the seriousness of sin? Our consciences need to be purged, "cleansed from acts that lead to death" (Heb. 9:14). Can an appetite for holiness and for God flourish if we are eating in the garbage dumps of our culture? Remember Jesus' words in Matthew 5:6: "Blessed are those who hunger after righteousness for they will be filled."

6

JESUS THE GOD-MAN

The Only Savior

For there is one God and one mediator between God and men, the man Christ Jesus, who gave himself as a ransom for all men.
—1 Timothy 2:5–6

For born Son-like, and led forth lamb-like, and slaughtered sheep-like, and buried man-like, he has risen God-like, being by nature God and man.
—Melito of Sardis (A.D. 150),
On the Pascha

But when the kindness and love of God our Savior appeared, he saved us, not because of righteous things we had done, but because of his mercy. He saved us through the washing of rebirth and renewal by the Holy Spirit, whom he poured out on us generously through Jesus Christ our Savior, so that, having been justified by his grace, we might become heirs having the hope of eternal life.
—Titus 3:4–7

Martin Luther, the great reformer, used to quote a Latin poet who addressed the rule in drama: a god is not to be introduced into the action of a play unless the plot has gotten into such a tangle that only a god could unravel it. Knowing the tangle of our own hearts, we can only concur with the Scripture: we need a Savior from sin, because we cannot save ourselves. Many pulpiteers in our time follow the early heretic Pelagius, who taught that we are born as innocent as Adam and, though we may of our own volition lumber into some difficulties, there is no need for any sort of divine intervention to extricate us from the consequences of our own folly. Augustine on the other hand said of God's requirement that we be holy in his sight and his provision to restore that holiness, "Give what thou commandest, and command what thou wilt."[1]

Thus, Christianity is Christ. The Old Testament gives us the promise of the coming Savior (beginning in Gen. 3:15, the prot-evangelium) and the New Testament records the fulfillment of more than three hundred prophecies about the Messiah, sharing with us the life, death, and resurrection of our Savior, "the Lord of Glory." His names are precious and reveal much of who he is and what he has done and will do.[2] Because of his centrality and indispensability in the divine plan, the doctrine of Christ requires unwavering fidelity (cf. 2 John 9–11). Many of the cults demean Jesus by denying his status in the ontological Trinity. Liberals and Unitarians demote him to great teacher and noble character. The Jesus Seminar participants cast votes by multicolored beads, identifying what of the divine in Jesus can be salvaged from higher criticism. But as Bishop Moule used to say, a Savior not quite God is a bridge broken at the farther end.

Elton Trueblood used to say that the Christ of God may be accepted or rejected, but he cannot be ignored. Some contemporary so-called scholars make Jesus out to be a "countercultural hippie," or even "a homosexual magician." But where is the evidence for any of this heretical nonsense? Sartre believed that the idea of Jesus as God encroached upon his own autonomy, and therefore he denied God altogether. Similarly, Ayn Rand, cultural icon to some, argued that altruism itself is our enemy, saying "I do not recognize anyone's right to one minute of my life." John Allegro went so far as to insist that Jesus was not a man but "a mass hallucination brought on by a species of mushroom." But even libertines who detest Jesus cannot elude or escape him. Norman Mailer's *The Gospel According to the Son* and Gore Vidal's blasphemous *Live from Golgotha* give no credence to the claims of Jesus. Yet even these writers cannot ignore him.

Rather than here debate doubters and unbelievers, we humbly and reverently bow before the Christ of God and worship him. Back in the early 1950s Billy Graham said,

> I made a commitment never to preach again without being sure
> that the gospel was as complete and clear as possible, centering on

Christ's sacrificial death for our sins and the Cross and his Resurrection from the dead for our salvation.

Think how God has blessed that commitment with the conversion of hundreds of thousands of souls. And this because Christ, as the Lamb of God who takes away the sin of the world, is the heart and essence of the everlasting gospel![3] *Jesus, yes!*

His Mission from Eternity

Christ Jesus came into the world to save sinners.
—1 Timothy 1:15

Now the Divine Being took upon Himself the seal of humanity, in order for humanity to be adorned by the seal of Divinity.
—Saint Isaac's
seventh century "Christmas Sermon"

Many deceivers, who do not acknowledge Jesus Christ as coming in the flesh, have gone into the world. Any such person is the deceiver and the antichrist.
—2 John 7

In the incarnation of Christ, we see the embodiment of the eternally begotten Son of God, who embarked upon a mission of salvation and redemption. Henry Stanley, the Welsh journalist, was commissioned by a London newspaper to go to darkest Africa to find Dr. David Livingstone, who had dropped out of sight. The British government once sent a small army to secure the release and safety of a British subject who had been detained thousands of miles from home. In our own time, astronauts have at great risk walked on the moon and probed outer space to fulfill a national mission. But no mission has ever been like that of Christ, for whom a body was prepared through his supernatural virgin birth, and in and through whom was to be effected the way back to God for sinful humankind (Heb. 10:5–10).

"Who do you say I am?" (Matt. 16:15) Jesus asked his disciples. The inhabitants of ancient Jerusalem considered Christ and asked, "Who is this?" (Matt. 21:10). Early in the twentieth century, Albert Schweitzer wrote about "the quest for the historical Jesus," in which some (such as David Strauss, a

German scholar whose work was translated into English by George Eliot) denied even the actual existence of Jesus of Nazareth and in other ways made Christ over in their own images. But even Schweitzer, who happily took seriously the words of Jesus about the Second Coming, saw Jesus as mistaken on the imminence of the event. John Stackhouse, in surveying the endless opinions that have been advanced about the identity of Jesus, comes to the one question that is at the heart of the Savior's mission: "What about the cross?"[4] In the mission of Christ, his person and work are conjoined. The cradle and the cross are inseparable.[5]

The relevancy and authenticity of the New Testament representation of Jesus Christ serves as a beacon to all who, still today, consider Christ and ask, "Who is this?" It remains so despite the Jesus Seminar's judgment, based on its own criteria, against the authenticity of New Testament documents; despite John Dominic Crossan's human Jesus, whose birth was conventional, who did no miracles and did not rise from the dead, and who, after his execution, was probably eaten by wild dogs. These views no doubt pique the curiosity of nonbelievers, but there is no evidence for these conclusions (which are really old heresies rehashed).[6] How much better to align with serious scholarship (such as that of Adolph Schlatter), which declares simply that "Jesus Christ appeared precisely as the Gospels record—with the claim to be the Son of God and Israel's Messiah."[7] The question is, as Professor Wallace saw so clearly, do a culture and an era judge the Bible or does the Bible judge the culture and the era? "In the end of the matter," said professor Wallace, "Jesus Christ must be recognized as the author of the entire Christian tradition, and we acknowledge him as Lord for the simple reason that he knew himself to have secured the right to this worship by his passion and his exaltation to the right hand of God."[8]

Scripture tells us that the Second Person of the Godhead, in whom "all the fullness of the Deity lives in bodily form" (Col. 2:9), had in fact lived eternally in the bosom of his Father (John 1:1–5). He has eternally lived in the form of God, that is, he is that of the eternal God which can be seen (Phil. 2:6). He is the Son who came from heaven (John 3:13, 6:62, 17:5). "God sent forth his Son," says Paul (Gal. 4:4). Jesus himself spoke of his being "before Abraham" (John 8:56–58). That "Christ is before everything" (Col. 1:15–17) and that he is "the alpha and the omega" buttresses the fact of his eternal preexistence. Indeed, that Jesus Christ is called "the Lamb that was slain from the creation of the earth" (Rev. 13:9) bespeaks a mission conceived and projected before the fall of our first parents in time/space history.

We should be loathe to do other than confess "the true historic Jesus," of
whom James M. Gray wrote so accurately and so appropriately:

> I know no other Jesus
> Than He who died for me;
> The Savior of lost sinners,
> The Christ of Calvary.
>
> I know no "ideal" Jesus
> That human minds invent;
> The only Christ I worship
> Is whom the Father sent.
>
> That human Christs could save me
> Is inadmissible;
> My Jesus is the image
> Of God invisible.
>
> My Christ became incarnate
> And of the Virgin born;
> He left a crown of glory
> To wear the platted thorn.
>
> The infant of the manger,
> The village carpenter,
> The Teacher sent from heaven
> To men to minister.
>
> The true historic Jesus,
> Who died and rose again,
> He only is the Jesus
> That I proclaim to men.

THE INEFFABLE MIRACLE

*But when the time had fully come, God sent his Son, born of a woman, born under
the law, to redeem those under law, that we might receive the full rights of sons.*
—Galatians 4:4–5

The incarnation is the sole way in which the Christian conception
of God becomes credible or even expressible.

—Donald Baillie,

God Was in Christ

*The Word became flesh and made his dwelling among us. We have seen his
glory, the glory of the One and Only, who came from the Father, full of grace
and truth.*

—John 1:14

An ancient Latin inscription found in Asia Minor shares the witness of
the Son of God to himself. Speaking of his becoming flesh, it says, "I am
what I was—*God*. I was not what I am—*Man*. I am now called both—*God
and Man*.[9] The preparations that God made among the Jews, the Romans,
and the Greeks for Christ's coming were carefully made over several thousands of years.[10] The body of prophecy concerning Messiah's coming consists of more than three hundred prophecies concerning small details as
well as the big picture.[11] God's preservation—at times miraculously so—of
the messianic line into which the Son of God would be born insured the
proper credentials, a necessity to rule on David's throne.[12] (It is of interest
to note that such a credentialing of Messiah became impossible after A.D.
70 when the genealogical records were destroyed with the temple and the
city. Anyone even suspected of being in David's lineage was marked out for
extinction by the Romans.[13])

Apparently, a small remnant in Israel was still "looking forward to the
redemption of Jerusalem" (Luke 2:40), including such as aged Anna and
Simeon, Zechariah and Elizabeth, and Joseph and Mary who were betrothed
to be married.

From the earliest messianic prophecy it was clear that the Messiah would
be humanly born and Isaiah, among others, foretold the birth of the child
(Isa. 9:6). "Conceived by the Holy Spirit, born of the Virgin Mary" is the
early creedal confession of the Christian church. Isaiah's great prophecy of
the Virgin Birth, or, more correctly, the virginal conception (7:14), was
fulfilled in the coming of Jesus two thousand years ago (Matt. 1:20–23)
and predicts the method for the bridging of the infinite gulf between a
Holy God and sinful humanity. How could Messiah properly and fully
represent God to man and man to God? He would have to be God-man.
How would this be possible?

In the Savior's supernatural birth, the human egg of Mary was divinely fertilized and formed the zygote, which grew as a fetus in Mary's womb until he, in the ordinary way, emerged from the birth canal. This supernatural conception and this very special birth are the divinely given sign to humanity that indeed God is with us. He is Immanuel. That the conception would be divine is clear in the Angel Gabriel's annunciation to Mary (Luke 1:26–38). Matthew tells us that Mary "was found to be with child through the Holy Spirit" (Matt. 1:18).[14]

The miraculous birth of the Lord Jesus lays the foundation for all of the ministry he was to perform and accomplish. He did not, as Bishop J. A. T. Robinson once remarked, "dress up like a man." His was genuine and total deity conjoined with genuine and total humanity. We are not surprised that the enemies of Christianity should so viciously attack the doctrine of the virgin birth of Christ since it is the foundation for all that Jesus came to be and do on earth and what he continues to be and do in heaven on our behalf. Even Karl Barth conceded that "no one can dispute the existence of a biblical testimony to the Virgin Birth" (*Dogmatics,* I, 2, 176). I well remember how, in my first year in seminary, Professor Wilbur Smith had us work through J. Gresham Machen's masterpiece *The Virgin Birth of Christ.* Machen grapples with all of the issues surrounding our Lord's birth, including the integrity of the narratives and the church's belief from the beginning in the Virgin Birth.[15] Machen concludes his brilliant and monumental four-hundred-page study by stating what is categorically the truth: "Only one Jesus is presented in the Word of God; and that Jesus did not come into the world by ordinary generation, but was conceived in the womb of the virgin by the Holy Ghost."[16] This we affirm and acclaim,

> Who is He in yonder stall,
> At whose feet the shepherds fall?
> 'Tis the Lord! O wondrous story!
> 'Tis the Lord, the King of glory!
> At his feet we humbly fall—
> Crown Him! Crown Him Lord of all!
> —Benjamin R. Hanby, 1866

THE SUPERNATURAL MERGING

Every spirit that acknowledges that Jesus Christ has come in the flesh is from God, but every spirit that does not acknowledge Jesus is not from God. This is the spirit of antichrist, which you have heard is coming and even now is already in the world.

—1 John 4:2–3

It is, in point of fact, extremely improbable, under existing conditions, that Jesus would have been permitted to be born at all. Mary's pregnancy, in poor circumstances, and with the father unknown, would have been an obvious case for an abortion; and her talk of having conceived as a result of the intervention of the Holy Ghost would have pointed to the need for psychiatric treatment, and made the case for terminating her pregnancy even stronger.

—Malcolm Muggeridge,
Jesus: The Man Who Lives

And we have seen and testify that the Father has sent his Son to be the Savior of the world.

—1 John 4:14

Martin Luther pictures baby Jesus on his mother's lap and suckling from her breast, and then Mary cleaning his bottom.[17] "God reduced to a span!" exclaimed John Wesley. Truly we are lost in "wonder, love and praise" as we contemplate the hypostatic union of perfect deity and perfect humanity mysteriously, perfectly, and eternally in our Lord Jesus Christ, as was affirmed at the Council of Chalcedon in A.D. 451. "Two whole, perfect, and distinct natures, the Godhead and the Manhood inseparably joined in one person, without conversion [i.e., one becoming the other], composition [not glued like plywood] or confusion."[18]

This supernatural fusion of natures in our Savior is both taught in Scripture and necessarily inferred from the fact that Jesus Christ is unequivocally God[19] (John 1:1, 18; 20:28; Acts 20:28, etc.) and unequivocally man (Heb. 2:9, 14–18, etc.). We thus place our confidence in his divine person and work and, because he truly "knows the way that we take" (Job 23:10), we also take comfort in his true humanity. Again and again the gospel narratives portray the mystery of two natures in simultaneous manifestation: Jesus at the age of twelve in the temple, speaks in obvious self-consciousness of his heavenly Father's business, and yet he returns to Nazareth subject to Mary and Joseph (Luke 2:46–51)[20]; at the marriage feast of Cana, described in John 2:1–11, he is the congenial guest but he also changes water into wine, thus "manifesting his glory"[21]; in John 4, he is exhausted at the well of Sychar, but tells the woman the secrets of her heart (cf. also John 2:25); Jesus fell asleep in the ship during the storm, but rose and rebuked the wind and the waves; he sobs convulsively at the grave of Lazarus, but then summons him forth from the dead (John 11)[22]; in his passion he thirsts, but also says to the penitent thief, "Today you shall be with me in paradise" (Luke 23:43). Jesus is most assuredly the God-man.

The conjoining of human and divine natures we cannot fully grasp, and as we hold the "oneness" and the "threeness" of the triune God in a tension-filled synthesis (an expression from the Swedish theologian Gustaf Aulen), so we must also hold both the deity and humanity of our Lord. Throughout church history and in our own time, believers are prone to tilt one way or another. The following four tendencies must be resisted, as failure to do so will distort our understanding and experience of the life that is in God:

1. *The tendency to rob Christ of his deity.* Anti-Trinitarian teachings will do this, of which Arianism is the chief example as it makes Christ a creature rather than the Creator God he is. The church has throughout its history confronted Arianism repeatedly and today faces it in the cults, Unitarianism, and religious liberalism.

2. *The tendency to rob Christ of his humanity.* Docetism saw the humanity of Christ as illusory or phantom-like. In Appolinarianism, Jesus has a body and mind, but the divine *vous* (mind) replaces the human *vous* (mind), giving rise to what we call an adoptionist Christology in which Jesus is a man adopted and endowed by God with extraordinary ability, but denying the hypostatic union and the true humanity of Christ. Adoptionism has been a persistent strain down to the present.[23]

3. *The tendency to overemphasize the difference between the two natures,* as in Nestorianism, whereby in order to preserve the humanity of Christ such stress was placed on the two natures that Jesus is like two different persons.

4. *The tendency to lose the distinction between the two natures* as in Eutychianism, whereby Jesus is totally unified to the point that he

has one nature and that is divine. The heresy of monophysitism (one nature) has plagued some of the eastern churches.

Jesus Christ as the eternally begotten Son of God "emptied himself" (Phil. 2:6), but the Christian hymn is mistaken in speaking of his "[emptying] himself of all but love." He did not empty himself of his deity, but rather of the insignia of his deity.[24] He laid aside the independent exercise of his divine attributes, living in total dependence on his Father and the Holy Spirit. He truly grew as an adolescent boy would grow (Luke 2:40, 52), and his were the common experiences of the race in everything but sin (Heb. 4:15; 7:26). Yet, in terms of his incarnate dependency, he did not know the date of the Second Coming (Mark 13:32), he used only the authority that was "given" to him (Matt. 28:18–20; 11:27; John 8:26; 28–29, 38, 42, 55). Let us worship the God-man as we contemplate his moral excellency and immeasurable love. Here is our model for total reliance on God.

THE BEAUTIFUL EXPOSITION

No one has ever seen God, but God the One and Only, who is at the Father's side, has made him known [i.e., led him out or, literally, exegeted him].
                                  —John 1:18

Veiled in flesh the Godhead see:
Hail th' incarnate Deity,
Pleased with us in flesh to dwell,
Jesus our Emmanuel.
             —Charles Wesley,
"Hark! the Herald Angels Sing"

But in these last days he has spoken to us by his Son, whom he appointed heir of all things, and through whom he made the universe. The Son is the radiance of God's glory and the exact representation of his being, sustaining all things by his powerful word.
                            —Hebrews 1:2–3

As the Reformers emphasized, Jesus Christ came into the world to fulfill a threefold office—prophet, priest, and king. Each shall be considered, but his prophetic office shall be examined first—Jesus came to disclose his Father's heart, to exegete God for humankind. Of his mission, Jesus stated, "For this reason I was born, and for this I came into the world, to testify to the truth. Everyone on the side of truth listens to me" (John 18:37). Even in his testifying before Pontius Pilate, he "made the good confession" (1 Tim. 6:13). Because he is "the image of the invisible God," he made it clear that "anyone who has seen me has seen the Father" (John 14:9), and he demonstrated his Father's attributes in three distinct ways:

1. His Teachings

Nicodemus, the Jewish theologian, acknowledged that Jesus was "a teacher who has come from God" (John 3:2). And while he was much more than that he was, indeed, a master teacher. Jesus spoke as "one with authority" (Matt. 7:29), teaching with great "wisdom" (Mark 6:2), and his theme was God and the kingdom. His parables both revealed and concealed, arresting the attention and appealing to his listeners.[25] Even the temple guards had to concede that "no one ever spoke the way this man does" (John 7:46). The breadth of his teaching is breathtaking.[26]

Professor Barclay notes that "Jesus did not see mankind through a golden and sentimental haze."[27] As presented in the four gospels, Jesus was aware his ministry of service was an introduction to his passion. As we shall subsequently see, Jesus spoke often about his impending death as a "ransom" for us sinners (Mark 10:45). And Jesus' sacrifice was necessary because we human beings are "evil" (Luke 11:13) and our hearts are full of many evil things (Mark 7:20–21); we need a Savior. "The Son of Man" (a title derived from Dan. 7:13–14 and probably the highest claim of divinity that Jesus made) "came to seek and to save what was lost" (Luke 19:10). In the parable of "the waiting father," Jesus taught of God's love and compassion toward his wayward and sinful creatures (15:11–32), and his teaching and preaching were the backbone of his public and private ministry. Are we listening?

2. His Miracles

His mighty works addressed those who suffered with pain (real or imagined), concretizing compassion and affection. His miracles clearly had evidential value, as Jesus indicated to John the Baptist, who found himself in doubt and depression (Matt. 11:4–6). Jesus cites his "mighty works" as prima facie evidence of the reliability of his truth-claims. Similarly, the procession of healed lepers who presented themselves to the priests in Jerusalem, as per the process stipulated in Leviticus 14, confronted the religious establishment with the undeniable evidence of the validity of Christ's claims. Apparently no one had ever thus presented himself or herself before the priesthood for this kind of an examination (Luke 4:27). The miracles of Jesus also had pedagogical value, in that Jesus makes tangible and vivid the truth about his Father. In healing the paralytic, Jesus demonstrates his power in ways accessible to his hearers; this was "that you may know that the Son of Man has authority on earth to forgive sins" (5:24), a spiritual reality not accessible to some of his hearers. Relative to Christ's intercessory miracles, N. T. Wright correctly points to "the modernist belief that history is a closed continuum of cause and effect." In contrast, Wright affirms his belief that "the God of Israel, the world's creator, was personally and fully revealed in and as Jesus of Nazareth. . . . If that's what God deemed appropriate, who am I to object?"[28] In my faith pilgrimage, when I came to believe that God raised Jesus Christ from the dead, I had no problem believing in his virginal conception or his ability to change water to wine. I still pray, "Lord I do believe; help me overcome my unbelief" (Mark 9:24).

3. His Life

Jesus exhibited the glory of the Father (John 1:14). Christians are indeed to "walk as Jesus did" (1 John 2:6). We are to "follow in his steps" (1 Peter 2:21), and let it be noted that these are the steps of one who "committed no sin." But Jesus is more than our example and model, and the Christian life is more than the imitation of Christ. We applaud the knowledgeable use of the question, "What would Jesus do?" proffered in Charles Sheldon's *In His Steps*. But recall that, in its day, this book was the expression of quintessential liberalism, which, without reference to the atonement for sin or regeneration, saw Jesus as our example, and living a Christian life as trying to do what he did. To reiterate, a better question would probably be, "What would the living Christ want me to do and be with and through his enabling power?" (John 15:5). But, in living his life in full dependency upon his Father, Jesus has embodied and exemplified the principle of true spirituality: "If anyone loves me, he will obey my teaching. My Father will love him, and we will come to him and make our home with him" (John 14:23). The key to living through Jesus is reciprocal indwelling: "If a man remains in me and I in him, he will bear much fruit" (15:5). Self-effort and undertaking the attainment of the complete life on our own is only to court failure. Our reach is higher than our grasp, and what we exult in as a momentary success cannot be long sustained.

Like the Twelve, we are to be disciples, or learners, who company with Christ and allow his word to dwell in us (Col. 3:16). Then, indeed, "the beauty of the Lord our God will be upon us and the work of our hands will be established" (Ps. 90:17 KJV). Then it could be said of us, "When they saw the courage of Peter and John and realized that they were unschooled, ordinary men, they were astonished and they took note that these men had been with Jesus" (Acts 4:13). The true Christian, then, is a person who belongs to Christ, who approaches God in Christ. The Christian is a follower of Christ, one who carries about in his or her body "the death of Jesus, so that the life of Jesus may also be revealed in our body" (2 Cor. 4:10). The Christian life is Christ "in us, the hope of glory" (Col. 1:27), Christ "living in us" through the Holy Spirit (Gal. 2:20). *All praise be to Christ.*

DESERVING ADORATION

That which was from the beginning, which we have heard, which we have seen with our eyes, which we have looked at and our hands have touched— this we proclaim concerning the Word of life. The life appeared; we have seen it and testify to it, and we proclaim to you the eternal life, which was with the Father and has appeared to us. We proclaim to you what we have seen and heard, so that you also may have fellowship with us. And our fellowship is with the Father and with his Son, Jesus Christ.

—1 John 1:1–3

The greatest problems in the field of history centre in the Person and Life of Christ. Who He was, and what He was, how and why He came to be it, are questions that have not lost and will not lose their interest for us and for mankind. For the problems that centre in Jesus have this peculiarity: they are not individual, but general, concern not a person, but the world. How we are to judge Him is not simply a curious point for historical criticism, but a vital matter for religion. Jesus Christ is the most powerful spiritual force that ever operated for good on and in humanity. He is today what He has been for centuries—an object of reverence and love to the good, the cause of remorse and change, penitence and hope to the bad; of moral strength to the morally weak, of inspiration to the despondent, consolation to the desolate, and cheer to the dying. He has created the typical virtues and moral ambitions of civilized man; has been to the benevolent a motive to beneficence, to the selfish a persuasion to self-forgetful obedience; and has become the living ideal that has steadied and raised, awed and guided youth, braced and ennobled manhood, mellowed and beautified age. In Him, the Christian ages have seen the manifested Good, the Eternal living in time, the Infinite within the limits of humanity; and their faith has glorified His sufferings into a sacrifice by the Creator for the creature, His death into an atonement for human sin. No other life has done such work, no other person been made to bear such transcendent and mysterious meanings. It is impossible to touch Jesus without touching millions of hearts now living and yet to live. He is, whatever else He may be, as a world's imperishable wonder, a world's everlasting problem, as a pre-eminent object of human faith, a pre-eminent subject of human faith.

—Andrew Fairbairn,
Studies in the Life of Christ

When my Lord Christ became a living and unutterably necessary Reality to me, I remember that one of my first sensations of profound relief was: "HE absolutely trusted in the Bible, and though there are in it things inexplicable and intricate that have puzzled me so much, I am going, not in a blind sense, but reverently, to trust the Book because of HIM."

—Bishop H. C. G. Moule,
Wilbur Smith's
Chats from a Minister's Library

Learning the facts about Jesus Christ and faith in Jesus Christ require focus on Christ.[29] The writer to the Hebrews urges us to fix our eyes on Jesus, "the author and perfecter of our faith" (12:2). Paul testifies to a passion for Christ: "I consider everything a loss compared to the surpassing greatness of knowing Christ Jesus my Lord, for whose sake I have lost all things. I consider them rubbish, that I may gain Christ and be found in him, not having a righteousness of my own that comes from the law, but that which is through faith in Christ—the righteousness that comes from God and is by faith. I want to know Christ and the power of his resurrection and the fellowship of sharing in his sufferings, becoming like him in his death, and so, somehow, to attain to the resurrection from the dead" (Phil. 3:8–10).

Contrary to religious liberals who speak of "the peril of worshipping Jesus," believers in the Savior know that it is proper and necessary to love and worship him. Consider the many hymns that exalt and magnify him. Immerse yourself in the many reverent works written on the life of Christ: H. P. Liddon's *The Divinity of our Lord,*[30] John Paterson's *The Greatness of Christ,*[31] H. C. Hewlett's *The Glories of Our Lord,* J. G. Bellet's *The Moral Glory of the Lord Jesus Christ.*[32] These and other fine works reinforce what Scripture tells us about Jesus.[33]

Meditate, too, on the names of Christ. A Muslim once boasted to General Clinton Howard in Civil War times that Allah had ninety-nine names. The Muslim challenged the Christian: "If your God has more than ninety-nine names I will believe in Him, because the number of names proves his superiority." Howard found that Scripture uses more than two hundred different names and titles for the Savior.[34] Praises be to his holy Name. And praise, too, his divine attributes.

His Beauty

How well I remember the evangelist Gypsy Smith teaching us to sing:

> Let the beauty of Jesus be seen in me
> All His wonderful passion and purity;
> O thou Spirit Divine, all my nature refine.
> Till the beauty of Jesus be seen in me.

Consider the seven metaphors for Jesus in the gospel of John ("I am the Bread of Life," etc.) or the Beatitudes of Matthew 5 as portraits of the Lord Jesus. How do we see Jesus? (Heb. 2:9). Although in his rustic humanity and in his passion "He had no beauty or majesty to attract us to him, nothing in his appearance that we should desire him" (Isa. 53:2b), still as George Bennard's wonderful hymn says, "that Old Rugged Cross has a wondrous attraction for me."

"He's the fairest of ten thousand, the bright and morning star" depicts the glory of Christ, motivation for joy and adoration. Several of Oswald Chambers's books focus on different stages of development in Christ's life,[35] and G. Campbell Morgan's *The Crises of the Christ* explores often neglected ways to worship our Lord.[36]

His Power

Visualize the people whom Jesus met and whose lives he changed so profoundly. Morgan's *The Great Physician* shows the compassionate and empathetic Christ at work.[37] The "He is able" texts trace through Scripture[38] the Savior's abilities. "Conversion" stories give glory to the Lord, evincing that "nothing is impossible with God" (Luke 1:37).[39]

Ponder John's vision of the living Christ in Revelation 1:9–20. This is an impressionistic portrait, but mark each description that is rooted in the Old Testament. Look at "the Lamb in the center of the throne" (Rev. 5:6). Join the great chorus in praise that resounds in the revelation of Jesus Christ![40]

His Singularity

Nothing is more galling to our pluralistic society than Christ's claim of exclusivity. Just as access to God was through one prescribed aperture in both the ancient tabernacle and in the temple in Jerusalem, so Jesus is the way and the only way. He is not the "way-shower"; he *is* the way. Notice in John 14:6 that we "come to the Father" through Christ, that is, Christ is identified with the Father so that we do not "go to the Father" but rather "come to the Father through Him." "There is no other name under heaven given to men by which we must be saved" (Acts 4:12). Exclusivity is seen in modern times as immoral, but this very insistence on what is or is not moral resembles exclusivity. Professor Ronald Nash, in *Is Jesus the Only Savior?*,[41] ably and aptly addresses a sagging on the part of certain so-called evangelical thinkers on the subject of Christ's absolute uniqueness as Savior and Lord. Several professors at a prominent evangelical college have called for our rethinking the Christian concept of "salvation only through Christ."[42] How tragic and how false. There is only *one way.* Let us worship Christ and praise him now and forever.

Appropriating the Excellencies of His Names

Consider some of the names of Jesus, such as Lord, Savior, Servant, Prophet, the Stone, the Bridegroom, the Mediator, the Last Adam, the Word, and the Head of the Body. Cite a biblical instance or narrative, or a happening in your own life or your church that demonstrates in a meaningful way the activity of this "wonderful name."[43]

7

THE HEALING CROSS

Our Bleeding God

The propitiation of Christ is the epoch and turning point in the world's history!

—H. A. W. Meyer,
Romans (1894)

The death of Christ on the cross is the centre of all Christian theology.

—Jurgen Moltmann,
The Crucified God

May I never boast except in the cross of our Lord Jesus Christ.

—the apostle Paul,
Galatians 6:14

Walking in downtown Chicago one day, I saw a crowd of people in front of the beautiful Chicago Temple building. They were looking up toward the lighted cross very prominently displayed on top of that structure. Someone volunteered: "There must be something wrong with the cross." Another party offered: "I guess the cross isn't working."

Now, almost two thousand years after the suffering and death of Jesus on the cross, some wonder about the relevance and effectivess of the Cross. But we may rest well-assured that there is nothing wrong with the Cross and that the cross of Christ is still working.

The cross of Christ—the scandal of Christianity. The work of our Lord Jesus Christ and the centrality of the cross in the divine plan of salvation for sinners is pivotal in our faith. Sir William M. Ramsay spoke of Christ's death on the cross as "the central fact in history."[1] J. I. Packer describes the cross of Christ as "the heart of the Christian gospel." John R. W. Stott testifies out of his own experience that "I could never myself believe in God, if it were not for the cross."[2]

The dominance of the Cross in Scripture and the priority of the Cross in the redemptive mission of the Savior are incontestable. The meaning of the atoning death of Jesus and the shedding of his blood is, therefore, an absorbing concern for theology and for all Christians. The message of Calvary and its song are crucial (from *crux, crucis,* Latin for the cross) in Christian proclamation and worship, with both baptism and the Lord's Supper being signs of the Lord's death.

Satan's antipathy for the Cross is apparent early on and throughout the biblical record. Opposition and criticism from "the enemies of the cross of Christ" (Phil. 3:18ff.) across the centuries bear witness to the importance of the finished work of the Savior. The Cross is still "a stumbling block" and "foolishness" and an affront to human intellectual pride (1 Cor. 1:18–25). The *New Yorker* once scoffed at the death of Jesus by emblazoning an Easter bunny crucified over an IRS 1040 tax form.[3] Ted Turner mocked Jesus, saying, "What's wrong with saying we're basically good? Nobody has to die on the cross for us, with blood sacrifice. You know, all that old stuff about blood sacrifice, all those ancient religions did it" *(The Humanist).* In a panel on Jesus, Union Theological Seminary professor Delores Williams argued, "I don't think we need folks hanging on crosses and blood dripping and weird stuff. . . . We just need to listen to the God within."[4] These comments and images are but echoes of what has been called in ridicule "the gospel of gore" and "the slaughterhouse religion" and contribute to a deep aversion to hymns about the blood of Christ.

A fixture in the American university scene and spreading like a poison in our time is the scholarship of the French Catholic thinker Rene Girard, who now teaches at Stanford. Girard argues against God requiring the death of Christ as a sacrificial offering, claiming such substitution would be scapegoating and immoral. Some evangelicals, too, are venturing down the same slippery slope.[5] The hatred for the cross is reflected in the views of another Catholic theologian, John Dominic Crossan: "If we are to believe that God deliberately sent his only son into the world to be brutally tortured and crucified, then I take that to be transcendental child abuse, and I will not have it."[6] Perhaps Crossan will not have it, but he does not have the last say. For "it pleased the Lord to bruise him" (Isa. 53:10).

The Cross is not only of concern to theologians and philosophers. Western history, culture, and the arts are pervaded, indeed obsessed, with the cross of Christ.[7] Gavin Bryars, the contemporary British composer, wrote an aria in which a London derelict intones again and again, "Jesus' Blood Never Failed Me Yet."[8] England's most noted painter in the twentieth century, Stanley Spencer, painted out of his spiritual vision *The Crucifixion.*[9] The theology of the cross of Jesus is inescapable. And so believers join to sing,

> O that old rugged cross, so despised by the world,
> Has a wondrous attraction for me;
> For the dear Lamb of God left His glory above
> To bear it to dark Calvary.
> —George Bennard

THE CROSS ANTICIPATED

To put it bluntly and plainly, if Christ is not my Substitute, I still occupy the place of a condemned sinner. If my sins and my guilt are not transferred to Him, if He did not take them upon Himself, then surely they remain with me. If He did not deal with my sins, I must face their consequences. If my penalty was not borne by Him, it still hangs over me. There is no other possibility. To say that substitution is immoral is to say that redemption is impossible. We must beware of taking up such a disastrous position.
—Leon Morris of Australia[10]

The atoning death of Jesus was in the mind and purpose of God from all eternity and "the Lamb was slain from the creation of the world" (Rev. 13:8). In speaking to the two disciples on the road to Emmaus about the necessity of his sufferings and about entering his glory, Jesus "explained to them what was said in all the Scriptures [only the Old Testament at this point] concerning himself" (Luke 24:27). From the moment of the Fall, when God slew innocent animals to clothe the nakedness of Adam and Eve (Gen. 3:21), the principle of substitutionary atonement was established. "Without the shedding of blood there is no forgiveness of sin" (Heb. 9:22) is the axiom by which Abel's bloody sacrifice was acceptable to God, whereas the work of Cain's hands was not (Gen. 4:2ff.; Heb. 11:4).

But how much of the atonement did the offerer in the Old Testament grasp as hands were placed on the head of the innocent animal sacrifice? How many looked forward to a perfect sacrifice yet to be offered? Clearly the blood sacrifice was accepted by God (cf. Gen. 15:7; Rom. 3:25–26) and was typical of "Christ [who] died for our sins according to the Scriptures" (1 Cor. 15:3). Thus we also sing,

> Nothing in my hand I bring,
> Simply to thy cross I cling.
> —Augustus M. Toplady

The elaborate sacrificial cultus of the Old Testament foreshadows and depicts aspects of the cross of Jesus. Each of the five sacrifices in Leviticus 1–7, and each of the different animal sacrifices stipulated, add nuances to the meaning of "the precious blood of Christ, a lamb without blemish or defect . . . chosen before the creation of the world" (1 Peter 1:19–20).[11] The shedding of Christ's blood is not a cosmic transfusion but a necessity to complete his sacrificial and vicarious death for sinners, because "the life of a creature is in the blood, and I have given it to you to make atonement for yourselves on the altar" (Lev. 17:11).

The Hebrew word *kipper* (to atone) carries the idea of covering over or wiping away and purging, but most importantly averting punishment by payment of a ransom, that is, propitiating the wrath of God (Num. 16:41– 50; 25:11–13).[12] God's illustration of the way of salvation is, of course, the Tabernacle in the wilderness, which, as Andrew Bonar shows, is "the token of God returning to mankind after the Fall."[13] Excluded from fellowship with a righteous God by the high white-linen fence, we come through the one door to the brazen altar. Access by shed blood is everywhere presented to us, even in the High Priest's entry into the Holy of Holies on the Day of Atonement.[14]

The Passover lamb (1 Cor. 5:7), the serpent lifted up in the wilderness (John 3:14), and the smitten rock (1 Cor. 10:4), all provide a glimpse of Christ's atoning work. Powerful prophecies like Psalm 22 and Isaiah 53 bring us to the very foot of the cross. The piercing of the hands and feet (Ps. 22:16) and the piercing through for our transgressions (Isa. 53:5) afford us portraits of the suffering Savior many centuries before his passion. The opening of a fountain of cleansing for Israel at the end of the age (Zech. 13:1ff.) brings us immediately to the Cross and the promise:

I will pour out on the house of David and the inhabitants of Jerusalem a spirit of grace and supplication. They will look on me, the one they have pierced, and they will mourn for him as one mourns for an only child, and grieve bitterly for him as one grieves for a firstborn son.

—Zechariah 12:10

Thus the Old Testament abounds with "early editions of the gospel," making very clear that "we have confidence to enter the Most Holy Place by the blood of Jesus, by a new and living way opened for us through the curtain, that is, his body" (Heb. 10:19). And so we worship the Lamb of God, the Savior of the world:

> Dear dying Lamb, thy precious blood
> Shall never lose its pow'r,
> Till all the ransomed church of God
> Be saved to sin no more.

> E'er since by faith I saw the stream
> Thy flowing wounds supply,
> Redeeming love has been my theme,
> And shall be till I die.
>
> —William Cowper,
> "There Is a Fountain Filled with Blood"

THE CROSS ACTUALIZED

We have to do in the New Testament with the person of Christ and the cross of Christ. And in the last issue with the cross of Christ, because it is the one key to his person.

—P. T. Forsyth,
The Cruciality of the Cross

> We may not know, we cannot tell,
> What pains He had to bear;
> But we believe it was for us
> He hung and suffered there.
>
> —Cecil F. Alexander,
> "There Is a Green Hill Far Away"

Called Jesus because he would save his people from their sins (Matt. 1:21), he was born to die. The four writers of the Gospels share with us narratives of the life of Jesus, which introduce the passion story. The descriptions of his suffering and death—what the Romans called *teterrimum et crudelissimum* (the most cruel death possible)—are related without detail or embellishment in the New Testament, de-emphasizing the physical anguish and stressing the spiritual agony.[15]

Jesus shared with his disciples extensive teaching on his impending death and subsequent resurrection, but they found this unappealing (cf. Matt. 16:22). On the way up to Jerusalem, he spoke explicitly about his passion, to the astonishment of the disciples (Mark 10:32–34). Indeed he "resolutely set out for Jerusalem" (Luke 9:51) and made clear that he would die in Jerusalem (13:35). The subject was uncongenial and "the disciples did not understand any of this. Its meaning was hidden from them, and they did not know what he was talking about" (18:34). Then, as now, the cross is anathema to the flesh. One seeker-focused evangelical did not want the cross on display in the "multimedia center," because it carried so much "excess baggage" and caused guilt. One homiletician urges us to proclaim the exalted and glorious Christ, an image more appealing to aspiring and upwardly mobile individuals. Living in the shadow of the cross, some argue, puts a damper on enthusiasm. One leader in spiritual formation speaks derisively of "Christian vampires, who want only a little blood for their sins and nothing more."[16]

The early followers of Jesus needed to have their eyes opened "so they could understand the Scriptures" (Luke 24:45). (The enemies of our Lord seemed, in fact, to have better memories than his devotees in regard to certain prophecies [Matt. 27:62ff.].) They had difficulty understanding that the Savior was dedicated to fulfill *all* the prophecies of him (Luke 22:37; Mark 14:27). John's gospel refers to Christ as "the Lamb of God taking away the sin of the world" (John 1:29), and Jesus received John's baptism as the conscious sin-bearer.[17] He spoke of his death as the destruction of "this temple" (John 2:19), as being lifted up like the brazen serpent (3:14). He would give his flesh for the life of the world (6:51–57) in the sense of "a priestly act of oblation."[18] He stated explicitly that "I lay down my life of my own accord. I have authority to lay it down and authority to take it up again" (10:18). He spoke clearly about his upcoming death as the supreme revelation of the Father's glory (12:23–28).

At the Last Supper, Jesus spoke of his death as the glorification of the

Son of Man (13:31–32),[19] as his body "given for you" (Luke 22:19), and as "the new covenant in my blood, which is poured out for you" (Luke 22:20). In the Garden of Gethsemane, Jesus prayed that the cup would be taken from him. Jesus prayed not that he be spared Calvary but rather the weight of our sins was so heavy and the "mystery of lawlessness" so grave that he was "overwhelmed with sorrow to the point of death" (Matt. 26:38). Luke, the physician, tells us that "his sweat was like drops of blood falling to the ground" (Luke 22:44). It may be that Jesus was in danger of dying prematurely in the garden and asked the Father to give him the strength to make it to the cross (Heb. 5:7; cf. Luke 22:43).

In Mark 10:45, our Lord clearly interprets the events described in the Gospels: the Son of Man is giving his life as "a ransom for many." Can it be doubted that his statement refers to substitution? Even a reluctant Vincent Taylor has to concede that "something is done for the many which they cannot do for themselves. . . . The saying means that, by the willing surrender of his life, Jesus comes to provide a means for the deliverance for men."[20]

Lest the theology of the cross be merely intellectual exercise, it would be enlightening to examine a work on the subject and thereby ponder the seven sayings of Jesus from the cross. His utterances complete the portrait of both crucified man and his work. What does each outcry teach us?[21]

Near the cross! O Lamb of God,
Bring its scenes before me;
Help me walk from day to day
With its shadow o'er me.
—Fanny J. Crosby,
"Jesus, Keep Me Near the Cross"

THE CROSS ANALYZED

Love and faithfulness meet together; righteousness and peace kiss each other.
—Psalm 85:10

The death of Christ satisfied the just and merciful will of God by a perfect obedience and was a real propitiation for the sins of all men.
—Episcopius, d. 1643,
(early Arminian theologian)

Bearing shame and scoffing rude,
In my place condemned He stood—
Sealed my pardon with His blood:
Hallelujah! what a Savior!
—P. P. Bliss,
"Man of Sorrows, What a Name"

With whatever subtlety such words as *propitiation* and *reconciliation* are explained away, in the lexicon of the New Testament they remain, to assert the stern element of sin-avenging justice in the character of God.
—G. G. Findley,
Fellowship in the Life Eternal

As recorded in Acts (2:23–24; 10:39–40, etc.) the death and resurrection of Christ were the prime elements in apostolic preaching (the *kerygma*). The epistles are extensive theological reflection and interpretation on the event that is the moral epicenter of the universe. What Luther called "the theology of the cross" is today often avoided in favor of a sentimental "stroking of today's religious psyche," making the Cross little more than an event to which contemporary victimology might consider itself an adjunct. In a brilliant volume titled *On Being a Theologian of the Cross,* Professor Gerhard Forde exposes today's emphasis on "the suffering God" and his identification with human misery as being continents away from the New Testament's teaching on our sin and separation from God, and our redemption as provided through Christ on the cross. "Preachers try to prop up our self-esteem with optimistic blandishments," Forde observes, "but more and more people seem to suffer from a deteriorating sense of self-worth. Perhaps a return to calling a spade a spade has its place."[22] Unless a clear "theology of the cross" is emphasized, notwithstanding "the official optimism of North America," the "theology of glory" will simply evaporate.

Throughout history, different interpretations of Christ's atonement have flourished. But clearly no one theory can grasp the fullness of what Christ wrought on Calvary, any more than any one type of Old Testament sacrifice can comprehend the totality of the saving act. Some in the early church spoke of Christ's death as a ransom paid to Satan. Christ's death is a ransom, as we have seen (Mark 10:45), but not paid to Satan.[23] Others, following Abelard, have seen Christ's death as essentially the great demonstration of love. This perception reflects the moral influence or exemplarist theory of the atonement, and does, in fact, constitute a strand of truth (see Rom. 5:8). Yet underlying this theory is the notion that man's problem is ignorance and he but needs to know the truth. Much thinking about the Cross is predicated on this false premise. A religion of insight and inspiration is not what brings mankind to salvation. We need divine redemption. Stanley Hauerwas' essay is correct: "Love's Not All You Need."[24]

The moral government theory, popularized by Grotius in the Netherlands and in New England theology, enlarges the role of God's righteousness and moral government but provides no transaction by which our sin is dealt with. Too, the governmental view provides for dealing with sin in the future, but how does it deal with the sins of our past? Gustaf Aulen's "Christus Victor" properly underscores Christ's cosmic victory on the cross over sin, death, and the Devil (Col. 2:13–15). But he omits involving Christ's humanity. Vincent Taylor shows that Christ is the representative man—which is true but not sufficient. When the apostle Paul speaks of "Christ who knew no sin being made sin for us in order that we might become the righteousness of God in Him" (2 Cor. 5:21) he is referring to a transaction.

Anselm in the Middle Ages, and more recently James Denney, recognized the transactional element of the Cross. The latter wrote,

> If I were sitting on the end of the pier on a summer day enjoying the sunshine and the air, and someone came along and jumped into the water and got drowned "to prove his love for me," I should find it quite unintelligible. I might be very much in need of love, but an act in no rational relation to any of my necessities could not prove it. But if I had fallen over the pier and were drowning and someone sprang into the water and at the cost of making my peril, or what, but for him, my fate his own, saved me from death, then I should say GREATER LOVE HAS NO MAN THAN THIS. I should say it intelligibly because there would be an intelligible relation between the sacrificial love in action and the necessity from which it redeemed.[25]

The causal connection between Christ's death and our pardon is seen in the satisfaction of both God's wrath and the demands of the law. "What the sin-offering was in the old economy, Jesus is for the sins of his people."[26] Drawing on understandings tracing back to the early fathers of the church,

Anselm posed the ultimatum: either punishment or satisfaction. The juristic understanding of the atonement of Christ, as found in both classical Calvinistic and Arminian thinkers (in which the wrath of God is balanced and honored with the love of God), has tended to yield in our time to philanthropism (in which the love of God eclipses the righteous anger of God). Such thinking exemplifies the triumph of romanticism over the scriptural reality that "Christ died for the ungodly" (Rom. 5:6).[27]

Ethelbert Stauffer states, "The act of reconciliation on the cross is what makes the justification of the sinner possible. No one has seen this point more clearly than Anselm of Canterbury. God is just, He does not cancel the hereditary sin of the centuries, but lays them upon the crucified. And at that point we have a revelation of God's forensic righteousness."[28] Christ is thus the vicarious sufferer of Isaiah 53: "Pierced for our transgressions, he was crushed for our iniquities; the punishment that brought us peace was upon him, and by his wounds we are healed. . . . The LORD has laid on him the iniquity of us all" (vv. 5–6). "He became a curse for us" (Gal. 3:13). "He himself bore our sins in his body on the tree" (1 Peter 2:24). "For Christ died for sins once for all, the righteous for the unrighteous, to bring you to God" (3:18).

Christ as "the atoning sacrifice for our sins" or "the propitiation for our sins" (1 John 2:2) is unpalatable in a time when it is unfashionable to proclaim doctrines of sin and judgment, heaven or hell, wrath and repentance. No one worked harder to excise any notion of the wrath of God demanding satisfaction than the late C. H. Dodd, particularly in his treatment of Romans 3:25ff. Any penal idea of atonement or of the placation of God's wrath is banished by Dodd (in which he is joined by a legion of thinkers such as Donald Baillie, William Neil, etc.), and this view has found its way, under Dodd's influence, into both the *Revised Standard Version* and the *New English Bible*. But Professor Roger Nicole's study shows from Old Testament and intertestamental data that Dodd's stand is untenable.[29] Expiation is not sufficient. Only *satisfaction* is sufficient, before which, as needy and condemned sinners, we can only praise God for "reconciliation through his blood" (Rom. 5:10; 2 Cor. 5:19; Col. 1:19–20, etc.).

> Jesus paid it all,
> All to Him I owe;
> Sin had left a crimson stain—
> He washed it white as snow.
> —Elvina M. Hall, 1868

THE CROSS APPLIED

It is only in the crucifixion of Jesus that all human ideas of God are totally shattered and all religious efforts become worthless. One does not invent such a God. In the story of His Son, God overturns all pretty, wishful images of God by showing total human weakness to be His strength.

—Helmut Thielicke,
The Faith Letters, 1978

How shall I think of the cross and God at the same time? Is it not precisely here that the answer is given, that stands over the whole Christian message: Christ goes through the cross, and only through the cross to life, to the resurrection, to victory? The wondrous theme of the Bible that frightens so many people is that the only visible sign of God in the world is the cross. Christ is not carried away from earth to heaven in glory, but he must go to the cross. And precisely there, where the cross stands, the resurrection is near; even there, where everyone begins to doubt God, where everyone despairs of God's power, there God is whole, there Christ is active and near.

—Dietrich Bonhoeffer

The atoning death of Jesus and his bodily resurrection are the wellspring of blessings to the life of a Christian and to the Church, "which is Christ's body." The applications of redemption shall be here examined, for so magnificently "the cross reveals the inner unity of God's judgment and grace" (G. Berkouwer) and all that they entail. Christ's death and resurrection are the fountainhead and the foundation of redemption, and no theory of salvation will stand that is not firmly fixed there. Certainly the cross is not all of the Christian life, but that life's inception and all of Christian experience are based on the threefold imputation of God's forensic reckoning:

1. the imputation of the sin of our first parents to the whole of their descendent race;
2. the imputation of the sin of the race to the sinless Son of God, who bore it to Calvary;
3. the imputation of the perfect righteousness of Christ to all who repent and believe.

The atonement wrought by Christ is sufficient for all, but efficient for only those who believe.

In chapter 4 it was argued that the love of God is inclusive and that Christ died for all. If this be so and if Christ has paid the debt for each of us, would not God be exacting a double payment from those who are eternally condemned because of unbelief? No one has written more helpfully on this point than A. A. Hodge, building on the foundations of his father, Charles Hodge. There are two kinds of satisfaction: (1) pecuniary or commercial satisfaction, in which the satisfaction is quid pro quo, that is, satisfaction for a debt of $5,000 would be $5,000, plus agreed upon interest. Mercy is not involved in this type of satisfaction; (2) penal satisfaction, in which the judge determines a just equivalent for crimes committed, such as libel, for example. On the satisfaction achieved through the atonement, Hodge writes:

> The penal satisfaction made by the sufferings of Christ to the law and justice of God is, in its own intrinsic value, a full equivalent in the strict rigour of justice for the penal sufferings of all men for ever, and that God accepts and acts upon this satisfaction in the justification of believers in his capacity of Judge, not in the exercise of sovereign prerogative, acknowledging its intrinsic value and full adequacy to the end designed, as a matter of fact, and not by any gratuitous acceptance or gracious estimation, arbitrarily raising the sacrifice up to the level of the law, nor by any sovereign relaxation letting down the law to the level of the substituted penal sufferings.[30]

Thus, "Jesus paid it all," but the application of forgiveness and justification is only efficacious in the lives of those who repent and believe.

A further application of the cross is to be seen in the believer's identification with Christ in his death (cf. Rom. 6:1ff.; Gal. 2:20). Christians are to follow in the steps of the Savior, whose profound sacrifice furnishes us with an example and a principle for living (1 Peter 2:21). "Whoever claims to live in him must walk as Jesus did" (1 John 2:6). It is a great truth, which shall be explored more fully in chapter 12, that the Christian life is a crucified life: "If anyone would come after me, he must deny himself and take up his cross and follow me" (Matt. 16:24). Because "Christ loved us and gave himself for us" (Eph. 5:2), "we ought to lay down our lives for our brothers" (1 John 3:16). The Cross becomes the paradigm of Christian experience (cf. Phil. 2:5ff.). As Christ was, so we must be, and we are privileged to respond,

> When I survey the wondrous cross
> On which the Prince of glory died,
> My richest gain I count but loss,
> And pour contempt on all my pride.
>
> Were the whole realm of nature mine,
> That were a present far too small:
> Love so amazing, so divine,
> Demands my soul, my life, my all.
>   —Isaac Watts, 1707

THE CROSS ACCLAIMED

You with all your elegant diction, do not hinder the teaching of Christ; but we, by mentioning the name of the crucified Christ drive away all the demons whom you fear as gods. Where the sign of the cross appears, their magic is powerless and sorcery ineffectual.

> —Anthony the Hermit, V. Ant. 78

There we leave you in that blessed dependency, to hang upon him that hangs upon the cross.

> —John Donne,
> the last sentence in his final sermon

I've heard a lot of sermons in the past ten years or so that make me want to get up and walk out. They're secular, psychological, self-help sermons. Friendly, but of no use. They didn't make you straighten up. They didn't give you anything hard. . . . At some point and in some way, a sermon has to direct people toward the death of Christ and the campaign that God has waged over the centuries to get our attention.

> —Garrison Keillor

After the bullet of an assassin had killed a secret service agent assigned to protect him, President Harry Truman was asked how he felt about the circumstance. He replied, "I never knew what it meant to have someone die in my place." Since Jesus Christ died for us, the same question could be addressed to us. The preaching of the Cross as "the power and wisdom of God" (1 Cor. 1:23–24) is persuasive when the preaching is authentically biblical. Yet Phillips Brooks, the famous pulpit orator, could give four presentations on *The Influence of Jesus* and never mention the death of Jesus or redemption. Martin Dibelius, the respected scholar, wrote a widely used book entitled *Jesus* that doesn't even hint that God's redemptive purpose sent Jesus to the cross that we might be saved from our sins. These are indeed grievous omissions, but ones that are becoming increasingly typical.

The effects that follow upon Christ's atonement are as follows:

1. Pardon

Sin is the cause of suffering—societal and personal. What can lift the burden of guilt? It is not the psychiatrist's couch but Christ's cross that takes away our condemnation. "Therefore there is now no condemnation for those who are in Christ Jesus" (Rom. 8:1). Pilgrim felt the chains snap and he was free from his unbearable load at Calvary, as Bunyan describes it in *The Pilgrim's Progress:* "His burden fell from off his back, and began to tumble, and so continued to do, till it came to the mouth of the sepulchre, where it fell in, and I saw it no more."[31]

> At the cross, at the cross where I first saw the light,
> And the burden of my heart rolled away—
> It was there by faith I received my sight,
> And now I am happy all the day!
> —Ralph E. Hudson, 1885

2. Purity

In our X-rated society how can we attain purity, which is not native to us? Walking with Jesus on the Calvary road, we can wipe the slate clean, for "if we walk in the light, as he is in the light, we have fellowship with one another, and the blood of Jesus, his Son, purifies us from every sin" (1 John 1:7).

> What can wash away my sin?
> Nothing but the blood of Jesus;
> What can make me pure within?
> Nothing but the blood of Jesus.
> —Robert Lowry, 1876

3. Peace

We live in a complex and turbulent world, but "we have peace with God through our Lord Jesus Christ" (Rom. 5:1). He "made peace through his blood, shed on the cross" (Col. 1:20). When we are reconciled to God, he "cleanses our consciences from acts that lead to death, so that we might serve the living God!" (Heb. 9:14). "He came and preached peace to you who were far away and peace to those who were near" (Eph. 2:17). What other source of peace is there?

> Peace, perfect peace, in this dark world of sin?
> The blood of Jesus whispers peace within.
> Peace, perfect peace, our future all unknown?
> Jesus we know, and He is on the throne.
> —Edward H. Bickersteth, 1875

4. An Obligation to Proclaim

"I am compelled to preach," Paul wrote. "Woe be to me if I preach not the gospel!" (1 Cor. 9:16). Jesus spoke of a vast movement—spiritual empowerment in which "repentance and forgiveness of sins will be preached in his name to all nations" (Luke 24:47). So while "the message of the cross is foolishness [an absurdity] to those who are perishing, to us who are being saved it is the power of God!" (1 Cor. 1:18). Indeed, Paul was constrained "to know nothing except Jesus Christ and him crucified" (2:2).

> Would you be free from your passion and pride?
> There's pow'r in the blood.
> Come for a cleansing to Calvary's tide—
> There's wonderful pow'r in the blood.
> There is pow'r, pow'r, wonder-working pow'r
> In the precious blood of the Lamb.
> —Lewis E. Jones, 1899

5. Opportunity to Praise

Orthodoxy means "right praise." The orthodox doctrine of the atonement naturally issues in songs of praise for the Lamb. The old Moravians spoke of "living in the wounds of Jesus," which meant they pondered the meaning and application of the sufferings of Jesus. The overriding theme of the worship in the book of Revelation is "Worthy is the Lamb, who was slain, to receive power and wealth and wisdom and strength and honor and glory and praise" (5:12).[32] In his great composition on the crucifixion, *The Passion According to Saint Matthew,* Johann Sebastian Bach repeatedly returns to simple four-part chorale tunes that resemble congregational hymns. The "Passion Chorale" appears in five variations, each in a different key and harmonized differently, representing the adoration and worship of deeply moved hearts:

> O sacred Head, now wounded,
> With grief and shame weighed down,
> Now scornfully surrounded
> With thorns Thy only crown;
> How art thou pale with anguish,
> With sore abuse and scorn!
> How does that visage languish
> Which once was bright as morn!
> —ascribed to Bernard
> of Clairvaux, 1090–1153

In awe of and gratitude to our Savior, we all raise our voices in a crescendo of praise:

> The cross it standeth fast,
> Hallelujah, hallelujah!
> Defying every blast,
> Hallelujah, hallelujah!
>
> The winds of hell have blown,
> The world its hate has shown,
> Yet it is not overthrown,
> Hallelujah for the cross!

'Twas here the debt was paid,
Hallelujah, hallelujah!
Our sins on Jesus laid,
Hallelujah, hallelujah!

So round the cross we sing,
Of Christ our offering,
Of Christ our living King,
Hallelujah for the cross!
　　　　　—Horatius Bonar,
　　　　　　　1808–1899

HEART SEARCH

Talk to some believers about the Cross, and gather anecdotes and testi-monies about the power of the cross of Christ. In my own pilgrimage, I was converted at the age of nine after reading family devotions out of Isaiah 53. The Holy Spirit brought Calvary very close. Charles Simeon and J. Hudson Taylor were both saved as the result of contemplating the transference of guilt to the sacrificial victim in the Old Testament. One elderly couple in a congregation I served remembered the ministry of Pastor August Erickson before World War I, because of his preaching of the cross of Christ. I loved to listen to them describe with tears the preciousness of Calvary to their hearts, as recalled so many years later. Bishop Lesslie Newbigin relates that "a vision of the cross" brought him to Christ while a student at Cambridge, "the cross spanning the space between heaven and earth, between ideals and present reality, and with arms that embraced the whole world." Now in advanced years, Newbigin testifies, "I still see the cross of Jesus as the one place in all of the history of human culture where there is a final dealing with the ultimate mysteries of sin and forgiveness, of bondage and freedom, of conflict and peace, of death and life."[33] Keep a notebook of quotes and memories gar-nered from your investigations and on your readings on the Cross. Gather a collection of hymns on the Cross, such as the one by Merrill Dunlop:

Lord, make Calvary real to me!
Jesus, dying in agony,
Thy great sacrifice let me see:
Lord, make Calvary real to me!

8

THE VACANT TOMB

The Groundbreaking

But Christ has indeed been raised from the dead, the firstfruits of those who have fallen asleep. For since death came through a man, the resurrection of the dead comes also through a man. For as in Adam all die, so in Christ shall all be made alive.

—1 Corinthians 15:20–22

In the darkness of this fallen world,
The church is an opening in the wall
Made by the triumphant Cross. . . .
The love of the Trinity never ceases to shine
Through the light of the Resurrection.

—Olivier Clement,
The Living God

This grace was given us in Christ Jesus before the beginning of time, but it has now been revealed through the appearing of our Savior, Christ Jesus, who has destroyed death and has brought life and immortality to light through the gospel.

—2 Timothy 1:9–10

John Wesley was right. The heart of the gospel is the atoning death of the Lord Jesus Christ. It must follow, then, that the resurrection of our Lord is the vascular system, carrying that life and vitality throughout the whole body. The resurrection of Jesus is the capstone of each gospel account. The preaching of the apostles was essentially their eyewitness to the Resurrection.

The proclamation of the apostle Paul was described as concerning "a dead man named Jesus who Paul claimed was alive" (Acts 25:19). Even in his sermon to the intellectuals in Athens, Paul focused on the resurrection of Christ as the guarantee of human accountability in the judgment (17:31). Of the 27 books in the New Testament, 23 attest to the primacy of the Resurrection. It is referred to 104 times in the 260 chapters of the New Testament.

The Resurrection links doctrine and experience; neither will survive without the other. The German scholar C. H. Auberlen demonstrated that the Reformers did not sufficiently emphasize the Resurrection, resulting in a moribund scholastic orthodoxy. By contrast is the ministry of R. W. Dale, longtime pastor of Carr's Lane Chapel in Birmingham in the nineteenth century. An avid student of the Cross, he published his famous lectures on the atonement.[1] While preparing his Easter sermon one year, the thought of the risen Christ broke in suddenly upon him:

> "Christ is alive!" he said aloud to himself. *"Alive! ALIVE!"* he exclaimed. "Can this really be true? How can I live and preach as I do if He is alive?" He got up and walked around saying over and over, "Christ is living! Christ is living!" It was a new discovery. "I had believed it all along but not until then was I sure. I then said: 'My people shall know it!'"[2]

This is the path we need to walk—the vital experience of the living Christ!

FOREGLEAMS OF THE RESURRECTION

Death was the first mystery, it started man on the road to the other mysteries.

—de Coulanges

For the wages of sin is death, but the gift of God is eternal life through Jesus Christ our Lord.

—Romans 6:23

Death as we know it, is both the symbol and the penalty of sin.

—L. S. Thornton

Scarcely into the Old Testament the human race faces the punishment of death as a consequence of its revolt against God. The Lord God had said to Adam and Eve in the garden, "But you must not eat from the tree of the knowledge of good and evil, for when you eat of it you will surely die" (Gen. 2:17), literally, "dying, you shall die." Death as the consequence of sin is to be seen not only as an event but as a state of being. As separation from God, death alienates humankind from God. Physical death is the sacrament of sin, the physical sign of the spiritual reality. Paul wrote, "Therefore, just as sin entered the world through one man, and death through sin, and in this way death came to all men, because all sinned" (Rom. 5:12).

It would seem that if Adam and Eve had obeyed God, they would have been confirmed in righteousness and immortality. In other words, the scourge of physical death is not a biological necessity but is the penalty for transgression. So we human beings throughout our lives "are held in slavery by our fear of death" (Heb. 2:15). Leon Morris observes, "Physical death is perhaps the most spectacular consequence of sin, but the really important thing is that man is now introduced into a different sphere spiritually as well as physically. The stamp of death is on all of his life."[3]

Humankind's loss of position is represented in shame and guilt, as Adam and Eve tried to hide their nakedness from God (Gen. 3:7). They were subsequently banished from the garden lest they eat of the tree of life and live forever in their fallen state (v. 22). Lost though they were, God did not want them to live forever in their lostness. They would have to face the alternative, and certainly, with the violent death of their son Abel, our first parents confronted the awful reality of "the king of terrors." John Milton vividly and graphically depicts the results of human rebellion when the angel shows to Adam subsequent human history and the diary of death (*Paradise Lost,* bk. 11, p. 423ff.). Genesis 5 is like a walk through an old world graveyard, punctuated with the reiterated sound of the death knell, "And he died. . . . And then he died." Every day, we turn a page in the book of our lives, and no one knows how close to the end of our volume this day may be. The clothes we wear to the grave may well be on our backs. As no respecter of persons, death may come suddenly or slowly, violently or softly, but whenever it comes and to whomever it comes, it comes with a sense of violation. Death is "something completely unnatural, an alien, a horror, an enemy."[4]

Yet throughout Scripture it is clear that death is never regarded as the cessation of being. Oscar Cullmann and others remind us that the emphasis of Scripture is not on the immortality of the soul but on the resurrection of the body.[5] Indeed, of the 129 occurrences of the word *resurrection,* 42 are of Christ's resurrection, 27 of the believer being raised with him (8 of miraculous raisings, 3 of the report that John had been raised, and the remainder having to do with "life in one way or another"[6]). It is thus demonstrated that "deliverance from death is associated with the death of Christ," and that the redemption was paid for and procured by the Savior. Thus, "the death of Jesus has been instrumental in delivering men from the sphere of death."[7]

As human beings, we are immortal, that is, the nonmaterial part of us continues to exist, and we enter an intermediate state after death. Belief in immortality and an existence after death is virtually universal,[8] as is the belief that we face judgment and accountability after death. The Vikings, for example, believed that there was a place called Niffleheim where cowards go, forever to sit naked on cakes of ice.

William Wordsworth grasped for "intimations of immortality," but immortality is far more certain than intimations; it is the clear implication in the biblical record. Enoch, who walked with God, was taken up to God before dying (Gen. 5:24). Of Abraham's death it is said, "he was gathered to his people" (25:8). This phrase could not refer to his being placed in the family burial plot, because his grave was a new burial place, which he had obtained for his wife. The death of the patriarch Jacob follows the formula of Abraham: "When Jacob had finished giving instructions to his sons, he drew his feet up into the bed, breathed his last and *was gathered to his people"* (49:33 emphasis added). King David recognized the truth of Scripture: When his and Bathsheba's baby died, David cried out, "I will go to him, but he will not return to me" (2 Sam. 12:23).

Still Job's question reverberates: "If a man dies, will he live again?" (Job 14:14). Job looks forward to a release and a renewal in the future: "All the days of my hard service I will wait for my renewal to come" (14:14). When Job's friends turn their faces against him, he looks death squarely in the eye and finds "a witness is in heaven, my advocate is on high, my intercessor is my friend" (16:19ff.). Beyond "the journey of no return" he sees light and hope (cf. 17:10–16), and in Job 19:25–27 the patriarch exults in his vision:

> *I know that my Redeemer lives, and that in the end he will stand upon the earth. And after my skin has been destroyed, yet in my flesh I will see God; I myself will see him with my own eyes—I, and not another. How my heart yearns within me!*[9]

The Psalms also indicate that the believer can anticipate dwelling forever with God in his house (23:6). There awaits the believer after death his or her seeing the face of God (17:15). Clear indications reinforce the believer's hope of a bodily dimension after death, which is so vital since we have been created body-spirits. So the psalmist rejoices that "my body also will rest secure" (16:9), and this because "you will not abandon me to the grave, nor will you let your Holy One see decay" (v. 10). Peter on Pentecost tells us that the psalmist David refers in the latter instance to Jesus Christ and how "God raised him from the dead, freeing him from the agony of death, because it was impossible for death to keep its hold on him" (Acts 2:24–25).

Of course various resuscitations of the dead, as well as Elijah's being carried to heaven in a whirlwind in a fiery chariot, bespeak the mighty power of God over death and its domain. The prophets speak of resurrection:

> *But your dead will live; their bodies will rise. You who dwell in the dust, wake up and shout for joy. Your dew is like the dew of the morning; the earth will give birth to her dead.*
>
> —Isaiah 26:19

Ezekiel, in his vision of scattered skeletal remains, sees a glorious rising up of the dry bones (37:1–14). This rising up is prophetic of the whole house of Israel, but suggestive of the living God and his predilection for bringing life out of death (which he will dramatically do for Israel in the last times, cf. Rom. 11:15). Daniel, too, paints a glorious picture of a resurrection to come:

> *Multitudes who sleep in the dust of the earth will awake: some to everlasting life, others to shame and everlasting contempt. Those who are wise will shine like the brightness of the heavens, and those who lead many to righteousness, like the stars for ever and ever.*
>
> —Daniel 12:2–3

The preceding passage seems to refer to a physical resurrection for Israel, as Michael (v. 1) stands for those whose names are written in God's Book, which I take as the Book of Life.[10] Although much more can be said about the intermediate and ultimate state after death, such is beyond the purview herein.[11] Yet it can be reasonably asserted that many "foregleams" in the Old Testament only fuel and fortify our hope. Only a rough outline of the hope of resurrection has been presented in Scripture, so we are left longing for a palpable and demonstrated resurrection event. It is all coming in the Lord Jesus Christ.

THE RESURRECTION AS FACT

After his suffering, he showed himself to these men and gave many convincing proofs that he was alive. He appeared to them over a period of forty days and spoke about the kingdom of God.

—Acts 1:3

The reason why the resurrection is so pivotal is that it validates and vitalizes all the other basic doctrines.

—Professor T. A. Kantonen,
The Theology of Evangelism

We did not follow cleverly invented stories when we told you about the power and coming of our Lord Jesus Christ, but we were eyewitnesses of his majesty.
—2 Peter 1:16

In anticipation of postmodernism, Friedrich Nietzsche argued that there are no facts, but only interpretations. Given that the bodily resurrection of Christ is the cornerstone of the Christian faith, it is no wonder that the enemy of our souls unleashes relentless attacks upon the factuality of the historical event. The Resurrection is, after all, the miracle of all miracles. When I came to believe that God raised Jesus Christ from the dead, I had no further doubts regarding the miraculous.

The Scottish empiricist David Hume's (1711–1776) argument against the Resurrection is predicated upon his rejection of all miracles. But what about the testimony of the witnesses? What about the historians at the time of the event? Hume would ask us, "Have you ever seen anyone rise from the dead?" I must answer "no," but I am not arguing for continuous resurrections; I am arguing for *the* Resurrection two thousand years ago, for which there were many witnesses—indeed 517, as cited, 500 of whom were present on one occasion (1 Cor. 15:6). But witnesses are irrelevant to Hume, because along with Renan, he believes that "miracles don't happen." But can we fairly treat any historical data with such scorn? Hume offers no explanation for the phenomena of the New Testament data.

Islam denies the Resurrection and argues, without evidence, that Jesus never really died but that he swooned and revived in the grave. One sect of Islam argues that Jesus prayed to be delivered from death, and that he was, in fact, spared only to die later and be buried in Srinagar in Kashmir. Rudolf Bultmann maintained that "the resurrection itself is not an event of past history. All that historical criticism can establish is that the first disciples came to believe in the resurrection" (in *Kerygma and Myth*), to which G. B. Caird responded, "The first disciples didn't believe that the resurrection is something which happened to them, but an event which happened to Jesus."[12] George Ladd said, "It was not the disciples' faith which created the stories of the resurrection; it was an event lying behind these stories which created their faith. They had lost faith. The fact of the resurrection and faith in the resurrection are inseparable but not identical. The fact created the faith."[13]

Some churchmen, like Donald Rowlingson, deny that the Bible is a valid body of evidence for the Resurrection. Paul Tillich held that the resurrection narratives contain symbols of eternal life, but no historical referent. The German theologian Wolfhart Pannenberg wants to affirm the historicity of Christ's resurrection, but sees the language as metaphorical and will not affirm that the gospel accounts are "fundamentally reliable historically." Because Pannenberg refuses to accept the historicity of the virginal conception of Jesus, and sees the infancy narratives as legend, and denies any propitiatory significance in the atonement, his views leave little more than a few shreds of the supernatural. These massive assaults of unbelief have neutralized much pulpit proclamation and nullified the hope of many people.

Even more radicalism was seen in Hugh Schonfield's *The Passover Plot,* with its convoluted contention that Jesus only feigned death on the cross by taking a drug; and in French Professor Charles Guignebert's argument (with what evidence?) that the body of Jesus was dropped in a ditch and thus disappeared; and in the forty members of the Jesus Seminar who joined behind the assertion of Professor Luedemann that "the resurrection accounts are historically worthless and the product of imagination and fantasy."[14] Such crass unbelief strips the supernatural from the gospel of Jesus, admitting of no hope for time or eternity.

William Willimon would lead us beyond any "objective truth" and propositions to some vacuous experience.[15] Kathleen Norris concludes that "to believe" is a matter of the heart, not the mind. But that statement presents a false dichotomy—believing is in both the mind and the heart. Believing that God raised Christ from the dead (Rom. 10:9–10) does stem from some propositional representations of fact. Alexander Maclaren said, "It is no exaggeration to say that the whole fabric of Christianity and all of Christ's worth as a Witness to God, stand or fall with the fact of his resurrection."[16]

The factual data of the Scriptures are impressive and cumulative:

1. Jesus predicted his resurrection on the third day (John 2:19–22; Matt. 26:61–62; 27:40; Mark 15:29; Luke 27:63–64). The disciples tended not to understand Christ's words and to forget his promises (John 20:9). How about us?
2. The stone at the tomb was displaced. "Who moved the stone?"
3. The tomb that had held the body of Jesus was empty.
4. The grave clothes were undisturbed. The shape of the body was apparent, and the napkin wrapped separately indicated that he was not done yet (John 20:7).
5. The first lie about the resurrection is shared in the New Testament (Matt. 27:64; 28:11–15). If the soldiers had slept, how did they know who came to take the body?
6. The eyewitness accounts of Jesus' appearing after his resurrection are embedded in documents that are told without embellishment and with no effort to describe Christ's appearance. Their unanimous testimony and changed lives strongly reinforce the credibility of the accounts.
7. The shift of the day of worship from Saturday to the first day of the week in the early church is a witness to the confidence of believers in the fact of the bodily resurrection.
8. The witnesses all went to their graves (many facing martyrdom) in unanimous confidence that Jesus Christ was indeed risen from the dead.

Although, as an orthodox Jew, Rabbi Pinchas Lapide does not accept Jesus as the Messiah, he does acknowledge the weight of the evidence for the resurrection. "I accept the resurrection of Easter Sunday, not as an invention of the community of disciples, but as a historical event."[17] Paul speaks for the orthodox Christian view: "And if Christ has not been raised, our faith is futile; you are still in your sins. Then those also who have fallen asleep in Christ are lost. If only for this life we have hope in Christ, we are to be pitied more than all men" (1 Cor. 15:17–18). Our assurance of Christ's resurrection has to be based on more than the sentiment: "You ask me how I know he lives? He lives within my heart." John Updike's lines bespeak fact:

> Make no mistake: if He rose at all
> it was as His body. . . .
> Let us not mock God with metaphor
> analogy, sidestepping, transcendence;
> making of the event a parable,
> a sign painted in the faded credulity of earlier ages:
> let us walk through the door.

FULLNESS OF SALVATION THROUGH THE RESURRECTION

The death and resurrection of Jesus must be seen together; his death is meaningless until God gives it significance by raising him to life. . . . The idea that God's glory is revealed in the death of Christ is perhaps the New Testament's most profound insight into its meaning.
—Morna Hooker,
Not Ashamed of the Gospel

He was delivered over to death for our sins and was raised to life for our justification.
—Romans 4:25

For if, when we were God's enemies, we were reconciled to him through the death of his Son, how much more, having been reconciled, shall we be saved through his life!
—Romans 5:10

God's great plan of salvation and deliverance is like an elegant arch—were one major piece of stone to be removed, it would all collapse and fall into fragments. In speaking of Christ's bodily resurrection, Professor Merrill C. Tenney said, "By this one great fact all theology can be integrated. Revelation, incarnation, redemption, sanctification and eschatology reach their fullest development in the demonstration of the divine triumph over death."[18] James Orr asserts the same: "It seems evident that, if Christ died for men—in atonement for their sins—it could not be that he should remain permanently in the state of death. That, had it been possible, would have been the frustration of the very end of his dying, for if he remained himself a prey to death, how could he redeem others?"[19]

In Romans 4:25 the coupling of the death and the resurrection of Christ as complementary underscores the unity of God's redemptive plan, a plan already suggested in Isaiah 53:11.[20] Death asserts the negative part of the plan and resurrection affirms the positive; they are two sides of the same coin. And they, with their concomitants, being "buried" and being "seen," constitute the heart of the gospel (1 Cor. 15:1–4). Thus the resurrection of Christ becomes the capstone to the work of Christ for us, as indeed he said: "When I am raised to life again, you will know that I am in my Father, and you are in me, and I am in you (John 14:20 NLT).

Thus Christ is the pattern for the Christian life, not only in an outward, but also an inward sense. When we are converted and baptized (which, in apostolic days, were not widely separated in time, cf. Acts 2:41, et al.), we are baptized into Christ's death and resurrection; that is, into a participation and union with Christ. Remember Paul's words:

> Don't you know that all of us who were baptized into Christ Jesus were baptized into his death? We were therefore buried with him through baptism into death in order that, just as Christ was raised from the dead through the glory of the Father, we too may live a new life?
>
> —Romans 6:3–4

Baptized by the Holy Spirit into Christ (1 Cor. 12:11), of which water baptism is the sign, we can walk and serve in "newness of life" (Rom. 6:4; 7:6). Our daily opportunity is thus "to live looking to Jesus," that is, to be exploring and investigating the depths of what it means to be "in Christ and he in us." Thus Tenney correctly speaks of the Resurrection as "the essence and pattern of Christian experience."[21] For Paul, the Christian life emanates from this vital union with the risen Christ: "Since, then, you have been raised with Christ, set your hearts on things above. . . . For you died, and your life is now hidden with Christ in God. When Christ, who is your life, appears, then you also will appear with him in glory" (Col. 3:1).

Thus, "Christ dying for us" and "raised for us" is the foundation of salvation, but our being "crucified with Christ" and being "raised with him" is the fullness. Many are happy that Christ goes to the cross, but how about our going to the cross? This question shall be probed more deeply in chapter 12. But Daniel Whittle's hymn relates the implications of assuming the cross:

> Dying with Jesus, by death reckoned mine;
> Living with Jesus a new life divine;
> Looking to Jesus till glory doth shine,
> Moment by moment, O Lord, I am thine.

THE FORCE OF THE RESURRECTION

I want to know Christ and the power of his resurrection.
—Philippians 3:10

To a man, the New Testament writers believed he had risen. This was indeed the very core of the apostolic *kerygma*. . .it was the theme of every Christian sermon; it was the master motive of every act of Christian evangelism; and not one line of the New Testament was written apart from the conviction that he of whom these things were written had conquered death and was alive forever.
—James Stewart of Scotland,
A Faith to Proclaim

Do not be afraid. I am the First and the Last. I am the Living One; I was dead, and behold I am alive forever and ever! And I hold the keys of death and Hades.
—Revelation 1:18

"May the Force be with you!" has become a familiar catchphrase, with the popularity of George Lucas and his new mythology in the *Star Wars* film series. The "Force" in this science fiction epic is a "mystical energy field from which the Jedi draw their power."[22] But the films present a cosmic conflict: the Jedi Darth Maul became evil, Anakin Skywalker is immaculately conceived, Qui-Gon makes some Zen-like comments about living in the now and counsels, "Feel, don't think." Yet the side of good, because "the Force" is with them, triumphs over evil. Still "the Force" continues to be vague, impersonal, ill-defined, and unknown. In *Phantom*

Menace, the prequel to the original trilogy, "the Force" is mentioned only perfunctorily.

If Lucas is reaching for a quasi-spirituality, it falls far short of the energy and dynamism that transformed the early followers of Jesus Christ and enabled them to make an impact that turned the world upside down (which is to say, right-side up).

The noun "resurrection" (to stand up) occurs 42 times in the New Testament, and with its Greek ex-prefix (to rise up) is found 41 times, for a total of 83 direct references for "resurrection," mainly in the book of Acts. Daniel Fuller insists that "to try to explain [the church] without reference to the resurrection is as hopeless as trying to explain Roman history without reference to Julius Caesar."[23] That Christ rose bodily is a basic doctrinal proposition, but it is more than that. It is also dynamic personal experience. The gospel is anchored, Fuller writes, "not in what happens inside a person, but in the ancient land of Israel 2,000 years ago." But the gospel, including the Resurrection and the Day of Pentecost, is also "Christ in us" through the Holy Spirit (Col. 1:27).[24] The Resurrection is sharing in the life of Christ (John 14:19). Christ bestows the gift of eternal life to all of those who will repent and put their trust in him (John 11:25; 12:24–25). In John's gospel, "eternal life" and "Christ" are virtual synonyms. "Now this is eternal life: that they may know you, the only true God, and Jesus Christ whom you have sent" (17:3).

In a recent book titled *Civility,* Professor Stephen Carter of Yale shows that our culture is decreasing in civility. But Professor Alan Wolfe of Boston University, while in agreement, raises the question, Is it enough to exhort people to be civil?[25] Certainly we need to be nice to each other, but how do societal and personal change take place? What is lacking is empowerment by an adequate moral force, the existence of which is shown in Christ's resurrection. But although Dr. Scott Peck acknowledges sin, if, as he believes, Christ is only a great model of how to live and die, and the Cross is unnecessary, and the Resurrection merely a symbolic story, how does spiritual change take place? Obviously, Scott Peck himself has not found even a modicum of morality in his celebration of relative truth and his claim that "I deviate from traditional Christianity."[26] The devotees of "possibility thinking" warble that "if it's going to be, it's up to me." But the key to change is not to "make your thinking big enough for God to fit in," nor is it "I can choose any dream I want and go for it!" The key is God and his will and his power through the Resurrection, as Richard Bewes of

All Souls, Langham Place, London, celebrated in a memorable sermon entitled "An Unstoppable Force." The messengers of the gospel initiated change, "def[ying] the prevalent mind-set and lifestyle of an entire continent."[27] We who are Christians are the sons and daughters, the children of the Resurrection. We are the heirs of a spiritual and moral detonation that occurred two thousand years ago, the vitality of which still reverberates around the world. Professor Tenney insists,

> God has introduced a new dynamic into the course of human existence, capable of transforming it from a purposeless round of failure into a progressive march toward triumph.[28]

All of the positive outcomes of this dynamic are contingent upon the Resurrection. Thus Jesus said in coming down from the Mount of Transfiguration, "Don't tell anyone what you have seen, until the Son of Man has been raised from the dead" (Matt. 17:9). Because after witnessing Christ risen, no one would be able stop them—they "filled Jerusalem with their teaching about Jesus" (Acts 5:28). And this "power of his resurrection" touches our mortal and frail bodies even now. Paul exults, "And if the spirit of him who raised Jesus from the dead is living in you, he who raised Christ from the dead will also give life to your mortal bodies through his Spirit, who lives in you" (Rom. 8:11). Not just then—but now!

To the Ephesians, Paul writes that "[God's] incomparably great power," operative in us and through us, is nothing less than "the working of his mighty strength, which he exerted in Christ when he raised him from the dead and seated him at his right hand in the heavenly realms, far above all rule and authority, power and dominion, and every title that can be given, not only in the present age but also in the one to come" (1:19–21).

So, indeed, our reliance is not on ourselves, "but on God, who raises the dead" (2 Cor. 1:9b).

THE FUTURE GUARANTEED BY THE RESURRECTION

Praise be to the God and Father of our Lord Jesus Christ! In his great mercy he has given us new birth into a living hope through the resurrection of Jesus Christ from the dead.

—1 Peter 1:3

Jesus always keeps his word. He said he would rise from the dead, and he did; he says that his people also shall rise, and they will.
                                        —Charles Haddon Spurgeon

The affirmation that Jesus rose bodily from the dead on the third day, and that consequently all believers will rise when He appears, is written into the major Christian creeds. It has been the faith of the martyrs and missionaries and is the core of evangelical preaching.
                                        —Merrill C. Tenney

Christianity is a religion of the Resurrection. Believers in Christ in this age experience "the powers of the age to come" breaking through into "this present evil age" (Heb. 6:5). Eternal life has begun (John 3:36; 5:24). Here and now we enter into life through Christ (5:25), but there is coming the full experience and deliverance when "all who are in their graves will hear his voice and come out" (vv. 28–29). Thus we live in expectation that we will "attain to the resurrection from the dead" (Phil. 3:10) and we confess in the Apostles' Creed that "we believe in the resurrection of the body." The resurrection of Christ is "our entry into eschatology," that is, our experience of the life to come. Christians are the people of the future. We are premature ambassadors, the "people before the time," those "on whom the fulfillment of the ages has come."[29]

Christ's resurrection bears on three aspects of our future:

1. Christ's Resurrection Provides the Pattern of Our Identity

"When he appears, we shall be like him, for we shall see him as he is" (1 John 3:2). Christ is "the firstfruits of those who are asleep," and after Christ, "those who are Christ's at his coming" (1 Cor. 15:20–23). At that time the power and deliverance of God will extend to an expression of itself in all of the material creation, which has been sullied by sin (cf. Rom. 8:18–25), even to the bodies of believers who shall be raised in likeness to Christ (Phil. 3:20–21). Any hedging on the bodily resurrection is not acceptable, including any view that argues that the resurrection body of Jesus is "invisible and immaterial."[30] His body had flesh and bones and was as palpable as the fish and honeycomb that he ate—as will be ours. Our new bodies will be raised imperishable, in glory, in power, a spiritual body like his (1 Cor. 15:42–44).

"The day is coming when every cemetery will be in utter disarray and every mausoleum left desolate. Every grave will be burst open and once hallowed crypts will be desecrated."[31] In a world that is "without God and without hope," in the rising of Jesus from the dead we celebrate the birthday of hope.

2. Christ's Resurrection Guarantees Our Moral Accountability

The evaporation of any moral absolutes in our time shows the necessity of the resurrection of Christ, for "if the dead are not raised, 'Let us eat and drink, for tomorrow we die'" (1 Cor. 15:32f.). The Resurrection provides the rationale for Christian morality, in that Christ "through the Spirit of holiness was declared with power to be the Son of God by his resurrection from the dead" (Rom. 1:4). In Jesus the standards for high morals are firm. When Luther was facing moral temptation he cried, *"Vivit! Vivit!"* (He lives! He lives!). Because the Father has committed all judgment to his Son (John 5:22), the fact of his resurrection stands as the guarantee that we are all accountable and responsible. Notice how both Peter in the house of Cornelius (Acts 10:40–43) and Paul in Athens (17:31) associate facing God in judgment with the Resurrection. The Resurrection is the moral linchpin.

3. Christ's Resurrection Provides the Certainty of His Lordship

The resurrection and the Lordship of Christ are interlocked (cf. Rom. 10:9–10). In the New Testament, Jesus is called *Savior* twenty-four times, but he is called *Lord* six hundred times. Because Christ is Lord we can give "the reason for the hope we have" (1 Peter 3:15). Without the resurrection of Christ, there would be no Great Commission (or command) and no promise of the Lord's presence with us "to the very end of the age" (Matt. 28:18–20). Because of the Resurrection, Christ is always contemporary with us, is always our Lord, always will be our Lord. Although persons may claim power over us and will deny the lordship of Christ, yet "everyone who trusts in [Jesus] will never be put to shame (Rom. 10:11). Eugene Peterson said, "everything in the New Testament is done under the pressure of the end—the Lord Jesus Christ is coming back!"[32] And he is coming back to rule as our Lord.

Vainly they watch His bed—
Jesus my Savior!
Vainly they seal the dead—
Jesus my Lord!

Death cannot keep his prey—
Jesus my Savior!
He tore the bars away—
Jesus my Lord!

Up from the grave He arose,
With a mighty triumph o'er his foes;
He arose the Victor from the dark domain,
And He lives forever with His saints to reign.
He arose! He arose! Hallelujah! Christ arose!
—Robert Lowry, 1874

CREATIVE MEDITATION

1. Write a one-page essay stating the case for believing in the bodily resurrection of Christ. Assume your audience is a totally secularized postmodern audience that denies there is such a thing as truth.
2. Try writing some poems and verses in which you sing the wonders and glories of Christ's resurrection. You can write about gospel scenes, a proclamation from the book of Acts, the interpretive passages in the epistles, or the songs of the Revelation.
3. Write a letter to a Jew, a Muslim, a New Ager, an atheist, and a religious liberal, indicating why everyone should believe that God raised Jesus from the dead.

9

THE ASCENSION

The Neglected Doctrine

*When he had led them out to the vicinity of Bethany, he lifted up his hands
and blessed them. While he was blessing them, he left them and was taken
up into heaven.*

—Luke 24:50–51

*After he said this, he was taken up before their very eyes, and a cloud hid him
from their sight. They were looking intently up into the sky as he was going.*

—Acts 1:9–10

The Ascension is that festival which confirms the grace of all the
festivals together, without which the profitableness of every festival would have perished. For unless the Savior had ascended into
heaven, his Nativity would have come to nothing . . . and his Passion would have borne no fruit for us, and his most holy Resurrection would have been useless.

—St. Augustine, *Sermo* 53.4

Thus the distance between the Infinite and the finite is bridged
over by the Incarnation and the Ascension. But the incarnate and
ascended Lord is also *the Lamb of God which taketh away the sin of the
world,* and therefore can mediate not only between the finite and
the Infinite, but between sinners and the all-holy.

—H. B. Swete,
The Ascended Christ

The Ascension can well be called the forgotten event. With Ascension Day following Easter by forty days and always falling on a Thursday, the yearly observance tends to pass largely unnoticed. It is thus one of the most neglected doctrines in theology. The Ascension of Christ, however, carries practical implications for the daily life of the believer in Christ. A fuller understanding of the Ascension will help believers grow in Christian maturity and spirituality.

The Ascension as historical event is described in the biblical accounts. Some have wondered if the cloud that received Jesus out of the sight of the apostles was the Shekinah cloud, which left the temple in 586 B.C., as described by the prophet Ezekiel (Ezek. 8, 10). However the means, Jesus returned to heaven. But where is heaven in what Hubble's Law describes as our infinitely expanding universe? Many have abandoned any idea of heaven or hell as actual locations, and even evangelicals have preferred to speak of heaven more as a person than as a place. The Russian cosmonauts, during their early space walks, said they had not seen God, and scientists write about "Outer Space: What is Out There?"[1] Jesus spoke of heaven as a place (John 14:2). Beyond the earth's atmospheric heaven, and the interplanetary or galactic heavens (all made by God, Gen. 1:1), there is the so-called third heaven, where the power and glory of the omnipresent God are manifested in a special manner and to the ultimate degree.[2] The removal of the spiritual body of Jesus (material enough to be displayed and touched and spiritual enough to pass through solid surfaces) from Earth to the right hand of God places something of this earth somewhere in this universe. Christ is there, although dwelling in the hearts of his own through the Holy Spirit.

The Ascension can be called "the finishing touch" in the work of redemption performed by our Lord (cf. John 16:28). Thus, in its essential bridging, completion, and initiation, we well concur with a medieval Christian who spoke of our Lord's ascension as "the most solemn feast of our Lord Jesus." Probing the doctrine of ascension will reveal its power and relevancy.

CHRIST'S POSITION IN HEAVEN: OUR RULER

> Crown Him with many crowns,
> The Lamb upon His throne:
> Hark! how the heavenly anthem drowns
> All music but its own!

Awake, my soul, and sing
Of Him who died for thee;
And hail Him as thy matchless King
Thru all eternity.

Crown Him the Lord of heav'n!
One with the Father known,
One with the Spirit thru Him giv'n
From yonder glorious throne.

To Thee be endless praise,
For Thou for us hast died;
Be Thou, O Lord, thru endless days
Adored and magnified.
—Matthew Bridges

The ascension of Christ is both end and beginning. The Savior has been received back into heaven, where he has been crowned and exalted. Peter on Pentecost declared that Christ has been "exalted to the right hand of God" (Acts 2:33). The apostle maintained that "God has made this Jesus, whom you crucified, both Lord and Christ" (v. 36). Jesus was certainly Lord and Christ from the Resurrection, but after ascension his universal Lordship is now demonstrated and fully claimed.[3] Jesus had once quoted from Psalm 110:1:

> The LORD says to my Lord:
> "Sit at my right hand
> until I make your enemies
> a footstool for your feet."

The ascension of Christ is another step in the exaltation of the Savior. Paul said, "Therefore God exalted him to the highest place and gave him the name that is above every name" (Phil. 2:9). Christ in his resurrection body arrived in heaven and is seen in heaven. He is back in the glory, the glory given the Son before the creation of the world (John 17:24). His return to glory was the "joy set before him," in terms of which he "endured the cross" (Heb. 12:2).

Jesus anticipated his ascension when he said to his disciples, "What if you see the Son of Man ascend to where he was before?" (John 6:62). When Jesus said to Mary after the Resurrection, "Do not hold on to me, for I have not yet returned to the Father" (20:17), he does not imply that he would ascend on Easter Sunday, but rather that their former relationship was not to be resumed; Jesus knew he was headed for heaven. So Peter asserted, "Jesus Christ, who has gone into heaven and is at God's right hand—with angels, authorities and powers in submission to him" (1 Peter 3:22). Christ has returned home![4] He was received into heaven, his proper destination.

The ascension of Christ is the sign that the Savior is glorified and triumphant. So Paul speaks of "Christ Jesus, who died, yes, who was raised from the dead, who is at the right hand of God" (Rom. 8:34). C. H. Dodd saw the Ascension as essential in the early preaching of the church, because, indeed, "Christ was raised from the dead and seated at (the Father's) right hand in the heavenly realms, far above all rule and authority, power and dominion, and every title that can be given, not only in the present age but also in the one to come. And God placed all things under his feet and appointed him to be head over everything for the Church, which is his body, the fullness of him who fills everything in every way" (Eph. 1:20–22). "He is the head of the body, the church" (Col. 1:18). In heaven he is the living head of the body, of which we are members (1 Cor. 12).

His humiliation is over, and although he still bears "rich wounds above," the Lamb is in the middle of the Throne (Rev. 5:6). Christ has gone into the far country (Luke 19:12), where he is now vice-regent, "sharing in all of the glory and authority and power of the Father."[5] His Ascension and his sitting down show that he is "first before all others" (Col. 1:18–19).

Jesus warned the religious establishment at his trial that they would "see the Son of Man sitting at the right hand of power" (Mark 12:36; 14:62). Believers now see Christ "crowned with glory and honor" (Heb. 2:9) and we "are seated with him in the heavenly realms in Christ Jesus" (Eph. 2:6). Even so, "at present we do not see everything subject to him" (Heb. 2:8).

This age is one of waiting "until." The promised kingdom has not yet been restored to Israel (Acts 1:6; Isa. 9:6–7).[6] But when Christ comes in power and glory, he will set up his kingdom and rule on the Throne of David (Luke 1:32–33). And someday, when we are bodily with Christ in heaven, we shall reign with him (Rev. 3:21).

He waits, seated at the Father's right hand. But although he waits he is not resting. Stephen saw him *standing* (Acts 7:56), thus he is reigning. So there is no excuse for pompous human rulers to be autocratic or assuming. The appropriate response of all persons should be humble submission and worship of our exalted Head. Jesus Christ is Lord, and ultimately "every knee shall bow in heaven and on earth and under the earth, and every tongue confess that Jesus Christ is Lord to the glory of God the Father" (Phil. 2:10–11). But as the "people before the time," we presently bow the knee and confess with our lips his Lordship, our hearts rejoicing in both the present privilege and the eternal prospect. "For he must reign until every enemy is put under his feet" (1 Cor. 15:25). Even now we sing "The Hallelujah Chorus":

> Hallelujah! For the Lord God omnipotent reigneth.
> The kingdom of this world is become the kingdom
> of our Lord and of His Christ;
> And He shall reign forever and ever.
> King of Kings, and Lord of Lords. Hallelujah!
> —G. F. Handel

CHRIST'S PROCESSION TO HEAVEN: OUR FORERUNNER

> When I die, Receive me, I'll cry,
> For Jesus has loved me, I cannot tell why;
> But this I do find, We two are so joined
> He'll not be in heaven and leave me behind.
> —Rowland Hill of London
> (1744–1833)

> Mighty Lord, in Thine ascension
> we by faith behold our own.
> —A. Skevington Wood

I go to prepare a place for you. And if I go and prepare a place for you, I will come again, and receive you to Myself; that where I am, there you may be also.
—John 14:2–3 NASB

The Christian life is from beginning to consummation the following of Jesus Christ. His invitation bids us, "Follow me" (Matt. 4:19; John 21:22).

His death for us left us "an example, that you should follow in his steps" (1 Peter 2:21). That we may "live a new life" (v. 4), in our justification at conversion we are identified with Christ, and in our sanctification we are united with Christ in his death, burial, and resurrection" (Rom. 6:1–11).

The writer to the Hebrews (12:2) speaks of Jesus as the "author" of our faith, or our file leader, our predecessor, the one who takes the lead *(archegos)*. As such, Jesus is our forerunner, leading a vast procession. He is, to use Moffat's translation of Hebrews 12:2, "the pioneer" who goes ahead of us (John 10:4; Matt. 28:7) with the objective of bringing many sons and daughters to glory (Heb. 2:10).

John Pearson, the English theologian who wrote on the Apostles' Creed, recalls what the ascension means for Christ:

> I am fully persuaded, that the only-begotten and eternal Son of God, after he rose from the dead, did with the same soul and body with which he rose, by a true and local translation convey himself from earth on which he lived, through all the regions of the air, through all the celestial orbs, until he came into the heaven of heavens, the most glorious presence of the majesty of God.[7]

Likewise, the Second Helvetic Confession of 1566 teaches the same:

> We believe that our Lord Jesus Christ, in his same flesh, ascended above all visible heavens into the highest heaven, that is, the dwelling place of God and the blessed ones at the right hand of the Father.[8]

Our Lord Jesus returned, then, to the glory in a human body, albeit a resurrection body. His ascension means that our Master has reached the destination to which we by his grace are headed. His arrival there is the guarantee we shall likewise make it there, "where high the heavenly temple stands" (Michael Bruce). Professor John Duncan of New College, Edinburgh—or "Rabbi," as his students called him—said, "The dust of the earth is upon the throne of the majesty on high!" That is, his ascending there and his working there are the guarantee of our being there. "Whoever serves me must follow me; and where I am, there will my servant be. My Father will honor the one who serves me" (John 12:26).

Picture a skilled guide scaling perilous cliffs. Those linked to him follow up the precipitous terrain. Then, at last, the goal is reached; the summit is scaled. What a joyous reunion when all have safely arrived. He is now the anchor of our souls, "firm and secure. It enters the inner sanctuary behind the curtain, where Jesus, *who went before us,* has entered on our behalf" (Heb. 6:19–20). He has gone ahead to prepare abiding places for us and will come to receive us to himself (John 14:2–3). And thus all believers will come at last to the Father's house.

G. Campbell Morgan argues that "the stoop of God to human form was not for a period merely."[9] That he is forevermore one with us is amazing. As the last Adam and founder of a new race, he has been welcomed into the glory (cf. Psalm 24). We never could have made it or qualified for entrance. We find inestimable comfort, as Morgan says:

> The comfort ever comes as we behold on the throne of the Eternal, One who bears amid the dazzling splendour, marks that tell of His having suffered and died for us men, that He might bring us into union with His unending joy and eternal Love.[10]

The early Greek church found great solace and strength in seeing Christ "as the firstfruits." Gregory of Nyssa (c. 330–395) commented on the Savior's words to Mary in John 20:17:

> For this cause, the Mediator between God and man, having assumed the firstfruits of all human nature, sends his brethren the announcement of himself, not in his divine character, but in that which he shares with us, saying: "I am departing in order, by my own self, to make to be your Father, that true Father, from whom you are separated; and by my own self, to make to be your God that true God from whom you had revolted; for by that firstfruits which I have assumed, I am in myself presenting all humanity to its God and Father."[11]

The "firstfruits" is the whole and is offered up to God, sanctifying the whole. So Chrysostom, the "golden-mouth" preacher, declared,

> So he offered the firstfruits of our nature to the Father so the Father admired the gift, and on account of the worth of the offerer and the blamelessness of that which was offered, he received it with his own hands and placed the gift next to him, and said "Sit thou on my right hand."[12]

Similarly, St. Augustine, the Bishop of Hippo, often emphasized that "the going before of the Head is the hope of the members."[13] Our living Head is now in heaven and his loving concern is ever to "feed and care for his church" (Eph. 5:29). Thus he functions for us as prophet and as priest and as king, "the Master behind the veil." B. F. Westcott said,

> The ascension of Christ is, in a word, His going to the Father—to His Father and our Father—the visible pledge and symbol of the exaltation of the earthly into the heavenly. It is emphatically a revelation of the heavenly life, the open fulfillment of man's destiny made possible for all men.[14]

And all of this is encapsulated in what is probably the greatest ascension hymn, that by Charles Wesley. Let us sing it and praise our Lord through it.

> Hail the day that sees Him rise,
> To His throne above the skies;
> Christ the Lamb for sinners giv'n,
> Enters now the highest heav'n.
>
> There for Him high triumph waits;
> Lift your heads, eternal gates,
> He hath conquered death and sin,
> Take the King of glory in!
>
> See, He lifts His hands above!
> See, He shows the prints of love!
> Hark! His gracious lips bestow,
> Blessings on His church below.
>
> Lord, beyond our mortal sight,
> Raise our hearts to reach Thy height,
> There Thy face unclouded see,
> Find our heav'n of heav'ns in Thee!

CHRIST PRAYING IN HEAVEN: OUR INTERCESSOR

Entered the holy place above,
Covered with meritorious scars,
The tokens of his dying love.

Our great High Priest in glory bears,
He pleads His passion on the tree,
He shows Himself to God for me.
—Charles Wesley

Therefore he is able to save completely those who come to God through him,
because he always lives to intercede for them.
—Hebrews 7:25

Five bleeding wounds He bears,
Received on Calvary;
They pour effectual prayers,
They strongly plead for me;
"Forgive him, O forgive" they cry,
Nor let that ransomed sinner die.
—Charles Wesley

The marvel and the mystery of prayer suffuse all of Scripture. This extraordinary, divine provision for living in God's presence and consciously walking before him is a remarkable opportunity for mortals to enjoy access into the very throne chamber and control room of the universe. Such an impressive succession of notable believers (leaders, but humble and obscure servants as well) is described in the Bible as practitioners of prayer, of wrestling and agonizing before God in the throes of what it means to "pray through" (Col. 4:12). Jesus our Lord lived a life of dependence on prayer as the power line to his Father as he, in terms of his subordination to the Father, trusted in him for all things. The invitations to significant and meaningful lives of prayer are found everywhere in Scripture. Hindrances to prayer that prevails are underscored and the efficacy of intercessory prayer in the economy of God are both indicated and empirically illustrated. Prayer is our buried weapon. Prayer is our neglected resource for encountering the enemy of our souls. When Ananias is told to go to the new convert,

Saul of Tarsus (now Paul), the Lord identifies the man by his behavior: "He is praying" (Acts 9:11). Prayer matters much to God and it ought to mean much to us if we truly aspire to the new life in God.

The dedication at the front of this book is to prayer warriors whose ministry, in part, has been to pray for my ministry and my family. With the passing of our parents we have been deprived of some virtually nonstop prayer support. I picture so clearly my ninety-five-year-old father on his knees, praying and pleading on behalf of his children and grandchildren. How we miss our dear parents. Who stands in their stead, who takes their place as a constant prayer warrior?

The importance of the ascension of Christ is his present ministry on our behalf. We need never be deprived of his intercessory support. Many believers, who cherish what Christ has done for them on Calvary and who anticipate with relish what Christ will do for them in the age to come, do not seem to know or appreciate the blessings of his present work for us. Our salvation includes Christ's present work: "For if, when we were God's enemies, we were reconciled to him through the death of his Son, how much more, having been reconciled, shall we be saved through his life!" (Rom. 5:10). *Through His life!*

A little boy asked "Mommy, what does Jesus do all day?" He does many things (including preparing abiding places for us in heaven, [John 14:12ff.]), but foremost among the roles emphasized in the New Testament is his continuous ministry as our great High Priest, interceding for us.[15]

Jesus prays for us as he prayed for Peter in the hour of his duress: "Simon, Simon, Satan has asked to sift you as wheat. But I have prayed for you, Simon, that your faith may not fail" (Luke 22:31). John 17 is sometimes called "the high-priestly prayer" because it is the outpouring of our Lord's intercession for the disciples and for "those who will believe in me through their message" (v. 20). The apostle John assures us that his writings are to encourage us to not sin, "But if anyone does sin, we have one who speaks to the Father in our defense, Jesus Christ, the Righteous One. He is the atoning sacrifice for our sins, and not only for ours but also for the sins of the whole world" (1 John 2:1–2). Christ functions as our advocate with the Father. What an attorney to have in our defense, and he has never once lost a case.

The three appearances of Christ on behalf of his own constitute his work of total redemption:

He entered heaven itself, now to appear for us in God's presence.
—Hebrews 9:24

He has appeared once for all at the end of the ages to do away with sin by the sacrifice of himself.
—Hebrews 9:26

He will appear a second time, not to bear sin, but to bring salvation to those who are waiting for him.
—Hebrews 9:28

We have already seen that Jesus has entered into the holiest of all "on our behalf" (Heb. 6:20). He "always lives to intercede for us" (7:25). In the Incarnation, he was made like us, "that he might become a merciful and faithful high priest in service to God" (2:17). Indeed his competency to perform as our heavenly intercessor is clear, in that "He himself suffered when he was tempted" and is therefore "able to help those who are being tempted" (2:18). We can rejoice in that "we do not have a high priest who is unable to sympathize with our weaknesses, but we have one who was tempted in every way, just as we are, yet was without sin" (4:15). The hairs of our head are numbered, and he is concerned with every aspect of our beings, temporal and eternal. He knows and he cares and he is able to help us.

> Praying for his children
> In that blessed place,
> Calling them to glory,
> Sending them his grace.
> —Frances Ridley Havergal

His priestly ministry of intercession is described aptly in the *Larger Catechism*:

> Christ maketh intercession, by his appearing in our nature continually before the Father in heaven, in the merit of his obedience and sacrifice on earth, declaring his will to have it applied to all believers, answering all accusations against them, and procuring for them quiet of conscience, notwithstanding daily failings, access with boldness to the throne of grace, and acceptance of their persons and their services.[16]

Romans 8:34 sets forth his intercessory work: "Who is he that condemns? Christ Jesus, who died—more than that, who was raised to life—is at the right hand of God, and is also interceding for us." Romans 8:35–39, read in light of Romans 8:34, grants to us further assurance and confidence. Everything that Christ accomplished for us at Calvary and in his resurrection is now daily applied and effected in our lives by virtue of his ascension, and he is seated in perpetually presenting himself before the Father on our behalf.[17] No need for the saints above or our Lady to pray for us. Is there any higher and holier intercession than that of the Son?

> In the hour of trial,
> Jesus, plead for me;
> Lest by base denial,
> I depart from Thee:
> When Thou seest me waver,
> With a look recall,
> Nor for fear or favor
> Suffer me to fall.
>
> With forbidden pleasures
> Would this vain world charm,
> Or its sordid treasures
> Spread to work me harm
> Bring to my remembrance
> Sad Gethsemane,
> Or, in darker semblance,
> Cross-crowned Calvary.
>
> Should Thy mercy send me
> Sorrow, toil and woe,
> Or should pain attend me
> On my path below,
> Grant that I may never
> Fail Thy hand to see;
> Grant that I may ever
> Cast my care on Thee.
>   —James Montgomery, 1834

CHRIST PARDONS FROM HEAVEN: OUR MEDIATOR

Day after day every priest stands and performs his religious duties; again and again he offers the same sacrifices, which can never take away sins. But when this priest had offered for all time one sacrifice for sins, he sat down at the right hand of God.

—Hebrews 10:11–12

The Father hears Him pray,
His dear anointed One,
He cannot turn away
The presence of His Son.
The Spirit answers to the blood
And tells me I am born of God.
—Unknown

He is not a man like me that I might answer him,
that we might confront each other in court.
If only there were someone to arbitrate between us,
to lay his hand upon us both.
—Job 9:32–33

That "Christ entered his new work as the last Adam in his resurrection from the dead"[18] is vital to every phase of Christian experience and growth.

He now functions as "the life-giving spirit" (1 Cor. 15:45). Indeed, after he had given up his spirit to his Father on the cross, he preached to the spirits in prison (1 Peter 3:18–20); that is, he went to announce his victory on Calvary, to both those in Hades and those in paradise in the lower parts of the earth. In his ascension, he transferred "the spirits of just men made perfect" (the Old Testament saints) to their new venue in the third heaven, whence deceased believers now go (Phil. 1:23; 2 Cor. 5:6–8). Paul tells us that when Christ ascended, "he led captives in his train" (Eph. 4:8ff.); that is, he both descended and then ascended with a host of saints. Is this the explanation of the cryptic reference in Matthew 27:51–53 to "holy people" who came out of the graves and appeared in Jerusalem after Christ's resurrection?

In Christ's sacrifice on the cross atonement for our sins was finished—completed (John 19:30; Heb. 9:26, etc.). Scripture refutes any notion of the perpetual sacrifice of the Mass, or any idea that Christ entered the heavenly sanctuary in 1844 to cleanse it by an investigative judgment of believers' sins, which had to be completed before the Second Advent. Such belief contradicts what the writer to the Hebrews makes plain in 9:12: "He entered the Most Holy Place once for all by his own blood, having obtained eternal redemption." This entrance he made upon his ascension to heaven, and, as we have seen, "When this priest had offered for all time one sacrifice for sins, he sat down at the right hand of God" (10:12). There is no doctrine that Satan detests more than that of the finished work of Christ on Calvary and the saving and sanctifying efficacy of his shed blood.[19]

Christ now functions in his mediatorial and priestly office from his throne. John Calvin agrees:

> The priestly office belongs to Christ alone because by the sacrifice of his death he blotted out our own guilt and made satisfaction for our sins. . . . We or our prayers have no access to God, unless Christ, our High Priest, having washed away our sins, sanctifies us and obtains for us that grace from which the uncleanness of our transgressions and vices debars us.[20]

Thus we pray, believing in the name of our Lord Jesus Christ, in recognition of his mediatorial office (1 Tim. 2:5). Notice again that he functions by virtue of the atoning sacrifice made for humankind. He makes our prayers acceptable to God and a sweet-smelling savor before God. He offers what we cannot offer (Rom. 8:26–27). As Toon makes clear, believers celebrate the "indivisible priesthood of Christ" by serving him "in and through His Spirit" (1 Peter 2:8), and we are therefore recipients of his blessing from heaven.[21]

Thus the ascension has been called "Christ's triumphant certification as the Savior of the world!" (J. Theodore Mueller). His is now "the joy set before him" (Heb. 12:3). "He will see the result of the suffering of his soul and be satisfied," or, as the Jerusalem Bible puts it, "and be content" (Isa. 53:11). It is his great pleasure to act on our behalf, delighting in every advance of his church and in every precious soul converted.

CHRIST'S PRESENCE IN HEAVEN: OUR SUSTAINER

And surely I am with you always, to the very end of the age.
—Matthew 28:20

When he ascended on high, he led captives in his train and gave gifts to men.
—Ephesians 4:8

Whoever believes in me, as the Scripture has said, streams of living water will flow from within him. By this he meant the Spirit, whom those who believed in him were later to receive. Up to that time the Spirit had not been given, since Jesus had not yet been glorified.
—John 7:38–39

Exalted to the right hand of God, he has received from the Father the promised Holy Spirit and has poured out what you now see and hear.
—Peter on Pentecost, Acts 2:33

One critical facet of the Ascension in relation to the Christian life remains to be surveyed—the ascended and glorified Christ who pours out the Holy Spirit on the Day of Pentecost and presides over the profusion of the Spirit throughout the church age. We must remember that the Holy Spirit is commissioned in this age to bear faithful witness to the Lord Jesus Christ. He is the heavenly photographer, who is ever presenting the image of the Savior (John 14:16–17, 26; 15:26; 16:13–15). But if the divine photographer is going to present the picture of Christ, Christ as the proper subject must be in his right place, and that place is seated at the right hand of the Father. Hence, the Holy Spirit could not pursue his mission until Jesus was in his rightful place.

Although Christ is bodily in heaven and awaits his bodily return to earth (1 Thess. 4:13–18), he is present in the world and indwells every believer (Col. 1:27) through the Holy Spirit (cf. Rom. 8:9). By virtue of his participation in the triune nature of God, Christ as God is omnipresent, but in his human nature he is limited in location, just as in his human nature he died, which as God he could not do.

John Walvoord quotes W. H. Griffith Thomas regarding Christ and the Holy Spirit:

It is essential to preserve with care both sides of this truth. Christ and the Spirit are different yet the same, the same yet different. Perhaps the best expression we can give is that while their Personalities are never identical, their presence also is.[22]

The Lord Jesus—himself overshadowed and undergirded by the Eternal Spirit through his earthly ministry from his virginal conception to the ascension, now glorified—pours out the promised Holy Spirit (Isa. 44:3–5; Joel 2:28–32). G. Campbell Morgan says:

> Having accomplished that mediatorial work through which man may in the value of His death be brought back to God, He now commences that Mediatorial work through which God the Holy Spirit may come back in relation to man, for the administration of the virtue of his life.[23]

Thus the ascended Christ pours out the Holy Spirit, who administers and applies all the benefits and blessings of the redemptive work of Christ. Captured by Lewis Sperry Chafer in his *Systematic Theology* and expounded upon by John Walvoord is Christ's relationship to his church through the Holy Spirit:[24]

1. the last Adam and the new creation;
2. the head and the body;
3. the shepherd and the sheep;
4. the vine and the branches;
5. the chief cornerstone and stones of the building;
6. the high priest and the royal priesthood;
7. the bridegroom and the bride.

Thus are all believers in relation to the Lord Jesus in this age. Jesus, then, is among his people (Matt. 18:20), and is among us in a special way when we remember him in the Lord's Supper (1 Cor. 10:16), a memorial whereby H. B. Swete feels we experience "our nearest approach to the worship of heaven."[25] In Revelation 1–3 we see the living Christ walking among the lampstands—his churches—and seeking admittance where he is excluded (Rev. 3:20). So our ascended Lord works all manner of good things for us from the throne, but is not absent from us. He will yet come again, but in the meantime, in the face of all adversity, he is the one "who gives me strength" (Phil. 4:13). What a glorious and overflowing provision for our every need.

F. B. Meyer used to tell a story about his dog. Dr. Meyer felt great affection for his dog, but Mrs. Meyer resisted the idea of the dog being fed from the table by family members. So Dr. Meyer trained the dog to sit underneath the dining room table just in front of the doctor's knees. When the dog wanted a little bite to eat, he would place his paw on Dr. Meyer's knee and eagerly await the distribution. Again and again, master and dog would interact, with choice morsels being supplied in the outwardly unseen transaction of grace. This is something like the believer's reliance on the daily and abundant distributions of the Lord's grace.

> Day by day Thy mercies, Lord, attend me,
> O what comfort in this hope to rest!
> All that Thou in love divine dost send me,
> Draws me Savior, closer to Thy breast.
>
> Thou does love more tenderly than ever
> Earthly father careth for his own;
> Sorrow's heavy burden Thou will never
> Suffer me to carry all alone.
>
> Thro' life's devious paths Thou e'er wilt guide me,
> For each need will give me plenteous grace;
> In temptation's storms wilt safely hide me,
> Till in glory I behold Thy face.
>
> Thou hast promised for each day and hour
> Grace to trust, and strength to do Thy will:
> 'As thy day is, so shall be thy power,'
> This the gracious word Thou speakest still.
>
> O what joy, beneath Thy heav'nly favor,
> Trustingly to rest my soul in Thee;
> Help me, Lord, that I may never waver,
> Nor forget Thy loving care for me.
>
> For I know, no matter what betide me,
> Thou wilt ever hold me by the hand;
> With Thy presence, Savior, here to guide me,
> I shall reach at last the goodly land.
>   —Lina Sandell (Swedish, 1865)

THINK AND THANK

Both verbs, *think* and *thank,* come from the same Anglo-Saxon root. Robert E. Coleman, in his beautiful *Singing with the Angels,* uses the hymns of worship in the book of Revelation to convey the praises heard around the throne (see 4:8, 11; 5:9–10, 12, 13–14; 6:10; 7:10, 12; 11:15, 17–18; 12:10–12; 15:3–4; 19:1–4, 6–7).[26] Look at each one and rejoice.

Enter his gates with thanksgiving and his courts with praise!
—Psalm 100:4

THE LIFE-GIVING SPIRIT

The Divine Barrister

But as for me, I am filled with power, with the Spirit of the LORD, and with justice and might, to declare to Jacob his transgression, to Israel his sin.
—Micah 3:8

The Holy Spirit is more than a synonym for warm feelings.
—Regin Prenter,
Spiritus Creator

The Spirit of life and of witness is the source and power of the Church's address to the world.
—Roland Allen,
Pentecost and the World

If you then, though you are evil, know how to give good gifts to your children, how much more will your Father in heaven give the Holy Spirit to those who ask him!
—Luke 11:13

For if you live according to the sinful nature, you will die; but if by the Spirit you put to death the misdeeds of the body, you will live, because those who are led by the Spirit of God are sons of God.
—Romans 8:13–14

The fifty days between the Resurrection and the Ascension were times rich in instruction and prayer. There is no record of a single convert during this time. But on the Day of Pentecost, when the Holy Spirit was poured out on the waiting believers, three thousand were converted and a glorious harvest of souls began in the flood tide of spiritual power.

The principle of the spiritual life is enunciated in Zechariah 4:6, "'Not by might nor by power, but by my Spirit' says the Lord Almighty." To better understand the implications of this passage, it is important that "the[se] word[s] of the Lord to Zerubbabel" are placed in their original context. Zerubbabel was the civil governor of the contingent of exiles who returned from captivity, as described in the book of Ezra. He had royal blood in his veins and, in contrast to his compatriot, Joshua the High Priest, had a Babylonian name. We see his name in the genealogy of our blessed Lord (Matt. 1:12).

The dilemma of Zerubbabel was his alleged incompetence. In 537 B.C. the exiles had renewed sacrifice and laid the foundations for the new temple in 536 B.C., but for sixteen dreary years, nothing else happened. Other priorities took over and, amid much criticism and carping against him, Zerubbabel was a desolate and defeated leader. Then the Lord gave Zechariah a dream of two beautiful olive trees, whose fragrant oil flowed down into a gigantic bowl from which a network of pipes carried the oil into the seven lamps and brought illumination and witness. The lampstand doubtless represents the witness and testimony of God's people; the great bowl, the fullness of the divine supply; the oil, the Holy Spirit. Marcus Dods comments:

> The multiplied channels speak not only of abundant, unceasing, spontaneous, free and inexhaustible supply, but of perfect fullness of communication.[1]

Out of his fullness, our Lord Jesus pours out the Spirit. We are the little wicks, unnoticed in the flame we yield. And like wicks, we are without any power in ourselves, smoking, charring, burning out, in regular need of trimming and in constant need of the oil that flows. Zechariah 4:7 shows how God's intervening empowerment would enable his drained and discouraged servant to see a mountain of difficulty reduced to a level plain. With God's power, Zerubbabel would see the project through to completion and hear the praises of God's people lifted to the Lord.

Are we sometimes appalled by our own sense of insignificance and spiritual impotence? Is our awareness of our own inability paralyzing us with a heavy sense of futility and frustration? We must come to the divine source for Christian service, the lifeblood of Christian holiness and character. Our total dependence on God the Holy Spirit needs to be underscored and reinforced in all of our lives.

> Moment by moment I'm kept in his love;
> Moment by moment, I've life from above
> Looking to Jesus till glory doth shine;
> Moment by moment, dear Lord, I am Thine.
> —Major D. W. Whittle

THE HOLY SPIRIT AND TRUTH

Surely it is God's Spirit within people, the breath of the Almighty within them, that makes them intelligent.
—Job 32:8 NLT

Jesus said, "If you hold to my teaching, you are really my disciples. Then you will know the truth, and the truth will set you free."
—John 8:31–32

I have much more to say to you, more than you can now bear. But when he, the Spirit of truth, comes, he will guide you into all truth.
—John 16:12–13

We have renounced secret and shameful ways; we do not use deception, nor do we distort the word of God. On the contrary, by setting forth the truth plainly we commend ourselves to every man's conscience in the sight of God.
—2 Corinthians 4:2

This is good, and pleases God our Savior, who wants all men to be saved and to come to a knowledge of the truth.
—1 Timothy 2:3–4

Pontius Pilate asked the question of the ages: "What is truth?" But Pilate then, as Francis Bacon noted, turned on his heel and didn't wait for Jesus to answer.

The search for truth and the claim of truth are the foundations of all of life. Our daily newspaper is running ads on television claiming that "we are committed to telling the truth." Without the truth, communication and commerce are impossible. Truth, by definition, is statements and words that correspond to reality; or, more ultimately, truth is statements and words that correspond to the mind of God.

Much in modern theology, however, depreciates the cognitive dimension of the gospel regarding truth. So the deity and personality of the Holy Spirit (the ontological) are neglected in favor of the work and purpose of the Holy Spirit (the functional). Process theology tends to be "vague, general, and abstract" with respect to the Spirit, and neo-orthodoxy, or existential theology, either ignores the Holy Spirit (as in Rudolf Bultmann) or freely expresses doubt and uncertainty about the metaphysical (as in Karl Barth and Emil Brunner).[2] Rather should we affirm that the Christian doctrine of the Holy Spirit is "the belief that there is a spiritual dimension to reality, and a supernatural as well as natural way to discern truth."[3] Even as our Lord Jesus is the truth as well as the life, so the Holy Spirit is "the Spirit of truth" as certainly as he is "the Spirit of life."

Since all truth is God's truth, the Holy Spirit, in "common grace," is concerned with humanity as a whole, and "maintains in a measure the moral order of the universe, and distributes in varying degrees gifts and talents among men, promotes the development of science and art, and showers of untold blessing upon the children of men."[4] But beyond manifesting the goodness and benevolence of God to all of his creatures, the Holy Spirit enhances and enriches insight and savvy in those who are his by way of redemption (cf. Ex. 28:3; 31:3; 35:31). This ministry of the Holy Spirit is "the divine spirit of wisdom and understanding and knowledge." This "wisdom which is from above" is, in fact, the practical knowledge of the will of God as applied to life's situations, that is, the best means to the divinely appointed end (cf. James 1:5). Such may well have been an original gift to humankind, but now, weakened by sin, is restored as part of the redemption of God (cf. Isa. 11:2–4; Luke 2:40; Acts 6:3, etc.).

While the Holy Scriptures possess clarity and convey meaning to every sincere reader (the doctrine of the perspicuity of Scripture), unregenerate readers have an inherent inability to grasp the larger and fuller meaning of the divine revelation. So Paul saw the Israelites as having a "veil remaining when Moses is read" (2 Cor. 3:14–15). The message of divine wisdom clashes with the wisdom of this world, but as the apostle notes, "whenever anyone turns to the Lord, the veil is taken away" (v. 16):

None of the rulers of this age understood it, for if they had, they would not have crucified the Lord of glory. However, as it is written: "No eye has seen, no ear has heard, no mind has conceived what God has prepared for those who love him"—but God has revealed it to us by his Spirit.
—1 Corinthians 2:8–10

In the above passage, Paul shows us how "the Spirit searches all things, even the deep things of God" (v. 10). There are, indeed, "Satan's so-called deep secrets" (Rev. 2:24), but the Holy Spirit alone "knows the thoughts of God." The truth as revealed by God as well as the rich insights into these truths are impossible for and inaccessible to "the man without the Spirit" (v. 4). In fact, "they are foolishness to him, and he cannot understand them, because they are spiritually discerned." But "the spiritual man makes judgments about all things" (v. 15). Indeed "we have the mind of Christ" (v. 16). The Holy Spirit is our teacher and we can thus always be in the presence of the divine author of Scripture as we search the Scriptures and express these truths "not in words taught by human wisdom but in words taught by the Spirit, expressing spiritual truths in spiritual words" (v. 13).

Nicodemus, a teacher in Israel, is a good example of humans needing the Spirit to divine truth. Nicodemus comes to Jesus (John 3:1ff.) with cautious compliments. Even though he probably knows much of the Old Testament by heart, he does not grasp the most elementary necessity for the spiritual life when our Lord insists on spiritual rebirth "through water and the Spirit" (cf. John 3:5; Ezek. 36:24–32). Nicodemus thinks Jesus is talking about obstetrics. Jesus tells him the truth about being born again, which is clear in the Scripture Nicodemus knew. But our Lord had to contend with Nicodemus's limitation: "I have spoken to you of earthly things," said Jesus, "and you do not believe; how then will you believe if I speak of heavenly things?" (3:12).

Do we know the Holy Spirit as our teacher, our guide into truth, the witness to the veracity and potency of the Word of God?[5] With the Reformers we affirm the ministry of the Spirit as the internal witness to our certainty that the Bible is the Word of God (John 15:26; 1 John 5:6–12). As Bernard Ramm shows,

> Therefore, the Sacred Scriptures are taken intimately into the very bosom of the testimonium so that he who says "Abba Father" will eventually say "this Book is God's truth." He who has the part shortly possesses the whole.[6]

Thus we earnestly pray,

> More about Jesus let me learn
> More of His holy will discern;
> Spirit of God, my teacher be,
> Showing the things of Christ to me.
> —E. E. Hewitt

So the Holy Spirit opens God's truth to us—and we are taught by God (Luke 7:40; John 8:28).

THE HOLY SPIRIT AND CONVERSION

And if anyone does not have the Spirit of Christ, he does not belong to Christ.

—Romans 8:9

The Holy Spirit adjusts us to God.

—Irenaeus

There is no more of *power* than of merit in man; but as all merit is in the Son of God, so all power is in the Spirit of God; and therefore every man, in order to believe unto salvation, must receive the Holy Ghost.

—John Wesley

The Holy Spirit is the ultimate fact of Revelation and the unique force in Redemption.

—Samuel Chadwick

But when the kindness and love of God our Savior appeared, he saved us, not because of righteous things we had done, but because of his mercy. He saved us through the washing of rebirth and renewal by the Holy Spirit, whom he poured out on us generously through Jesus Christ our Savior, so that, having been justified by his grace, we might become heirs having the hope of eternal life.

—Titus 3:4–7

The conversion of the sinner who is "dead in trespasses and sins" (Eph. 2:1–4) consists of "turning from idols to serve the living God" (1 Thess. 1:9–10); of "crossing over from death to life" (John 5:24); of becoming "a new creation in Christ" (2 Corinthians 5:17); of "being rescued from the dominion of darkness and brought into the kingdom of the Son he loves, in whom we have redemption, the forgiveness of sins" (Col. 1:13). Conversion is bridging the chasm from eternal lostness to the new life in Christ. It is repenting of our sins and entering into eternal life.[7] It is receiving the gift of God.

Though the format of the conversion experience may vary, the theology of conversion is the same for every person who comes to Christ. The Holy Spirit without exception initiates and applies the new life in salvation. At every step in the process of conversion, the Holy Spirit is involved and proactive.

1. The Holy Spirit Convicts of Sin

Even in Old Testament times (where the ministry of the Spirit is referred to in at least eighty-eight passages), the Holy Spirit wrestles and contends with the power of sin in humans (Gen. 6:3). Stephen indicated that God's people had always "resisted the Holy Spirit" (Acts 7:51ff.). In the New Testament, the Holy Spirit is seen as the one who restrains "the secret power of lawlessness" (2 Thess. 2:7). The Lord expressly spoke of the Holy Spirit's ministry of conviction in our age:

> *When he comes, he will convict the world of guilt in regard to sin and righteousness and judgment: in regard to sin, because men do not believe in me; in regard to righteousness, because I am going to my Father, where you can see me no longer; and in regard to judgment, because the prince of this world now stands condemned.*
>
> —John 16:8–11

Three solemn activities preoccupy the Holy Spirit in dealing with human hearts: He convinces, reproves, and supplies conclusive evidence regarding 1) the criminality of unbelief, 2) the availability of righteousness, and 3) the finality of Satan's defeat.[8] An example of the convicting work of the Holy Spirit (in collusion with conscience) is seen after Peter's preaching on the Day of Pentecost. In Acts 2:37, we read that "when the people heard this, they were cut to the heart and said to Peter and the other apostles: 'Brothers, what shall we do?'" The moral consciousness of the listeners was pierced with "the sword of the Spirit which is the Word of God." Even the word used to describe how the soldier pierced the body of Jesus on the cross is not as strong as the word used here in Acts 2:37. This word means to utterly penetrate. True enough, Peter reasoned and sought to persuade, but "afterwards there was the divine penetration that went straight through—beyond their reasoning power into their being."[9]

While we dipped into the Calvinistic vocabulary for the term *common grace* to describe the generic work of the Spirit in enabling and enhancing humankind, so we may profitably dip into the Arminian vocabulary for the term *prevenient grace* to describe that presoteric work of the Spirit, what John Owen, the ardent predestinarian, called "the work of the Holy Spirit preparatory to regeneration."[10] The Spirit is "in, with, and under the Word" as it works on the sinner's heart, sometimes over a period of many years. Consider the case of the apostle Paul, who found it hard "to kick against the goads" (Acts 26:14). Similarly, Augustine resisted the Spirit's many gracious and pain-inducing overtures until he, too, at last yielded.

2. The Holy Spirit Facilitates Repentance and Faith

The Christian urges hearers "that they must turn to God in repentance and have faith in our Lord Jesus Christ" (Acts 20:21); that is, one must come to the Lord with true penitence and sorrow for sin, and trusting completely and with one's whole soul in the sufficiency of the Lord Jesus Christ and his saving work. A reduction of this call for response occurs only when the listener is in such manifest, broken helplessness as to make insistence on repentance superfluous, as in the case of the desperate jailer in Philippi (Acts 16:31).

Given our moral and spiritual deficiency, it would be folly to think that, unaided, we would respond to the call in repentance and faith. Saving faith, involving insight, consent, and commitment, is a big order for the likes of us. Yet Warfield is correct in defining such faith as "trustful appropriation of Christ and the surrender of self to Him."[11] This reliant trust and its complement, repentance—our profound admission of need and sorrow for our sins—are not of our own making. True, we are called to repent and believe, but it does not follow that we are capable of doing so; Scripture calls us to do many things of which we are not capable. If we were capable,

"How shall we account for the asserted fact, that the will inalienably able to turn at its option from its sins to God, in point of fact never does and never will so turn, *except under the persuasive action of the Holy Spirit?*"[12] Thus, repentance must ultimately be seen as an unmerited gift (Acts 11:18; Rom. 2:4). So also faith (Eph. 2:8).

Yet as the Holy Spirit works on us through the Word, we are clearly responsible and culpable in the decision-making process (Rom. 10:17). Even John Owen concedes that "there are some things required of us in a way of duty, which are so in the power of our natural abilities, as that nothing but corrupt prejudices and custom in sinning keep men from the performance of them."[13] Being dead in sin does not mean that we are incapable of deciding whether to drive according to the speed limit or be faithful to our spouses. So Jesus said, "You refuse to come to me to have life" (John 5:40), and he wept over Jerusalem and said "but you were not willing" (Matt. 23:37). Jesus did not weep crocodile tears. I concur with John Owen: "Common illumination and conviction of sin have a tendency to conversion; and whereas this end is not attained, it is from the willfulness and stubbornness of the mind."[14]

3. The Holy Spirit Regenerates the Sinner

Professor Timothy Smith of Johns Hopkins University has shown how George Whitefield and John Wesley, as well as evangelical Lutherans and Anglicans, hold to "the same basic stance on the primacy of the experience of the new birth."[15] Jesus promised life to the languishing and this new life is nothing less than the very life of God given to us in Christ through the Holy Spirit. It is nothing less than "the morally transforming experience of saving grace"; it is "participation in the divine nature" and thereby escaping "the corruption in the world caused by evil desires" (2 Peter 1:4). Eternal life is thus actually the present possession of the child of God. Notice the present tense in John 3:36 and 5:24 and elsewhere. We are new creatures in Christ with a new nature. Have you been born "from above"?

4. The Holy Spirit Indwells Us

Christ is "in us" in that the Holy Spirit has taken up residence "down deep in our hearts by faith" (Eph. 3:17). "Do you not know that your body is the temple of the Holy Spirit, who is in you, whom you have received from God?" (1 Cor. 6:19).

Andrew Murray, writing on "The Temple of the Holy Spirit," exhibits awe:

> I will meditate and be still, until something of the overwhelming
> glory of the truth fall upon me, and faith begin to realize it: I am His
> Temple and in the secret place He sits upon the throne. I do now
> tremblingly accept the blessed truth: God the Spirit; the Holy Spirit;
> who as God Almighty dwells in me. O my Father, reveal in me what
> it means, lest I sin against Thee by saying it and not living it.[16]

5. The Holy Spirit Certifies Our Salvation

While many of the Puritans denied immediate assurance of salvation (feeling it was presumptuous), it seems clear that knowing we belong to Christ is a birthright of the believer and a singular ministry of the Holy Spirit.[17] Again, the Holy Spirit through the Word "testifies with our spirit that we are God's children" (Rom. 8:16). John wrote his first letter that his readers "might know" that they have eternal life (1 John 5:13). Ridout is correct that "God does not leave His work without his stamp upon it."[18] God's stamp is the sealing of the Holy Spirit. The ministry of Jesus had the seal of God's approval upon it (cf. John 6:27), and upon regeneration the believer is sealed with the Spirit (Eph. 1:13; 4:30; 2 Cor. 1:21–22). The presence of the Holy Spirit in the believer's life is the guarantee, the pledge, of our everlasting inheritance.[19] "Come Holy Spirit, with all thy quickening powers!"

THE HOLY SPIRIT AND THE COMMUNITY OF GRACE

And on this rock I will build my church, and the gates of Hades will not overcome it.
                                                        —Matthew 16:18

For we were all baptized by one Spirit into one body—whether Jews or Greeks, slave or free—and we were all given the one Spirit to drink.
                                                        —1 Corinthians 12:13

In him the whole building is joined together and rises to become a holy temple in the Lord. And in him you too are being built together to become a dwelling in which God lives by his Spirit.
                                                        —Ephesians 2:21–22

> *. . . and the fellowship of the Holy Spirit.*
> —2 Corinthians 13:14

When sinners become children of God (John 1:11–12), they are simultaneously incorporated into the spiritual body of which Christ is the head. Lewis Sperry Chafer has shown that thirty-eight or so different states of being are realized at conversion—we are justified, adopted, reconciled. . . . The Holy Spirit was active in Old Testament times, touching the life of every creature (Abraham Kuyper) and yet not indwelling individuals as in our age or creating a spiritual organism such as the church.[20] Certain Old Testament saints were temporarily endued for specific ministries, but our Lord plainly foresaw, as he did the Pentecostal effusion (fulfilling part of Joel 2:28ff.), a new relationship with the Spirit, "for he lives with you and shall be in you" (John 14:17).[21]

A very special and unique ministry of the Holy Spirit began at Pentecost with the birth of the Christian church, which has extended now for almost two thousand years and will reach until the translation of the Bride of Christ (1 Thess. 4:13–18). As was discussed in the previous chapter, with the completion of the terms of Christ's earthly incarnation, in his sinless life, substitutionary death, and victorious resurrection, he returned to heaven. Christ had fully expounded and exhibited the truth of God in time and space. As he said, "I came from the Father and entered the world; now I am leaving the world and going back to the Father" (John 16:28). In the power of the Holy Spirit, he now constitutes the church, which is Christ's body, of which he is the living head in heaven. Now the Holy Spirit multiplies the impact of the living Christ through believers everywhere in the world. The exhibition and exposition of God's truth are now scattered everywhere and "greater works than these" will be possible in and through the church.[22] What Jesus began to do and to teach continues in the book of Acts (cf. 1:1), which must be regarded as an unfinished volume. His actual life is in us through the Holy Spirit. As Paul exclaimed,

> *I have been crucified with Christ and I no longer live, but Christ lives in me. The life I live in the body, I live by faith in the Son of God, who loved me and gave himself for me.*
> —Galatians 2:20

On the Day of Pentecost the waiting and praying followers of Jesus were empowered and baptized by the Spirit of God into the New Covenant community, the church (1 Cor. 12:13). It is accurate, then, to speak of the baptizing by the Holy Spirit as initiating one into the body of Christ. Unlike the filling of the Spirit, initiation is not repeatable. One baptism, but many fillings, seems to be God's order.[23] Because, in the early church, believers were baptized in water almost immediately upon their conversion, it is often difficult to distinguish in a given passage whether it is the baptizing work of the Spirit or water baptism that is under discussion, but there is really "one baptism" (Eph. 4:5), the baptizing work of the Spirit, of which the baptism in water is concomitant.

> How beautiful the union of souls redeemed and free,
> Who hold with God communion in faith and purity!
> While songs of praise are filling their sacred place of rest,
> Who then can be unwilling to join their circle blest?
> —J. L. Runeberg (Swedish)

This fellowship in the family of God is constantly being enriched by the sovereignly bestowed gifts of the Spirit (1 Cor. 12:11). The gifts, which are a function of the Spirit's ministry (cf. John 16:13–15; 15:26–27), are legion, and each one precious and "for the common good" (v. 7). We are to testify as the Spirit testifies, about Christ.

THE HOLY SPIRIT AND THE CHARACTER OF CHRIST IN US

For those God foreknew he also predestined to be conformed to the likeness of his Son.
—Romans 8:29

Now the Lord is the Spirit, and where the Spirit of the Lord is, there is freedom. And we, who with unveiled faces all contemplate the Lord's glory, are being transformed into his likeness with ever-increasing glory, which comes from the Lord, who is the Spirit.
—2 Corinthians 3:17–18

This is how we know we are in him: Whoever claims to live in him must walk as Jesus did. . . . Those who obey his commands live in him, and he in them. And this is how we know that he lives in us: we know it by the Spirit he gave us.
—1 John 2:5–6; 3:24

When floodlights shine on a beautiful building, we do not say, "What a lovely floodlight." Rather we say, "What a magnificent building!"[24] The "floodlight effect" aptly describes, too, the continuous dedication of the Holy Spirit to glorify Christ (John 16:14).

The Christian should live "looking to Jesus" (Heb. 12:1–2). Our focus needs to be on his glory and perfection, his moral excellence, his purity, his character, for he is truly "the image of the invisible God" (Col. 1:15; Heb. 1:3). We also were once in God's image and likeness, that is, reflectors of God's moral and spiritual being, but that image has been severely distorted and defaced (although not completely effaced). In redemption, it is God's purpose to restore the image in us. Paul writes,

> *Do not lie to each other, since you have taken off your old self with its practices and have put on the new self, which is being renewed in knowledge in the image of its Creator.*
>
> —Colossians 3:9–10

The Holy Spirit is the craftsman of character. That God is interested in our becoming holy is clear in the Old Testament: "Be holy because I, the Lord your God, am holy" (Lev. 19:2; cf. also 1 Peter 1:15–16). The product of redemption is a God-centered and God-pleasing life as set forth in Micah 6:8:

> *He has showed you, O man, what is good. And what does the LORD require of you? To act justly and to love mercy and to walk humbly with your God.*

The depths of the doctrine of sanctification will be plumbed further in chapter 12, but it will here be registered in the role of the Spirit in reproducing the character of Jesus in the life of the believer. Our culture has little interest in character. We seem more interested in reputation, which is what people *think* we are. Character is what we really are, and that is of primary concern to God.

The Holy Spirit, when in control of the believer's life, produces fruit in the form of admirable character traits (Gal. 5:22–23). When we become more interested in the graces of the Spirit than in the gifts of the Spirit, we know that the Spirit is dwelling in us, that we are living by the Spirit and keeping in step with the Spirit (see v. 25). So we are commanded, "Keep on being filled with the Spirit" (Eph. 5:18).[25] As Christians, we are filled with the Spirit to the degree that we are controlled by the Spirit. And, as the Spirit is ungrieved in a life of continued yieldedness to God,[26] every day we need to be filled again with the Spirit, as is the pattern in the book of Acts. The Spirit-filled life is overflowing with usefulness and fruitfulness, and many testify of the joys and blessings of such a life.[27]

Are you filled with the Spirit? Do you daily seek the filling of the Spirit? Let us remember that the Spirit's priority is always the re-creation of Christ in us. Is there a higher aspiration conceivable than that of the song,

> O to be like Thee! O to be like Thee,
> Blessed Redeemer, pure as Thou art;
> Come in Thy sweetness, come in Thy fullness;
> Stamp Thine own image deep on my heart.
> —Thomas Chisholm

THE HOLY SPIRIT AND OUR ABILITY TO SERVE

His divine power has given us everything we need for life and godliness through our knowledge of him who called us by his own glory and goodness.
—2 Peter 1:3

But you will receive power when the Holy Spirit comes on you; and you will be my witnesses in Jerusalem, and in all Judea and Samaria, and to the ends of the earth.
—Acts 1:8

I began to experience a growing dissatisfaction with the results of my work. Restless, discontented, I was led to a more intensive study of the Scripture. Every passage that had any bearing upon the price of, or the road to, the accession of power became life and breath to me.
—Jonathan Goforth of China

There is no reason why a man should not immediately from the moment of regeneration enter into all the blessedness of the Spirit-filled life: that is the Divine intention and that is the Divine purpose.
—G. Campbell Morgan,
The Spirit of God

The promise of the Spirit for the church age, and the gifts of the Spirit as poured out on believers, are calculated to fulfill the Great Commission before the Lord's return. Some of these specialized enduements are

1. the sealing of the Holy Spirit, establishing our assurance of salvation;
2. the anointing of the Holy Spirit, enlarging our knowledge and understanding (1 John 2:27);
3. the filling of the Holy Spirit, enhancing our ability and opportunity to proclaim and serve.

One of the great miracles on Pentecost was the transformation of the apostle Peter. Recall how ignominiously he had failed the Lord in his discipleship and denial. He had quailed before a little servant girl and swore with an oath that he did not know the Lord. Now, on the Day of Pentecost, facing the insinuations and insults of Christ's enemies that the disciples were inebriated, Peter and company were all "filled with the Holy Spirit" (Acts 2:4). Then Peter stood before the vast array in the temple court and spoke with courage and discernment of what had happened. He used scriptural illustration with mastery. He was poised and more than adequate for the occasion, for his message, and for his handling of questions. What had happened to him? How do we explain the transformation of the disciples from a timid and hesitant band of doubters into effective ministers and communicators of the "everlasting gospel"?

The answer then, as now, is the inworking of the power of the Holy Spirit, which finds available vessels and channels and then pours out the power of God. How well I remember early seasons in my ministry that were spiritually sterile, and then my discovery of S. D. Gordon's book, *Quiet Talks on Power*.[28] The passage he opened for me was cool water, a spring in my desert.

> *On the last and greatest day of the Feast, Jesus stood and said in a loud voice, "If anyone is thirsty, let him come to me and drink. Whoever believes in me, as the Scripture has said, streams of living water will flow from within him." By this he meant the Spirit, whom those who believed in him were later to receive. Up to that time the Spirit had not yet been given, since Jesus had not yet been glorified.*
>
> —John 7:37–39

The Lord Jesus promised "another Counselor to be with you forever" (John 14:16); that is, all that Jesus was to his followers in the days of his flesh, the Holy Spirit will be to every believer, infilling each with divine empowerment and enablement suited to each individual.

Another critical turning point in my early Christian life came when at Christmas my mother's Sunday school teacher gave her a little book entitled *Christ-Life for the Self-Life* by F. B. Meyer. In one of his sermons, Meyer described how, at the Keswick Convention one year, Hudson Taylor had challenged him to seek the filling of the Holy Spirit.[29] After a prayer meeting, Meyer went out alone to receive what the Lord had promised. He testifies,

> I turned to Christ and said: "Lord, as I breathe in this whiff of warm night air, so I breathe into every part of me Thy blessed Spirit." I felt no hand laid on my head, there was no lambent flame, there was no rushing sound from heaven; but by faith, without emotion, without excitement I took, and took for the first time, and I have kept on taking ever since.

What would happen if every believer in the United States were filled with the Holy Spirit?

We all need to most earnestly pray,

> But though I cannot sing, or tell, or know
> The fullness of Thy love, while here below,
> My empty vessel I may freely bring;
> Oh Thou, who art of love the living spring,
> My vessel fill.
>
> I am but an empty vessel, not one thought
> Or look of love I ever to Thee brought,
> But I may come and come again to Thee
> With this the empty sinner's only plea,
> Thou lovest me.
>
> —Mary Shakleton

And so when filled and serving, we go forth into each day to discover the surprises of the Spirit.

On the Scent of the Spirit

Meditate on each of the following names of the Holy Spirit: the Holy Spirit, the Comforter or Counselor, the Spirit of Life, the Spirit of Power, the Spirit of Truth, the Spirit of Wisdom, the Spirit of Promise, the Spirit of Holiness. From the Bible, or from your experience in the Church, or from your own or others' contemporary pilgrimages recall appropriate illustrations that apply for each of the Holy Spirit's names.

Ponder also Eldad and Medad (Num. 11:25–29) and Moses' wish: "I wish that all the Lord's people were prophets and that the Lord would put his Spirit in them" (11:29). How does this passage relate to a pastor's intention: "In this new season I hope to learn more deeply what it means to live under the direction of the Holy Spirit."

JUSTIFICATION BY FAITH ALONE

The Final Acceptance

What is man, that he could be pure, or one born of woman, that he could be righteous? If God places no trust in his holy ones, if even the heavens are not pure in his eyes, how much less man, who is vile and corrupt, who drinks up evil like water!

—Job 15:14–16

How then can a man be righteous before God? How can one born of woman be pure?

—Job 25:4[1]

I delight greatly in the LORD; my soul rejoices in my God. For he has clothed me with garments of salvation and arrayed me in a robe of righteousness, as a bride-groom adorns his head like a priest, and as a bride adorns herself with her jewels.

—Isaiah 61:10

By justification we mean—man's acceptance with God, or his be-ing regarded and treated as righteous in his sight—as the object of his favor, and not of his wrath; of his blessing, and not his curse.

—James Buchanan,
The Doctrine of Justification

A few years ago I visited Ellis Island in New York City harbor. There, from 1892 to 1954, countless immigrants presented themselves for admis-sion to the land of their dreams. And there my grandparents came, filled with apprehension and anxiety, not speaking the language of the new land. *Would they be accepted?*

I stood in the long hall that they had entered. At the far end were desks where the immigration officials would have sat to render judgment on the hopeful immigrants. I imagined my grandparents stepping forward tremulously to present their documents. Behind and above them, watchful agents examined them. Would there be an evident deficiency that would disqualify them and send them back to their port of origin? I wept as I thought of how much had hung suspended on the verdict rendered at those battered wooden tables. Would they be admitted? Would they be received?

It's not difficult to draw an analogy between the position of my grandparents on Ellis Island and our position as sinners who stand before a righteous and holy God. Will we be received? We have nothing to commend us to him. But there is one who speaks for us, if we trust him. Jesus Christ is the justifier, and we can have admission and acceptance through him. Though we have "sinned and fall short of the glory of God," we can be "justified freely by his grace through the redemption that came by Christ Jesus. God presented him as a sacrifice of atonement, through faith in his blood. He did this to demonstrate his justice. . .so as to be just and the one who justifies those who have faith in Jesus" (Rom. 3:23–26).

The Reformers regarded the doctrine of justification as "the article of a rising or falling church." Justification is the legal foundation and basis for all of the saving work of God on our behalf through the Lord Jesus Christ. All that ensues therefrom is possible because satisfaction has been made for the broken law and the wrath of God abated through Christ's atoning work. God begins his healing work in us by accepting us wholly and fully through Christ. Failure to grasp the reality of God's acceptance fosters problems in assurance and confidence. Many otherwise insightful medieval writers in Christian spirituality (such as Thomas à Kempis in his powerful *Imitation of Christ*) desperately needed this truth, which was so pivotal in the Reformation. That we are declared righteous before God (justification) is preliminary to our being made righteous by God (sanctification). The two are inseparable yet logically and chronologically distinct.

Under the Death Sentence

Sin entered the world through one man, and death through sin, and in this way death came to all men, because all sinned.
—Romans 5:12

Those who are yet without any fear of God's wrath, who are secure and hardened and yet unyielding, must be strongly admonished and urged to repentance by the threats and terrors of that wrath, that is, to them no gospel is to be preached, but only the Law and Moses.

—Martin Luther

The wages of sin is death.

—Romans 6:23

Horace, the Latin playwright of ancient times, held that a deity was to be introduced into a drama only when all human effort had failed and there was no other recourse. Failure and a dearth of recourse is surely the predicament of humankind—by nature and by choice. We are spiritually bankrupt, having fallen into a gulf that separates us from God (cf. Gen. 3:3), and we cannot lift ourselves up by our own bootstraps. We are found guilty in the court of God's righteous judgment and are under the sentence of eternal death (cf. Rom. 3:9–20). The guilt of original sin has been imputed to us: "By the trespass of the one man, death reigned through that one man" (Rom. 5:17). We are lost and have nothing with which to commend ourselves to a holy God. We are infected with an incurable malady, and "all of us have become like one who is unclean, and all our righteous acts are like filthy rags" (Isa. 64:6a).

The illusion that we can rectify our situation is called "Pelagianism," after a Welsh monk who in the days of St. Augustine argued for the ability of human beings to save themselves. Something of Pelagianism resides in all of us. We would like to do something meritorious before God and have some claim for auto-salvation. The American Religion of Ralph Waldo Emerson, with its emphasis on "self-reliance," has been exceedingly durable in American religious life and can be seen even in the books of fantasy that are widely read and loved in our country. "The little engine that could," for example, finally made it because of its dogged determination: "I think I can; I think I can." *Jonathan Livingston Seagull* is another embodiment of the same premise. In contrast to C. S. Lewis's *Chronicles of Narnia* and their belief in God as the spiritual path to "the real paradise" is J. K. Rowling's popular *Harry Potter* series, with its counsel: "Believe in yourself . . . the most important magic comes from inside each of us."[2] Such sentiments are none other than the patently American power-of-positive-thinking now being popularized by Oprah Winfrey and her philosophy that all we need is within us. Notwithstanding current thoughts and trends, the Bible insists, as it has for thousands of years, that we need a reality *ab extra,* that is, something beyond us and above us. The way to spiritual peace is found only through salvation, and we cannot save ourselves. And that is the paralyzing and enervating sentence of death hanging like the Sword of Damocles over our heads.

The argument for the necessity of forensic justification (which addresses the legal problem of the human race and the need to satisfy the wrath and retributive justice of God) is relevant only if we take seriously the peril of our condemnation before God. Evidence of some evangelicals hedging about forensic justification is to be seen in Roger Olson's questioning of the necessity of forensic images of salvation (imputed righteousness as opposed to the infused righteousness of Catholicism).[3] Similarly, Gabriel Fackre frets about an overemphasis by evangelicals on "the penal and the personal in this too simplistic substitutionary view."[4] N. T. "Tom" Wright and James Dunn recast the whole theological tilt toward "national righteousness" rather than our personal righteousness and thus construe justification to be "God's declaration that we belong to the covenant community."[5] Likewise, Alistair McGrath broadens forensic justification until it is virtually unrecognizable.[6] These defections and the resultant lack of clarity on the imperativeness of forensic justification clearly stem from a reluctance to take seriously the human predicament. If, in fact, we are condemned to die, then the charges—"the written code, with its regulations, that was against us and that stood opposed to us" (Col. 2:14)—must be satisfactorily addressed and resolved by a holy God without any compromise of his own integrity. To fail to do justice to "the sternness of God" is as much a travesty as failing to do justice to "the kindness of God" (Rom. 11:22). We must face our actual crisis: "The soul who sins is the one who will die" (Ezek. 18:4). "The Evangelical Celebration of the Gospel of Jesus Christ" lays the foundation for the Good News with an unequivocal statement of the bad news: "We affirm that the Gospel diagnoses the universal human condition as one of sinful rebellion against God, which, if unchanged, will lead each person to eternal loss under God's condemnation."[7] We desperately need help as we sit on spiritual death row.

Some "respectable" Bible scholars today argue that God's wrath is impersonal and thereby ignore what Paul teaches in Romans 1:18ff. In fact, God, in "justifying the ungodly" (Rom. 4:5), does not turn a blind eye to our sin. Miroslav Volf, in a refreshing claim for legal justification, shows that "reconciliation is not inclusion of the enemy and justification is not acceptance of injustice. . . . A God of most radical grace must be a God of wrath—not the kind of wrath that burns against evildoers until they prove worthy of being loved, but the kind that resists evildoers because they are unconditionally loved. . . . God's wrath is nothing but God's stance of active opposition to evil."[8] At the juncture of wrath and love stands the cross of Christ.

The Perfect Sacrifice

God made him who had no sin to be sin for us, so that in him we might become the righteousness of God.
—2 Corinthians 5:21

Christ redeemed us from the curse of the law by becoming a curse for us, for it is written: "Cursed is everyone who is hung upon a tree." He redeemed us in order that the blessing given to Abraham might come to the Gentiles through Christ Jesus, so that by faith we might receive the promise of the Spirit.
—Galatians 3:13–14

For him [Martin Luther], the real Reformation breakthrough did not come until Staupitz directed his attention to the Crucified and thus away from himself, thereby changing the direction of his gaze and taking away his pious egocentricity. When Luther learned that in Christ Jesus he was righteous in the sight of God and accepted by God—that this God wanted to be his God even though he was unworthy—he became in a sense indifferent to himself and ceased being the subject of his self-observation.

—Helmut Thielicke,
Between Heaven and Earth

The apostle Paul argues in Romans that God is righteous, that he requires righteousness of us, that he provides righteousness for those who repent and believe, and this through the perfect sacrifice of Jesus offered on the cross. The work of Christ on Calvary involved an exchange, a transaction. He took our guilt and shame and offered us his perfect righteousness. Note, too, the further argument of Paul in Romans 4, where he shows that Abraham and David in the Old Testament are examples of this same principle of justification. Genesis 15:6 states, "Abraham believed the Lord, and he credited it to him as righteousness." Any human being in any age who has been right with God has been so on the same and essential basis. *"Justification by faith alone, apart from observing the Law!"* (Rom. 3:28). Then Paul states, "The words 'it was credited to him' [by forensic imputation, surely] were written not for him alone, but also for us, to whom God will credit righteousness—for us who believe in him who raised up Jesus our Lord from the dead. He was delivered over to death for our sins and was raised to life for our justification" (4:25).

Thus there inheres in the cross of Christ the disclosure of the marvelous love and mercy of God. A little girl said to her mother, "Mommy, I want to go to the cross," referring to a lighted cross high on a hill, overlooking a lake. It is not that the four-year-old grasped the intricacies of atonement theology, but she knew "it stood for something special about the love of Jesus."[9]

Some today derogate the cross as "divine child abuse" or obnoxious scapegoating. Others argue that the merit in Christ's death is in its selfless example, but how this fits in with satisfaction for sin and with the Resurrection is hard to see. A prominent evangelical scholar says that he finds no meaning in gazing upon the cross with all of its brutality. He depreciates the kerygma (that Jesus died, rose again, and is coming back) and insists that we must not "shame people by thrusting the cross in their faces"; indeed he sees the cross as psychological battering.[10] This view appears to bypass the necessity of repentance and of convicting by the law (cf. Gal. 3:24–25). Facing sin, and repenting of sin, must precede justification by faith. If resolving the matter of sin is of no importance, then there is little point to wrath, repentance, the Cross, or heaven and hell. The Cross underscores the enormity and seriousness of our sin in that the sinless Son of God died there to take away all of our sins. The problem of sin must have been of the greatest magnitude to require such a radical solution.

The cross of Christ is the moral epicenter of the universe. Here God upholds both the moral character of the universe and his own righteousness, as well as expresses his goodness and mercy. That he was able to achieve both ends in the saving death of Jesus Christ is, of course, *prima facie* evidence of the moral genius and creativity of God. The Word tells us that God detests those who "acquit the guilty and condemn the innocent" (Prov. 17:15). For God to declare by divine fiat that the ungodly are justified would mean that God himself is unjust and unrighteous. The English scholars who spoke of forensic justification as a "legal fiction" would embroil our God in reprehensible impropriety. The challenge is summed up by the apostle Paul in Romans 8: 33–34:

> *Who will bring any charge against those whom God has chosen? It is God who justifies. Who is he that condemns? Christ Jesus, who died—more than that, who was raised to life—is at the right hand of God.*

In a vicarious and substitutionary act Christ took our actual sins and their penalty upon himself in his death (Isa. 53:5–6). He then bequeaths his actual righteousness to all who believe (Rom. 5:18). What he has done is adequate for all humanity for he has dealt with "the sins of the whole world" (1 John 2:2).[11] Thus it is imperative that each of us "be found in him, not having a righteousness of our own that comes from the law, but that which is through faith in Christ—the righteousness that comes from God and is by faith" (Phil. 3:8–9).[12]

Christ's sacrifice was a perfect sacrifice to "cleanse our consciences from acts that lead to death, so that we may serve the living God!" (Heb. 9:14). "But now he has appeared once for all at the end of the ages to do away with sin by the sacrifice of himself" (v. 26). "We have been made holy through the sacrifice of the body of Christ once for all" (10:10). "By one sacrifice he has made perfect forever those who are being made holy" (v. 14). Christ's perfect sacrifice—not our own recommendation—has made us righteous and holy. And that is why the blood of Jesus is so precious, and the cross of Christ so dear to the believer, and why we resonate with the apostle Paul in exclaiming, "May I never boast except in the cross of our Lord Jesus Christ" (Gal. 6:14). So it is not self-esteem that we need, but Christ esteem.

And we need to say earnestly,

> Guilty, vile, and helpless we;
> Spotless Lamb of God was he.

or

> I need thee, precious Jesus, for I am full of sin;
> My soul is dark and guilty, my heart is dead within.[13]

During Holy Week in 2000, Johnny Hart, the well-known cartoonist and creator of *B.C.,* met severe criticism for his Easter Sunday comic. In fact, some papers wouldn't carry it. Hart shows B.C. and Cute Chick watching the sun set behind a very large cross. "As the sun dipped, the cross's shadow enveloped them. . . . The shadow was done in blood red to indicate Christ's sacrifice on the cross." The Chick and B.C. are then drawn in white because "His blood has made us white as snow." In the last panel, B.C. says, "I stand corrected"—"Jesus' blood has washed away their sin."[14] Hart maintains that he could do nothing else as a Christian but put his beliefs in his work. And belief in the atoning work of the Cross is at the very center of the gospel.

> What Thou, my Lord, hast suffered
> Was all for sinners' gain;
> Mine, mine was the transgression,
> But Thine the deadly pain.
>
> Lo, here I fall, my Savior!
> 'Tis I deserve Thy place;
> Look on me with Thy Favor,
> Vouchsafe to me Thy grace.
> —Bernard of Clairvaux

Healing Through Acceptance

For if, by the trespass of the one man, death reigned through that one man, how much more will those who receive God's abundant provision of grace and of the gift of righteousness reign in life through the one man, Jesus Christ.
—Romans 5:17

Catechism question: What is justification?
Answer: Justification is the work of God's grace whereby God freely pardons all our sins and accepts us as righteous in his sight, only for the perfect righteousness of Christ imputed to us and received by faith alone.

Christianity is not the sacrifice we make, but the sacrifice we trust; not the victory we win but the victory we inherit.
—P. T. Forsyth

By "accepting the unacceptable," God offers us healing in Christ. We who are by nature and choice distanced from a holy God "are brought near through the blood of Christ" (Eph. 2:13). The ultimate eschatological verdict of acquittal and acceptance is rendered now, in that "there is therefore now no condemnation for those who are in Christ Jesus" (Rom. 8:1). Indeed, "who will bring any charge against those whom God has chosen? It is God who justifies" (v. 33). Christ takes our guilt and gives to us his perfect righteousness. All we need do is accept the gift, and thus we are "accepted in the beloved" (Eph. 1:6 KJV). Christ offered up to the Father both his active and passive obedience (the life he lived vicariously and the death he died vicariously). On this point all evangelicals are of virtually unanimous opinion, as Buchanan, quoting Arminius, shows:

> I believe that sinners are accounted righteous solely by the obedience of Christ; and that the righteousness of Christ is the only meritorious cause on account of which God pardons the sins of believers, and reckons them as righteous as if they had perfectly fulfilled the law.[15]

In God's sight, then, we are clothed with the spotless righteousness of Jesus Christ. On this basis we have access to God in prayer, coming always in Jesus' name, and is as well the sole basis upon which we are accorded entrance into heaven when we die or the Lord returns for us. And thus it is that we sing,

> Dressed in his righteousness alone,
> Faultless to stand before the throne.
> —Edward Mote

and

> Jesus, thy blood and righteousness,
> My beauty are, my glorious dress;
> 'Midst flaming worlds, in these arrayed,
> With joy shall I lift up my head.
> —Count Zinzendorf,
> tr. by John Wesley

In a widely acclaimed "Evangelical Celebration of the Gospel of Jesus Christ," evangelicals across the spectrum present a statement that clarifies the way in which Jesus saves. Considering the fuzziness of some among us as to what the gospel really is, the statement is timely and trenchant. The sharply focused statement specifies "the key to our Christian identity and our continued effectiveness in God's mission."[16] In a world where the struggle for a sense of identity is increasing and for many is a source of pain, the statement iterates how one can achieve a profound and eternal sense of our acceptance by a holy and a loving God. It was said of Biff in Arthur Miller's *Death of a Salesman* that he "never knew who he was." We can know who we are, because of the provision and grace of God, who created us and who has paid the price for our redemption. The evangelical statement attributes all initiative for salvation to the grace of God, affirming that

As our sins were reckoned to Christ, so Christ's righteousness is reckoned to us. This is justification by the imputation of Christ's righteousness. All we bring to the transaction is our need of it. Our faith in the God who bestows it, the Father, the Son and the Holy Spirit, is itself the fruit of God's grace. Faith links us savingly to Jesus, but inasmuch as it involves an acknowledgment that we have no merit of our own, it is confessedly not a meritorious work.[17]

It is sad and disappointing that some evangelicals protested, arguing that the statement should have included some provision for sanctification—or at least not ruled out salvation—outside of a commitment to the Lord Jesus Christ.

But they protest too much. All of the Reformers who had been earnest Roman Catholics struggled to achieve assurance that they were right with God. Luther was typical in his frantic quest as he studied and lectured on Romans and Galatians and had what Roland Bainton called "his Damascus Road experience." He repudiated papal indulgences that forgave sin and emphatically proclaimed "justification by faith alone apart from the works of the law."[18] Official pronouncements of the Roman Catholic Church define justification as "the remission of sin and the infusion of sanctifying grace at baptism." The Council of Trent, after the Reformation, denounced Luther and his teaching on justification. Canon XI from 1545 says,

If anyone says that men are justified either by the sole imputation of the justice of Christ, or by the sole remission of sins to the exclusion of the grace and the charity which is poured forth in their hearts by the Holy Ghost, and remains in them, or that the grace by which we are justified is only the good will of God, let him be "Anathema."[19]

Roman Catholics have always insisted on infusion and impartation rather than imputation, which seems to miss the apostolic point.

In recent years, various denominations have entered into dialogue with the Roman Catholic Church and the impression has been conveyed that the Roman Catholic position has altered. Indeed, even some evangelicals have advanced the idea that a truce should be called in "proselytizing" each other's members, citing concurrence on the essential matter of how a person is made right with God.

Yet a recently issued update from the Vatican on indulgences offers new ways of "winning forgiveness" through the use of indulgences. Good works such as giving up smoking accrue merit for the earning of forgiveness. And although the Associated Press is not necessarily a source of sound theology, their conclusion is significant: "For Lutherans, salvation depends on God's grace; for Catholics, good works also figure in." But what does the Bible say?[20]

Compromise language on justification is neither desirable nor commendable. Whether it is the sacrifice of the Mass in Catholicism or the 1844 cleansing of the inner sanctuary through the blood of Jesus in Seventh Day Adventism, these events fall grievously short of the work Jesus finished on the cross of Calvary. With Oswald Chambers we are jubilant!

The greatest note of triumph that ever sounded in the ears of a startled universe was that sounded on the Cross. . . . "IT IS FINISHED!" That was the last word in the Redemption of man.

As prospectors for God's truth wherever it is, we have often sung hymns from the medieval period (like "Jesus the Very Thought of Thee") and found these theologically sound. Bernard of Clairvaux was biblical for the most part. But in mining the writings of Thomas à Kempis, Ignatius Loyola, Francois Fenelon, Madam Guyon, Teresa of Avila, and others, one must exercise caution, as they did not always have full appreciation for what the

Bible teaches about justification. Some writers on biblical truth have avoided use of the Roman Catholic writers entirely,[21] while others claim, almost without caution, that treasures indeed lie there.[22] A middle ground seems preferable wherein nonevangelical sources are used with extreme caution, but truth is appreciated wherever it can be found. The liberating reality of our acceptance in Christ must always be the bottom line.

> No condemnation now I dread;
> Jesus, and all in Him, is mine!
> Alive in Him, my living Head,
> And clothed in righteousness divine,
> Bold I approach th' eternal throne,
> And claim the crown, through Christ my own.
> —Charles Wesley

OUR SPIRITUAL ONENESS

It is the Sovereign LORD who helps me. Who is he that will condemn me?
—Isaiah 50:9

By his knowledge my righteous servant will justify many, and he will bear their iniquities.
—Isaiah 53:11

He has clothed me with garments of salvation and arrayed me in a robe of righteousness, as a bridegroom adorns his head like a priest, and as a bride adorns herself with her jewels.
—Isaiah 61:10

I have lost all things. I consider them rubbish, that I may gain Christ and be found in him, not having a righteousness of my own that comes from the law, but that which is through faith in Christ—the righteousness that comes from God and is by faith.
—Philippians 3:8–9

The Lord Jesus said that he was in the Father and that the Father was in him (John 14:11), and that "you are in me and I am in you" (v. 20). The believer's union with Christ is positional, but it is actual, just as the branches abide in the vine (15:4). The letters of the apostle Paul state 164 times that the believer is "in Christ" or "in Christ Jesus" or "in the Lord." Our position in Christ is one of the most profound and tender themes in the gospel, the virtual monogram of the apostle Paul, and the seal and signature of our salvation. A saint named Edward Arthur Litton put it aptly:

> Union with Christ is the distinctive blessing of the gospel dispensation in which every other is comprised—justification, sanctification, adoption and the future glorifying of our bodies; all these are but different aspects of the one great truth, that the Christian is one with Christ.[23]

As Christians we are "found in Christ." The preposition *in* conveys sphere and location as well as fixedness and solidity. To be "found in Christ" means that what water is for fish and air is for birds and the forest is for the living creature, so Christ is the essential environment for the child of God. Christ surrounds us, engulfs us, and inundates us. He is the vital element in which we exist. No longer are we "in Adam" with all the debilitating and death-producing effects of that enslavement. Our home is now Jesus Christ, and he was "delivered over to death for our sins and was raised to life for our justification" (Rom. 4:25).

The believer has a connection with the living Christ, which differentiates true Christianity from moralism. Much of religion is striving after morality without resting in Christ, but Christianity, as Henry Drummond used to say, works from the center while moralism works from the circumference. Canon Wilberforce put it,

> If you were to tie half a dozen branches of grapes on your old umbrella, that would not make it a vine. You may tie them on very carefully, but they will not grow. But that is just what multitudes of people are trying to do.

Frenetic effort at morality apart from knowing the living Christ is futile (Matt. 7:21–23). That which is merely external to us must yield to that which is internal. Adolph Deissmann argues in his great work on the apostle Paul that the phrase "in Christ" denotes "the most intimate possible fellowship of the Christian with the living Spiritual Christ." W. D. Davies, in his *Paul and Rabbinic Judaism,* points out,

To be "in Christ" involves an identity of experience with Christ. The union of the individual with Christ is such that the experiences of Christ are re-enacted in the experience of the individual Christian. The life, death, resurrection and glorification of Jesus cease to be mere external facts of history but living realities in the Christian's own life. The latter appropriates to himself the past events of the historical and risen life of Jesus so that they become his own. Thus it is that Paul could speak of Christ being formed in a person (cf. Galatians 4:19).[24]

Thus, being "joined to Christ" (1 Cor. 6:17 AV) or "united with the Lord" (1 Cor. 6:17) impels everything subsequent to conversion. Everything hinges on our being structurally "one" with Christ our Lord, an intensely personal position. Do you and I have a personal relationship with Christ? Have we been "grafted in among the others to share in the nourishing sap from the olive root" (Rom. 11:17)? And while oneness with Christ is an individual experience—and necessarily so—it is also a corporate and shared experience with both Jews and Gentiles, as Paul argues in Romans 11. We can be transplanted into new soil and into a new climate. James S. Stewart, in his Cunningham Lectures, published as *A Man in Christ: The Vital Elements of St. Paul's Religion,*[25] shows that this "wonder-working power of attachment to Christ" is truly "the mainstay of [one's] theology" and the "sheet-anchor of [one's] ethics."[26]

Then, out of our union with Christ, there properly follows our communion with Christ. The question is, Do we commune in the outer court or in the Holy of Holies? Entering into the interior of true Christianity opens the opportunity of deeper fellowship and communion (1 Cor. 1:9; 1 John 1:3–7). The psalmist talks about dwelling "in the secret place of the Most High" (Ps. 91:1 AV), an impossibility unless we are "found in him." Saints over the centuries have reveled in what the justifying grace of God has opened up for us in Christ.[27] The beauty of life in Christ is set forth in the following lines inscribed by an Indian Christian:

In the secret of his presence
How my soul delights to hide!
Oh, how precious are the lessons
Which I learn at Jesus' side!

Earthly cares can never vex me,
Neither trials lay me low;
For when Satan comes to vex me,
To the secret place I do.
—Ellen Lakshmi Goreh

THE IMPERATIVE OF FORGIVENESS

Blessed is he whose transgressions are forgiven, whose sins are covered. Blessed is the man whose sin the LORD does not count against him and in whose spirit is no deceit.

—Psalm 32:1–2

"The days are coming," declares the LORD, "when I will raise up to David a righteous Branch, a King who will reign wisely and do what is just and right in the land. In his days Judah will be saved and Israel will live in safety. This is the name by which he will be called: The LORD Our Righteousness."

—Jeremiah 23:5–6

Be kind and compassionate to one another, forgiving each other, just as in Christ God forgave you.

—Ephesians 4:32

Bear with each other and forgive whatever grievances you may have against one another. Forgive as the Lord forgave you.

—Colossians 3:13

There is a defect in our belief in the freeness of divine grace . . . to exercise unshaken confidence in the doctrine of gratuitous pardon is one of the most difficult things in the world.

—Archibald Alexander,
Thoughts on Religious Experience

The biblical doctrine of justification by faith translates into the full and free forgiveness of all of our sins through Christ, which D. L. Moody called "the greatest blessing this side of heaven." When we confess in the creed that "we believe in the forgiveness of sins," we stake out considerable ground, not only in our own personal relationships with God, but in our forgiveness of ourselves and others. All true forgiveness is predicated upon our grasp of the adequacy and thoroughness of the Lord's forgiveness of us. That we forgive because we are forgiven is foundational.

Holy Scripture strains at the leash of language to convey the competence of the Lord in dealing with the problem of our sins. John the Baptist twice (in John 1:29, 36) calls attention to "the Lamb of God, who takes away the sin of the world." Under the old covenant, sin was covered, but under the new covenant, sin is carried away, as foreshadowed in the scapegoat ceremony on the Day of Atonement (Lev. 16:20ff.). "The goat will carry on itself all their sins to a solitary place; and the man shall release it in the desert" (v. 22).

Referring to the disposition of our sins, the psalmist David rhapsodizes, "As far as the east is from the west, so far has he removed our transgressions from us" (Ps. 103:12). Had the passage said from north to south, that would be a calculable distance (from the north magnetic pole to the south magnetic pole), but it speaks of infinite direction with no possibility of computation. Similarly, the prophet Micah indicates that the Lord who delights in mercy "hurls all of iniquities into the depths of the sea" (Micah 7:19). To illustrate those depths, Chicago's mighty Sears Tower reaches 1,727 feet in height, but the depth of the sea exceeds 35,000 feet (in the Marianas Trench in the South Pacific). The writer to the Hebrews also stretches metaphor in quoting Jeremiah: "Their sins and lawless acts I will remember no more" (Jer. 31:34; Heb. 10:17). Thus is the glory of "redemption through his blood, the forgiveness of sins, in accordance with the riches of God's grace which he has lavished on us" (Eph. 1:7–8).

> My sin—oh the bliss of this glorious thought—
> My sin not in part but the whole,
> Is nailed to the cross and I bear it no more,
> Praise the Lord, praise the Lord, O my soul.
> —Horatio B. Spafford

If God can thus forgive me and accept me as righteous, what hinders my forgiving myself and accepting myself as a forgiven sinner? Vertical forgiveness—of us from God—provides a basis for horizontal forgiveness—of ourselves and others.

Forgiveness does not mean, however, immediate and automatic forgiveness of everyone for all evil perpetrated. Even God requires confession and repentance. Restitution is clearly part of the biblical pattern of forgiveness. If you steal a horse, you can be forgiven, but you must return the horse. Dennis Prager, a thoughtful Jewish writer, laments that "over the past generation, many Christians have adopted the idea that they should forgive everyone who commits evil against anyone, no matter how great and cruel and whether or not the evildoer repents."[28] Convinced that an earnest Christianity is necessary to reverse America's moral decline, Prager pleads that automatic forgiveness destroys "Christianity's central moral tenets," and that we must recognize that "even by God, forgiveness is contingent upon the sinner repenting, and [repentance] can be given only to the one sinned against." Dietrich Bonhoeffer insisted that preaching forgiveness without repentance is cheap grace.

Jesus made it plain, though, that an unforgiving spirit is the sign of an unforgiven spirit. He said, "But if you do not forgive men their sins, your Father will not forgive your sins" (Matt. 6:15). An anguished mother cried out, "Do I have to forgive the man who murdered my four sons?" when the murderer wrote to tell her he had found Christ and wanted her to forgive him. A man in Scotland who had murdered his mother and served his time, matriculated in theological education. He was forgiven according to his own testimony, but placement was impossible because congregations couldn't accept him as their pastor. Clearly, if there is repentance, we must forgive.[29] But both Jesus and Stephen asked forgiveness for their executioners even when the transgressors displayed not the faintest shred of repentance (cf. Luke 23:24; Acts 7:60). The root word translated "forgiveness" really means "to hold off." Perhaps, then, Jesus and Stephen called upon God to hold off his judgment on their oppressors. In effect they said, "As far as I am concerned, I release this to you," recognizing that "vengeance is mine, says the Lord" (Rom. 12:18–20).

To harbor resentment and bitterness toward those who have wronged us is to allow acid to penetrate and destroy the inner life. How much better and how much more blessed to allow the Lord to flush out of our spirits all such gall. Think what we have been forgiven! Even if the guilty person does not repent, we can release him or her to God for his judgment in due time. Praise be to God for fully pardoning us for all of our sins.

To provide an illustration of how the believer can be severed from the sin-stained past, recall that used in chapter 7 from John Bunyan's *Pilgrim's Progress*. Pilgrim, laboring under the burden of sin and guilt, comes to the cross, where he beholds the One who suffered for him. The straps of the heavy pack break and it slips into an open sepulchre beside the cross. Forgiven and now forgiving.

> I must needs go home by the way of the cross,
> There's no other way but this;
> I shall ne'er get sight of the Gates of the Light,
> If the way of the cross I miss.

> I must needs go on in the blood-sprinkled way,
> The path that the Savior trod,
> If I ever climb to the heights sublime,
> Where the soul is at home with God.
> —Jessie Brown Pounds

PAUSE FOR PARDON AND TO SURVEY YOUR POSITION IN CHRIST

If there are any unconfessed sins in your life, seek now to be forgiven (1 John 1:7, 9). Assay also the wonders of what it means to be "in Christ." Consider and then jot down the aspects of your relationship to Christ that correspond to the following unique metaphors from Scripture:

1. *The Architectural Figure:* living stones built on the foundation (Gal. 3:28; Eph. 2:11–22; Col. 2:7; 1 Peter 2:4–5)
2. *The Marital Figure:* the Bridegroom and the bride (Rom. 7:4; 2 Cor. 11:2; Eph. 5:31–32; Rev. 19:7; 22:17)
3. *The Horticultural Figure:* the vine and the branches (John 15:1–7; Gal. 5:22–23)
4. *The Physical Figure:* the body and its members (1 Cor. 12; Eph. 4:11–16; Col. 2:16–19)

SANCTIFICATION BY GRACE

Crisis and Growth

Be holy because I, the LORD your God, am holy.
—Leviticus 19:2

By one sacrifice he has made perfect forever those who are being made holy.
—Hebrews 10:14

God had planned something better for us so that only together with us would they be made perfect.
—Hebrews 11:40

But God disciplines us for our good, that we may share in his holiness.
—Hebrews 12:10

Make every effort to live in peace with all men and to be holy; without holiness no man will see the Lord.
—Hebrews 12:14

And so Jesus also suffered outside the city gate to make the people holy through his own blood.
—Hebrews 13:12

Sanctification is just taking justification seriously!
—Emil Brunner

C. B. Hedstrom was prepared to sacrifice. When he emigrated from Sweden to the United States, he paid heavily for his passage on a ship. He resolved to economize on his meals, eating only crackers and cheese for break-fast, lunch, and dinner all the way across the Atlantic. Finally, his last night on board, he went to the ship's dining room and celebrated with a hearty roast beef dinner. When he asked for the check the waiter appeared sur-prised and said, "But sir, the price of meals is included in your ticket."

This true story illustrates the relationship between the doctrine of justifi-cation and the doctrine of sanctification. Included in Hedstrom's passage were his meals—nourishment for the long journey. We, too, as justified believers, "heirs of God, co-heirs with Christ" (Rom. 8:17), receive nour-ishment for our spiritual journey—"the riches of God's grace that he lav-ished upon us" (Eph. 1:7), "the riches of his glorious inheritance in the saints" (v. 18), and "the unsearchable riches of Christ" (3:8). Thus the power of God includes everything we need to achieve sanctification, that is, a "life and godliness through our knowledge of him who called us by his own glory and goodness" (2 Peter 1:3).

It is God's purpose that we as Christians should be "conformed to the likeness of his son" (Rom. 8:29), thus restoring the image of God, defaced by the Fall. God himself is holy (Col. 3:9–10). *Holy* means "to be separated" and "set apart" from any sinful use. Inanimate objects—such as the vessels and utensils used in the tabernacle in the wilderness (Ex, 30:29; Lev. 8:10; Num. 7:1) and in the temple in Jerusalem (2 Chron. 7:16)—are sanctified, or set apart for the specific purpose of serving God. In this sense, also, our sinless Savior, the Lord Jesus Christ, was sanctified (John 10:36; 17:19).[1]

It is unthinkable, given redemption and its purpose, that a believer should "go on sinning" (Rom. 6:1). In justification we are declared righteous, and in sanctification we are made righteous through a lifelong process of crises and growth. Justification and sanctification, then, are not states of being in isolation from each other. They are complementary and symbiotic. Justifi-cation is the prelude to sanctification and the foundation upon which sanc-tification is built. In the moment of justification, the process of sanctification commences. "We are created in Christ Jesus to do good works, which God prepared in advance for us to do" (Eph. 2:10). Dietrich Bonhoeffer, in his *Ethics,* demonstrates that ethics for the Christian are "embedded in the reality of God the Creator, Reconciler, and Redeemer. What is of ultimate importance is now no longer that I should become good, or that the world may be made better through my action, but that the reality of God should show itself everywhere to be the ultimate reality. . . . It is the reality of God as he reveals himself in Jesus Christ."[2]

The practical application of the doctrine of sanctification is, however, sorely neglected by many in the church today. Those of us who profess Christ seem little different from those who do not know Christ. Looking at many contemporary Christians, the suspicion that the Reformation doctrine of justification would lead to antinomianism—the disregard for "the righteous requirements of the law as fully met in us" (Rom. 8:4)—seems well founded. Yet focusing solely on rules and regulations to change behavior is akin to starving oneself during a long sea voyage. During our long journey to achieve a godly life we may miss essential nourishment—the supernatural provision for achieving godliness that comes with justification. Our problem, then, is not that we don't know what we ought to do (cf. Rom. 7:14ff.); our problem is doing what we know we ought to do. The Galatian Christians apparently grasped the gratuitous nature of grace in justification, but did not see that as justification is wrought by God for us, sanctification is every bit as much wrought by God in us. Thus Paul chided them, "After beginning with the Spirit, are you now trying to attain your goal by human effort?" (Gal. 3:3).

In sanctification, God's complete redemption addresses sin and its rule over our lives. Christ came "to save his people from their sins" (Matt. 1:21). By examining "the inheritance of the saints in the kingdom of light" (Col. 1:12), the riches bequeathed to us through Christ will become evident. Come, then, to the banquet table and feast on what is spread before us. For God's repast will strengthen us for the journey.

Confrontation with Sin

This is the victory that has overcome the world, even our faith.

—1 John 5:4

Those who belong to Christ Jesus have crucified the sinful nature with its passions and desires.

—Galatians 5:24

Your enemy the devil prowls around like a roaring lion looking for someone to devour. Resist him, standing firm in the faith.

—1 Peter 5:8–9

As for you, you were dead in your transgressions and sins, in which you used to live when you followed the ways of this world and of the ruler of the kingdom of the air, the spirit who is now at work in those who are disobedient. All of us also lived among them at one time, gratifying the cravings of our sinful nature and following its desires and thoughts.

—Ephesians 2:1–3

We are reassured by Scripture that God never seeks our downfall by tempting us (James 1:13–15), and that with his help we can overcome temptations (1 Cor. 10:13). The enemies of our souls prior to our conversion, however, continue to be our foes after conversion. There is still great danger around and within us; hence, "if you think you are standing firm, be careful that you don't fall!" (v. 12). The ranks of believers on the front line in the war against the minions of evil are hard hit. We continue to sustain terrible losses among both ministers and laity. That believers in Christ are not more distinct from secular persons is at once a matter of concern and consternation.

Every believer is engaged in vicious spiritual battle (Eph. 6:10–18), and not one of us can remain on the sidelines in the war between good and evil, that is God and the Devil. We wage war on three fronts, "the trinity of temptation," and we need to be aware who comprises our antagonists— the world, the flesh, and the Devil.

The World

Over against the world of humanity, which God loves (John 3:16), is the world as a system of evil, violence, and sin, which we as believers are not to love (1 John 2:15). This world system (the *kosmos*, or cosmos, from which we get the word *cosmetic,* meaning "the attempt to bring order") is totally at variance with the plans and purposes of God. We are told in Scripture that "everything in the world—the cravings of sinful man, the lust of his eyes and the boasting of what he has and does—comes not from the Father but from the world" and is doomed to futility and destruction (vv. 16–17). Believers are not to be "conformed any longer to the pattern of this world" (Rom. 12:2a), and "friendship with the world is hatred toward God" (James 4:4). The followers of Jesus have been given to him "out of the world" (John 17:6), and although we are "in the world," we are not to be "of the world anymore than [Jesus is] of the world" (vv. 11, 14). We will indeed be hated by the world (v. 14), but Jesus does not pray that we will be taken "out of the world," but rather that we will be sent into the world and protected from the world (vv. 15, 18).

"The world is too much with us," Robert Browning observed, and many contemporary evangelicals are all too captive to a culture of materialism, narcissism, and pragmatism. With the "raunch factor" in the media increasing exponentially, how shall we remain pure in our minds and hearts in an X-rated society? The Bible commands us to "purify ourselves from everything that contaminates body and spirit, perfecting holiness out of reverence for God" (2 Cor. 7:1b). The grime of the world is all too much upon us. And yet Christians can, praise God, overcome the world.

The Flesh

Although *flesh* can refer to the physical life of humankind (as in the expression "flesh and blood"), most commonly it refers to the life of humankind in sin, and is synonymous with the fallen nature. F. B. Meyer has suggested that we spell *flesh* backward and drop the "h," leaving *self*.[3] Romans 7:18 says, "In me, that is, in my flesh, is no good thing" (av). The essence of our revolt against God is dethroning God and making self the point of reference in our lives. Our age's preoccupation with self-fulfillment, self-assertion, and self-reliance is the embodiment of Satan's offense against God (Isa. 14:13–14). The axiom of Scripture is clear: "The one who sows to please his fallen nature, from that nature will reap destruction" (Gal. 6:8). The deeds of the flesh are itemized in Galatians 5:19–21—"sexual immorality, impurity and debauchery; idolatry and witchcraft; hatred, discord, jealousy, fits of rage, selfish ambition, dissensions, factions and envy; drunkenness, orgies and the like." What a thatch of noxious weeds![4]

The very first characteristic of the flesh, which will increasingly typify the last days, is self-love (2 Tim. 3:1). We are not to have confidence in the flesh (Phil. 3:3) but to deny ourselves (Matt. 16:24). Epitomizing the "selfism" of our times is the famous German mountain climber, Reinhold Messner. He never planted his nation's flag on a summit but rather exclaimed, "I do things only for myself."[5] John Lennon crooned, "I believe in me . . . that's reality." How many of us suffer from acute inflammation of the ego. Walt Whitman captures the typical American mood when he sings of "himself" and celebrates himself in *Leaves of Grass*. (You may recall that President Clinton gave a copy of *Leaves of Grass* to Monica Lewinsky.)

Selfism has become a kind of contemporary religion that is little more than old-nature culture, devoid of the transcendent God and dedicated to "making people feel good about themselves." Tina Turner testified that she loved her Buddhist altar in her home and her new religion because, "in this religion, you decide for yourself what is wrong." Immediate enjoyment is "in" and deferral of gratification is "out." Max Stirner, in *The Ego and His Own,* is disturbingly candid:

> Nothing is more to me than myself. . .whether what I think and do is Christian, what do I care? Whether it is humane, liberal or inhumane and illiberal—what do I care about that?[6]

In the face of such a cultural current how can anyone buck the tide? Christ proposes that the Christian do just that. "For it is God who works in you to will and to act according to his good purpose" (Phil. 2:13). The "I" is to be replaced with the "yet not I" (Gal. 2:20) as we "by the Spirit put to death the misdeeds of the body" (Rom. 8:13). Then we shall live.

The Devil

The Bible clearly teaches the evil agency of the Devil—Satan—who with his legions of fallen angels—or demons—designs to thwart the purposes of God and defeat, mutilate, and destroy as many human beings, Christian or non-Christian, as he can. Our enemy is clever and crafty, shrewd and seductive. His batting average is high—he failed only to bring down our Lord Jesus Christ, who triumphed over him in the wilderness (Heb. 4:15). He is a murderer, a liar, the accuser of God's people, and the archdeceiver.[7] Thus the apostle John tells us,

> *He who does what is sinful is of the devil, because the devil has been sinning from the beginning. The reason the Son of God appeared was to destroy the devil's work.*
> —1 John 3:8

We see Satan's nefarious strategy used against Adam and Eve in Genesis 3. He brings them first to the place of doubting the Word of God, then denying the Word of God, and then disobeying the Word of God. Doubt, denial, and disobedience are the Devil's perennial occupation.

The pretensions and deceptions of the Devil have never been more effectively depicted than by John Bunyan in his *Holy War*. If in *The Pilgrim's Progress* Bunyan uses the journey as a paradigm of the spiritual life, in *Holy War* he uses the battle. (These two volumes constitute somewhat the *Iliad* and the *Odyssey* of Christianity). Coming through Eye-gate and Ear-gate in particular, Diabolus argues,

> Therefore let us assault them in all-pretended fairness, covering our intentions with all manner of lies, flatteries, delusive words; feigning things that will never be and promising that to them that they shall never find. This is the way to win Mansoul, and to make them of themselves to open their gates to us; yea, and to desire us too to come in to them.[8]

But the Evil One has been defeated at Calvary. Jesus announced, "Now is the time for judgment on this world; now the prince of this world will be driven out" (John 12:31). We can sing with Martin Luther and the saints of the centuries,

> And tho this world, with devils filled,
> Should threaten to undo us,
> We will not fear, for God hath willed
> His truth to triumph thru us.
>
> The prince of darkness grim—
> We tremble not for him;
> His rage we can endure,
> For lo, his doom is sure—
> One little word shall fell him.

For indeed it is ever true, "They overcame him by the blood of the Lamb and by the word of their testimony; they did not love their lives so much as to shrink from death" (Rev. 12:11).

Conflict with Sin

I urge you, as aliens and strangers in the world, to abstain from sinful desires, which war against your soul.

—1 Peter 2:11

For the sinful nature desires what is contrary to the Spirit, and the Spirit what is contrary to the sinful nature. They are in conflict with each other, so that you do not do what you want.

—Galatians 5:17

When I want to do good, evil is right there with me. For in my inner being I delight in God's law; but I see another law at work in the members of my body, waging war against the law of my mind and making me a prisoner of the law of sin at work within my members.

—Romans 7:21–23

In the civil war that rages within us, we cannot evade our responsibility by saying "The Devil made me do it!" Nor can we find immunity from blame by pointing to our gene pool or our upbringing. The Christian never moves completely or all at once out of Romans 7—all manner of evil desire—into Romans 8—walking only in the Spirit—but rather has agonizing moments of "What a wretched man [or woman] I am" quickly yielding to a glorious affirmation of "Who will rescue me from this body of death? Thanks be to God—through Jesus Christ our Lord!" (Rom. 7:24–25).

To understand this inner turmoil and its resolution in Christ, we should avoid the teaching of two extremes. Some have taught that our position is a kind of split personality or dual personality in which believers are schizoid, like two different people. On the other hand, David Needham and others have taught that the believer is an entirely new person with sin eradicated ("nothing inside me is essentially evil").[9] This surely is not the truth, as we all know about ourselves; to the last step we take in the Christian life there is "a radical need for mortification of the flesh."[10]

Borrowing from Charles Hodge and Renald Showers, a preferable explanation is derived from the definition of *nature*—"that inherent disposition of a being or thing that affects the conduct and character of that being or thing."[11] Both before and after the new birth, believers possess a human nature as homo sapiens. Before conversion, however, our disposition is to stray from God and his ways. But even the Old Testament prophets spoke of God giving us "a new Spirit" and "a new heart" (Ezek. 36:26). In the miracle of regeneration, the divine nature is implanted (2 Peter 1:4), which is the seed of a new life that energizes us and germinates into a new disposition to govern us. As Showers quotes Louis Berkhof,

> Regeneration consists in the implanting of the principle of the new
> spiritual life in man, in a radical change of the governing disposi-
> tion of the soul, which, under the influence of the Holy Spirit,
> gives birth to a life that moves in a Godward direction. In principle
> this change affects the whole man.[12]

Thus begins the process of being renewed in God's image (Titus 3:5–6; 2 Cor. 3:18; Col. 3:10). To be other than yielded to the Holy Spirit and subject to his control is to backslide and revert once again to the domination of the old disposition, the old way of self-effort. Shall we live the self-life or shall we live the Christ-life? Which disposition shall govern? With the Holy Spirit of God empowering and enabling, believers cannot live habitually in the grip of sin (1 John 3:9). God has provided deliverance from the power of sin in our daily lives, and does so in a fashion that is more than sufficient to effect holiness. The means is a new and transforming disposition, "the spirit of holiness" (Rom. 1:1–4) made potent through the Holy Spirit. There is victory through what Jesus did for us on the cross and through what the Holy Spirit does in us by his love and power.

"Walking in the light" describes the surrendered Christian life (1 John 1:7). Through the Word we seek the light of God's holiness (Ps. 119:105) to shine into our hearts and judge our thoughts and deeds. An old Keswick preacher described how he dusted the living room early one day. Yet, upon entering the room in the brightness of noonday, he saw a lot of dust that he had missed earlier. As more light shines into our hearts, we become aware of dust we had not seen earlier. As many have pointed out, the apostle Paul seemed to become more and more aware of the wickedness of his old disposition. In his earlier writings he spoke of himself as "the least of the apostles" (1 Cor. 15:9); then later he described himself as "the least of all God's people" (Eph. 3:8); and then, shortly before the end, he speaks of himself as "the worst of sinners" (1 Tim. 1:16). He seems to have experienced an increasing sense of his own sinfulness and a growing sense of the wonder of God's redeeming grace.

The basis for victory over sin is the work of Christ for us, our *positional* union with him in his death and resurrection, and our *practical* empowerment through the Holy Spirit, beginning with a transformation known as regeneration or the new birth. Discussion about sanctification and holiness apart from Romans 6:1–23 is unimaginable. Preserving a balance between the positional and the practical beckons us to the moral high ground.

As you and I face the onslaught of temptation from the world, the flesh, and the Devil, we need first to take our stand at Calvary as those who are in Christ and dead to sin: "Sin shall not be your master, because you are not under law but under grace" (Rom. 6:14).

But how can we be properly energized to

1. "know that our old self was crucified with him so that the body of sin might be done away with"?
2. "count [our]selves dead to sin but alive to God in Christ Jesus"?
3. "offer [our]selves to God as those who have been brought from death to life. . .offer the parts of [our] bod[ies] to him as instruments of righteousness"?
4. "wholeheartedly [obey] the form of teaching to which [we] were entrusted" (Romans 6:1–23)?

As you and I encounter the temptation to display temper, irritability, and rage; participate in sexual impurity and surrender to lust; be self-serving in carelessness with the truth (we may call it terminological inexactitude); surrender to the desire to be controlling, and so forth, we have the basis to resist all temptation—both the legal basis (through the Cross) and a basis within our lives (through the Holy Spirit).

F. B. Meyer endeavored one day to study for his Sunday sermon, but the house was full of noisy grandchildren. A rising sense of resentment choked him until he realized how inappropriate was his response. Seeing the reality of the situation, he saw the "light." As one joined to Christ, he called to the Lord, "Your patience, Lord, your patience, Lord" (asking, in a sense, to be "crucified with Christ"), but this through the power of the indwelling and infilling Spirit. He experienced a calmness and quietness in his spirit.[13] It is not necessary to capitulate to sin and, indeed, Christians need not sin. We are under no fatal necessity in the hour of temptation.

CONQUEST OVER SIN

Holiness, holiness is what I long for.
Holiness is what I need.
Holiness, holiness is what you want from me.

> Take my heart and form it.
> Take my mind, transform it.
> Take my will, conform it
> To yours, to yours, Oh Lord.
> —The Vineyard hymnody

Therefore, since Christ suffered in his body, arm yourselves also with the same attitude, because he who has suffered in his body is done with sin. As a result, he does not live the rest of his earthly life for evil human desires, but rather for the will of God. For you have spent enough time in the past doing what pagans choose to do—living in debauchery, lust, drunkenness, orgies, carousing and detestable idolatry. They think it strange that you do not plunge with them into the same flood of dissipation, and they heap abuse on you. But they will have to give account to him who is ready to judge the living and the dead. For this is the reason the gospel was preached even to those who are now dead, so that they might be judged according to men in regard to the body, but live according to God in regard to the spirit.

> —1 Peter 4:1–6

This much is clear: The Lord Jesus came that we might live the abundant and overcoming life (John 10:10). God's grace is adequate and in every way sufficient (Rom. 5:20b). Our endowment in Christ is superlative, our assets unlimited.

The French aviator Antoine de Saint-Exupery tells of taking some Bedouins from the parched Sahara to the French Alps. There, they saw a waterfall for the first time. They stood transfixed, eyes bulging and jaws agape. He couldn't move them away. They couldn't imagine such a copious supply of water. When he brought them into a hotel, he couldn't get them out of the bathroom, where they kept turning the faucets on and off. The next morning, they unscrewed all the faucets, wanting to take them home with them![14] Praise be to God for the bountiful supply in Christ—the living water (John 4:14), gushing forth as "rivers of living water" (7:37–39). Is this not the promise of God to his people from of old?

> For I will pour water on the thirsty land,
>   and streams on the dry ground;
> I will pour out my Spirit on your offspring,
>   and my blessing on your descendants.

> They will spring up like grass in a meadow,
> like poplar trees by flowing streams.
> —Isaiah 44:3–4

Thus the apostle Paul represents Christians as being "more than conquerors through him who loved us" (Rom. 8:37). He exults, "But thanks be to God who always leads us in triumphal procession in Christ" (2 Cor. 2:14). He prays for the Thessalonian believers: "May God himself, the God of peace, sanctify you through and through. May your whole spirit, soul and body be kept blameless at the coming of our Lord Jesus Christ. The one who calls you is faithful and he will do it" (1 Thess. 5:23–24). We sing,

> He breaks the pow'r of cancelled sin,
> He sets the prisoner free.

We sing,

> O for a heart to praise my God,
> A heart from sin set free.

In the catechism, we recite, "Sanctification is the work of God's Spirit whereby he renews the whole person after the image of God and enables us more and more to die to sin and live for God." Precisely what this means and how it is worked out is, of course, subject to interpretation.[15]

Some believers overstate the experience of sanctification, speaking in terms of eradication of the sinful disposition, or they redefine so as to attain perfection, although John Wesley himself did not care to use the word *perfection* and never claimed to have had the experience. The Westminster Catechism, on the other hand, precludes any possibility of real victory: "No man is able, either of himself, *or by any grace received in this life,* perfectly to keep the commandments of God; but doth daily break them in thought, word, and deed."

Certainly, by ourselves we cannot keep the commandments of God, before or after conversion. As has already been discussed in chapter 5, in the giving of a commandment or injunction, God is not implying that we are able to do what he tells us to do. Paul, in later Christian maturity, conceded,

Not that I have already obtained all this, or have already been made perfect,
but I press on to take hold of that for which Christ Jesus took hold of me. . . .
I do not consider myself yet to have taken hold. . . . but one thing I do:
Forgetting what is behind and straining toward what is ahead, I press on
toward the goal to win the prize for which God has called me heavenward in
Christ Jesus.

—Philippians 3:12–14

But while maintaining that sanctification is both positional and progressive—that is, in a series of crises and growth the believer makes steady strides toward an increasing conformity to Christ and likeness to him—we must succumb to neither an unbiblical idealism that overstates what Christian experience should be (and weighs us down with a heavy legalism), nor an unbiblical pessimism that understates what Christ is willing and able to do in us (and impales us in an oppressive antinomianism). The latter seems to be a danger in our time. The kind of moment-by-moment faith and victory that I see in the New Testament, however, could be encapsulated in the following:

1. before conversion: not able not to sin;
2. subsequent to conversion in the normal pattern of crisis and growth: able in temptation not to sin;
3. in glory with the Lord forever: not able to sin.

The New Testament will not allow us to languish in resigned defeatism. In any given day, I am to expect by God's Spirit to be more of a victor than I was yesterday. John Wesley asked, "Can God do nothing with sin but forgive it?"[16] Have we not the scriptural basis for expecting and for praying

> O that I now, from sin released,
> Thy word may to the utmost prove,
> Enter into the promised rest,
> The Canaan of Thy perfect love!
> —Charles Wesley

> Take myself, and I will be
> Ever, only, all for Thee.
> —Frances Ridley Havergal

How well I remember my conversion at age nine, after the postsupper family Bible reading. I had read from Isaiah 53:

> *All we like sheep have gone astray; we have turned every one to his own way;*
> *and the Lord hath laid on him the iniquity [sic] of us all.*
>
> —verse 6 KJV

I came under the conviction of sin and asked my dad if I could be saved. He responded in the affirmative and helped me pray to receive Christ as my Savior. But there were many dimensions of Christian experience that I did not yet grasp, including the fullness of the Holy Spirit and the life of yieldedness and consecration. At age thirteen, while reading a book that my mother's Sunday school teacher had given her (F. B. Meyer's *The Christ-Life for the Self-Life*), I came to the first in a series of spiritual crises in which I experienced brokenness and surrender. Aspects of service and obedience that I had never before imagined became essential, even critical. Still, what is considered the normal Christian life—yieldedness, prayer, Bible study, fellowship, participating in church sacraments—is not the average Christian experience. Why such a dearth in true Christian living and what can we do about it? It is a compelling concern for all of us.

THE CONUNDRUM OF SIN AND SANCTIFICATION

> *For God did not call us to be impure, but to live a holy life.*
> —1 Thessalonians 4:7

> *For he chose us in him before the creation of the world to be holy and blameless in his sight.*
> —Ephesians 1:4

> *I could not address you as spiritual but as worldly—mere infants in Christ. I gave you milk, not solid food, for you were not yet ready for it. Indeed, you are still not ready. You are still worldly. For since there is jealousy and quarreling among you, are you not worldly? Are you not acting like mere men?*
> —1 Corinthians 3:1–3

Persons that are well affected to religion, that receive instructions of piety with pleasure and satisfaction, often wonder how it comes to pass that they make no greater progress in that religion which they much admire. Now the reason of it is this: it is because religion lives only in their head, but something else has possession of their heart.

—William Law,
A Serious Call
to a Devout and Holy Life

In both the Old and New Testaments, it is clear that God intends for his people to be his "holy ones," reflecting his beauty and character (cf. Matt. 5:16; 1 Peter 2:9). God's objective in the regathering of Israel from the nations is "to show himself holy among them in the sight of the nations" (Ezek. 28:25). Further, he will "show himself holy through them before their eyes" (36:23; 39:27). Even in the millennial kingdom, the Lord has made provision that his people will be taught "the difference between the holy and the common" and be able "to distinguish between the clean and unclean" (44:23). The holiness of his people is obviously a top priority for God. Scandal and sullied living among believers encourage the wicked not to repent (13:22).

God's enabling grace and power have been evident in the lives of many men and women across the centuries, and in our time as well. The existence of spiritual giants from varied walks of life—Enoch, Noah, Joseph, Abraham, Moses, Joshua, Ruth, Daniel, and the apostle Paul—demonstrates that God does not have favorites—he has intimates. While we celebrate the overcomers, many in the church today settle for forgiveness but do not avidly desire holiness. Where is our "hunger and thirst after righteousness?" (Matt. 5:6). Paul Rees observed that in today's theological climate "justification has easy breathing, while sanctification gasps for breath."[17] Beyond deliverance from "natural man" status *(psukikos),* we must ask, Why are so many Christians stranded at the level of "carnal" *(sarkikos),* rather than living "as spiritual" *(pneumatikos)?*[18]

1. The New Morality

The church tends to take sin far less seriously in an age of relativism and "the new morality," which is another name for the old immorality. The very notion of divine prohibition is, to many, laughable in our time of moral anarchy. The Ten Commandments are, in large part, optional, and that Judaism and Christianity are of a "command ethic" is immaterial to many. Religious liberals long ago dismissed the biblical idea of sin as being "a relic in the theological jungle," and even evangelicals apologize, saying, "Now, I don't want to make you feel guilty." But we *are* guilty before God and need to repent. The Holy Spirit convicts of sin (John 16:8–11) and so must we. Unless we face sin head-on, there will be no call for repentance and the Cross becomes irrelevant. Unless sin is "exceeding sinful" (AV), or "utterly sinful"—compelling discipline by church or secular authority— we are left unmolested to live inconsistent and deeply flawed lives. But "I'm OK, you're OK" is an insufficient moral touchstone.

Our daily newspaper recently told of a man who had a huge pet boa constrictor. This powerful reptile was an amusing pastime and conversation piece until it crushed one of the man's children to death. If we tolerate sin and play games with sin, we shall come to tragedy. We need to hate sin and confess our sin and teach and preach on sin. The gradual loss of sensitivity to sin and our predilection for rationalizing and excusing sin will bring us to grief, as they have over the centuries brought so many others to grief.

2. A Moral Vacuum

We are living in a time of "moral vacuum," the bankruptcy of the Enlightenment experiment being painfully apparent. We are seeing the harvest of the sexual revolution of the 1960s and its "anything goes" philosophy. No one has analyzed this fallout with more precision than David Wells in his study *Losing Our Virtue: Why the Church Must Recover Its Moral Vision.* Wells shows how our generation has lost its moral bearings. Any sense of self-restraint has yielded to "self-gratification," and the preference is to live without moral boundaries. Tracing how we have lost our way morally, Wells perceives "the repeal of reticence, the loss of shame. In our becoming the therapeutic society [in which 'I feel' triumphs over 'I believe'], we are witnessing the secularization of the moral life."[19]

Thus we live without any cultural or societal reinforcement for biblical and traditional mores and may even be bereft of any help from the spiritual community of which we are a part. Any age has, of course, experienced its morass of evil, but Christians today are seeking scriptural holiness in a very unholy age: "Where there is no revelation, the people cast off restraint; but blessed is he who keeps the law" (Prov. 29:18).

3. The Days of Noah

The Bible tells us that as the age draws toward a close, the times shall become increasingly like in "the days of Noah" (Matt. 24:37) and like the days in which Lot left Sodom (Luke 17:28–29). "The terrible times in the last days" are described in 2 Timothy 3 and center around an unparalleled moral and ethical collapse. Those things that sinners have loved through the ages will culminate in an epidemic of love of self (narcissism), love of money (materialism), and love of pleasure (hedonism) rather than the love of God. The ethical and moral behavior at the end times will unravel, becoming what could be called "the world's Saturday night." In this setting, God's people will seek to respond to the divine mandate:

> Depart, depart, go out from there!
> Touch no unclean thing!
> Come out from it and be pure,
> you who carry the vessels of the LORD.
> —Isaiah 52:11

The course is not easy but it has, nonetheless, been laid out for us.

THE COURSE OF SANCTIFICATION

To enable us to serve him without fear in holiness and righteousness before him all our days.
—Luke 1:74–75

Therefore let us leave the elementary teachings about Christ and go on to maturity.
—Hebrews 6:1

And we, who with unveiled faces all reflect the Lord's glory, are being transformed into his likeness with ever-increasing glory, which comes from the Lord, who is the Spirit.
—2 Corinthians 3:18

But grow in the grace and knowledge of our Lord and Savior Jesus Christ.
—2 Peter 3:18

It is to a new life that God is calling us; not to some steps in life, some new habits or ways or motives or prospects, but to a *NEW LIFE.*

—Horatius Bonar,
God's Way of Holiness

Regarding spiritual growth, some absolutize crises and neglect growth while others absolutize growth and overlook the need for catalysts that lead to growth. The truth is we both go forward and slip backward in the Christian life. If we have ever been closer to Christ than we are at present, we are backsliders. The Hebrew Christians (clearly born-again, cf. Heb. 6:4–5) had fallen back, regressing into infantile behavior. Forward progress in the Christian life could not be resumed "as long as they kept on crucifying Christ all over again and putting him to public disgrace" (Heb. 6:6, taking the force of the present participle). We need to face any disobedience that hinders spiritual progress.

By giving the Spirit free course in our lives to help us benefit from the daily reading of the Word of God, the life of prayer, and intercession; by entering into the fellowship of other believers in the Christian community, partaking of the sacraments or ordinances of the church we experience milestones of spiritual progress. These attitudes and behaviors are "by faith from first to last" (Rom. 1:17) and are what Watchman Nee called "the normal Christian life."[20] Too, we need relationships with other Christians who will help us be accountable in living with short accounts before God. *Short accounts* entails what Brother Lawrence called "practicing the presence of God," or what Fredrik Franson terms "constant, conscious communion with the Lord." Helpful as well are role models such as those found in J. Gilchrist Lawson's sketches, *Deeper Experiences of Famous Christians.*[21] Such forays into the spiritual biographies and autobiographies of individuals are enriching, as long as we recognize that God formats spiritual experience in various ways according to each individual, and that the only One we are to slavishly imitate is the Lord Jesus himself.

Steady growth in the Christian life is predicated on the use of God's provisions for holy living:

1. Constant cleansing by the blood of Jesus, which washes away guilt and shame as we walk in the divinely given light of the Word (1 John 1:7).

2. Daily application of the "washing with water through the word" (Eph. 5:26), in which we are continually rinsed from the defilement caused by simply living in a fallen world.[22]

3. Enduring a deeper cleansing from inborn and inbred impurity, which comes through the refinement of fire (1 Peter 1:6–8). Isaiah's lips (the vehicle of his prophetic ministry) were touched by a live coal from the altar (Isa. 6:6ff.), in all likelihood a little piece of burnt lamb from a sacrifice. Daniel speaks of some of the wise ones who stumble "so that they may be refined, purified and made spotless until the time of the end" (11:35).

Thank God that there occurs restoration and healing when we have failed. We have all experienced cleansing by fire, and is it painful as "he sits as a refiner's fire or a launderer's soap" (Mal. 3:3).

Pouring over the testimonies of many who have been overcomers, I am struck by two particularly poignant factors in "the life that wins":[23] first, a growing sensitivity to sin—hatred of it—and an entering into the benefits of Calvary. When Dr. John Gerstner realized he was driving over the speed limit in a little Pennsylvania town, he drove to their police station and insisted on paying the traffic fine. It is necessary to deal with "the little foxes."

Second, overcomers understand the necessity of a fully surrendered life. When the temple was dedicated in the days of Solomon, the ark was brought into the Holy of Holies, set in its place, and then the priests went out, intending not to return. Their commitment was conclusive and complete. And so should be our surrender to Christ and his will—total and absolute.[24] We are to live looking to Jesus (Heb. 12:1–3). We first pray, "Take my life and let it be"; and we need then to pray, "Keep my life and let it be." We sing, "Turn your eyes upon Jesus, look full in his wonderful face"; we should continue to sing, "Keep my eyes upon Jesus." That concentration upon Christ through the Holy Spirit is the key to life in God. Oswald Chambers put it well: "Sanctification is allowing the perfections of the Lord Jesus to express themselves in human personality."

We look for the time when faith becomes consummated, when "we shall see him as he is" and become "like him" (1 John 3:2). And even the hope of that time contributes to our motivation to be holy, for "everyone who has this hope in him purifies himself, just as he is pure" (1 John 3:3). "Blessed are those who wash their robes, that they may have the right to the tree of life and may go through the gates into the city" (Rev. 22:14).

"You ought to live holy and godly lives as you look forward to the day of God and speed its coming" (2 Peter 3:11b). "Even so, come quickly, Lord Jesus!"

HELPS TO HOLINESS

Remember, God is more interested in our being holy than in our being happy. List the ninefold fruit of the Spirit (Gal. 5:22–23) on a page. Identify one biblical character from either the Old Testament or the New Testament who epitomizes or exemplifies this trait. Then, in another column, identify someone in the history of the Church or in contemporary society who likewise embodies these virtues. How can we appropriate these virtues for ourselves?

BELOVED COMMUNITY

The Divine Commonwealth

And on this rock I will build my church, and the gates of Hades will not overcome it.

—Matthew 16:18

For we were all baptized by one Spirit into one body—whether Jews or Greek, slave or free—and we were all given the one Spirit to drink.

—1 Corinthians 12:13

And in him you too are being built together to become a dwelling in which God lives by his Spirit.

—Ephesians 2:22

We are not Christ's because we belong to the Church—but we are of the Church because we belong to Christ.

—Peter Taylor Forsyth

Being the people of God in the world is a privilege and a risk. One of my former students was serving a large ethnic congregation in this country as associate pastor. One Lord's Day morning, a member pulled out a gun in the middle of the service and shot to death the senior pastor and the lead elder. As the armed man walked back up the aisle, searching for others to kill, a county sheriff's deputy, who was visiting that morning (and uncustomarily carrying his own gun), rose and shot the armed man. The congregation was, of course, in deep shock.

My former student became the interim pastor in that church and described, in his doctoral work, the ministry of prayer into which he led the congregation in the troubled days that followed the shootings. In a beautiful example of God's grace, the widow of the lead elder reached out to the family of the killer. Within the next several years, the gunman's eldest daughter was elected leader of the collegians at the church. Here we see in action both the privilege of God's care and provision for his own, along with the peril in which the people of God always find themselves (John 16:33). The church, although not always under the threat of weapons, is nonetheless "hard pressed on every side but not crushed" (2 Cor. 4:8).

In the moment of conversion (an individual event), the new believer is baptized into the Body of Christ (a corporate entity) and thereby fulfills the biblical injunction regarding the one and the many (Gal. 3:26–28). The exaggerated individualism in our country is totally antithetical to the meaning of Christian community; but there is also a collectivism prevalent in some contemporary thinking that totally obscures and eclipses the individual as a unique, unrepeatable personal event. From Pentecost to the return of Christ, the Lord is doing a new thing in creating the church, that is, "adding to their number daily those who were being saved" (Acts 2:47). Although the prophets of the Old Testament were clear that Gentiles would come to the Lord in great numbers (Mal. 1:11; 3:12), the nature and uniqueness of the church were mysteries not revealed until the apostleship of Paul (Rom. 16:25–27; Eph. 3:6, 8–11). Although, as Paul argues (Gal. 3:6–9), believers in Christ are truly descendants of Abraham and are sustained, as was Israel, by the nourishing supply of God (Rom. 11:17); the church is not Israel and Israel is not the church. Each retains its distinctive identity and special purpose in God's plan of salvation.

THE CHURCH AS THE FAMILY OF GOD

I kneel before the Father, from whom his whole family in heaven and on earth derives its name.
—Ephesians 3:14

His purpose was to create in himself one new man out of the two, thus making peace, and in this one body to reconcile both of them to God through the cross, by which he put to death their hostility.
—Ephesians 2:15b–16

There is one body and one Spirit—just as you were called to one hope when you were called—one Lord, one faith, one baptism; one God and Father of all, who is over all and through all and in all.

—Ephesians 4:4–6

And God placed all things under his feet and appointed him to be head over everything for the church, which is his body, the fullness of him who fills everything in every way.

—Ephesians 1:22

The word *church* in the New Testament *(ekklesia)* means literally "the called out ones," and in a generic sense is used variously to refer to an assembly of Greek citizens (Acts 19:39), a riotous mob (vv. 32, 41), and, indeed, Israel (7:38). In a specific sense, *Church* is used in the New Testament to describe the new people of God who are baptized into the Body of Christ. The church is not an aggregation of persons, but a congregation, the living organism comprising all who belong to Christ and are knit together in a supernatural fellowship.[1] The church is the redeemed community, both a coming together and a being together, and although never replacing Israel in the great plan and purpose of God, the church is "built on the foundation of the apostles and prophets" (Eph. 2:20) and lives as the people of God in this present age, which is called the church age (cf. Matt. 21:43).[2] Beginning with her birth on the Day of Pentecost, the church in her essential constitution recognizes no difference between Jew or Gentile, slave or free, male or female (Gal. 3:28). In the calling of the twelve apostles, Christ did a new thing, although not unrelated to God's ancient covenant with his people. But while the bonding of believers in the public ministry of Christ is, in a sense, the church in miniature or the anticipation of the church, Johnston's claim is legitimate that "the word 'church' should be reserved for the society that gathered into vital fellowship as the result of Christ's resurrection."[3]

Often, *church* is used to describe the whole household of faith in all of the centuries of her existence (Matt. 16:18). So this usage underscores not only the *unity* of the church but of all the individuals who ever have or ever will comprise the church. *Church* is also used, in the plural, of a number of congregations in a geographic area (Acts 15:41; Rom. 16:16) and in this sense emphasizes the *diversity* of the church. But, in more than fifty instances, *church* is used to identify a local congregation, as in "the church which is at Cenchrea" (Rom. 16:1) and stresses the *solidarity* of the church. In other words, Christ's great church has its necessary local outcroppings. So, while the church is a living organism, it does have organizational structure and offices for its ministry. There is no evidence in the New Testament, however, for the organizational union of churches or of a uniform liturgy for worship.[4] Such associations have arisen geographically, ethnically, and historically, and are viable options within the openness of the church in general under the sovereign guidance of the Holy Spirit.

A brother from a free-spirited church rebuked a member of a highly structured church: "You must be careful, lest you have a body without the spirit—that would be a corpse." The other responded, "And you must be careful, because a spirit without a body is a ghost." Although schism and division are reprehensible, the richness in the church's diversity appeals to different tastes and perceived needs. Many of the historic denominational differences are becoming insignificant while differences within denominations are becoming greater. For many, particularly younger believers, the idea of denominations is becoming increasingly outmoded. The more urgent question for them is, Where in our community is there an alive assembly of believers? A vital identification with a local body of believers is not optional, but essential for the nurture of the Christian life. The redemption that reconciles us to God also involves us in a community of believers reconciled to each other.

More than eighty different images are used in Scripture to depict the relationship with one another in the Body of Christ. "Branches in the vine" conveys the organic nature of our relationship; "shepherd and sheep" describes organization; "the Head and parts of the body" depicts functional aspects, and so on. The church is a covenant community bound together with "the unity of the Spirit through the bond of peace" (Eph. 4:3). We celebrate our covenantal bond in both baptism and in the Lord's Supper (Luke 22:20). F. W. Dillistone argues that some historic models of the church in Christendom have been defective, such as the monastic, the imperial, and the sectarian. He shows how the covenantal or federal church most satisfies the scriptural model, as "out of his gracious self-limitation God commits himself to man so that man may in an act of self-transcendence commit himself to God: and the Covenant form must ever bear witness to this dialectical movement."[5] The marks, then, of a living church are to be a gathering of believers where the Word of God is preached, the sacraments are administered, and discipline is enforced.

Christians are those "on whom the fulfillment of the ages has come" (1 Cor. 10:11). We live in this age, but the "powers of the coming age" (Heb. 6:5) have broken in upon us. The church is never to be seen in static terms, but rather as always on the move "in the power of the end," because the future has begun in Christ. "Christ is in us, the hope of glory" (Col. 1:27), which is to say, "Our incorporation into Christ and his body has an eschatological dimension in which we say, 'The Church can never be defined just as it is now!'"[6] Gordon Fee speaks of the church as "the people of God, the sphere of God's eschatological salvation in Christ" (i.e., the fulfillment of the promises of God concerning salvation).[7] The end is held back until the mission of the church is fulfilled, as Newbigin demonstrates. Indeed, in Christ we have "a new selfhood," the mutual losing of selfhood to find it again in our Beloved. Newbigin shows how "the eschatological tension between faith and hope finds its ultimate meaning in love."[8] We are to be Christ's community of love in a world bent on seeking its own selfish way. For this totally new identity we should indeed praise God.

The Church: Successes and Failures

You are the salt of the earth. But if the salt has lost its saltiness . . .
—Matthew 5:13

You are the light of the world. . . . Let your light shine before men, that they may see your good deeds and praise your Father in heaven.
—Matthew 5:14, 16

As it is written: "God's name is blasphemed among the Gentiles because of you."
—Romans 2:24

The church must be forever building, for it is forever decaying within and attacked from without.

—T. S. Eliot,
The Rock

God's ancient covenant people, Israel, experienced glory as well as ignominy. The message of God was delivered and was inscripturated in our Old Testament; the Messiah was promised and born; Israel's witness, though incomplete, was offered. Still, apostasy and idolatry were rampant, and only a godly remnant survived (Isa. 1:9). The nation's indictment was that she had profaned "the holy name of God among the nations" (Ezek. 36:20). Nevertheless, God's final word for this people is one of hope and victory (Rom. 11:25–26).

Similarly, the church, of which Christ is the Head (Col. 1:18), has had its moments of glory and its moments of shame. The book of Acts should not be romanticized, but it does depict the dynamics of a Spirit-filled church before, as J. B. Phillips put it, she "became fat and short of breath through prosperity or muscle-bound through over-organization."[9] The letters from the living Christ to the seven churches of Asia Minor (in Revelation 2 and 3) disclose that they consisted of a mixture of the virtuous and the villainous. In the same way, the seven local congregations addressed by the apostle Paul in his letters sharply contrast the carnality of Corinth with the vitality of Thessalonica, the heresy in Galatia with the fidelity of Ephesus.

Looking down the corridor of church history, we marvel with Daniel Jenkins at the extent and influence of the church, her "spectacular failure," and her renewal through the Spirit. The bush is not consumed.[10] But as Christians we are sometimes embarrassed by the gracelessness of the Church, what Richard John Neuhaus calls "the thus-and-so-ness" of the Church. Swinburne, the English poet, lamented that he would be able to worship the "Lamb of God" were it not for his "leprous bride." Many around us say, "Jesus, yes; the church, no." Someone remarked that the church reminded him of Noah's ark: If it weren't for the storm outside, you couldn't stand the stink inside. Another suggested that if Jesus came back to the North American church today, he would vomit (cf. Rev. 3:16).

The purpose of the church, however, is to glorify God by winning and discipling men and women, and by challenging "the principalities and powers"—the supernatural evil that dominates the world (1 John 5:19) and tyrannizes its cultural structures, traditions, and institutions.[11] As salt and light, we are to give our witness, but there is no indication that the church will transform the world in the old postmillennial sense. Indeed, the increasing secularization of the Western church seems to fulfill what Christ and the apostles intimated about the spiritual trends as time-space history draws toward a close (cf. Luke 18:8; 1 Tim. 4:1–3; 2 Tim. 3:1–9; 4:3–4; 2 Peter 3:3–7, etc.). Again, as in Israel, a true remnant will persist and be translated, but the ultimate victory will be Christ's at his coming in power and great glory (cf. Revelation 19:11–21). An overview of the church's undulations through the centuries will provide perspective.

On the Positive Side

1. The very survival of the Church is a miracle. There was nothing in the Graeco-Roman world like Christ's community of believers. She should be moldering by now in the dust, but she thrives. One of the greatest threats to the Church was at one time Marxist state socialism. It has collapsed, yet the Church lives.
2. With the "celestial gale" of the Spirit, the singularly unimpressive band of apostles was empowered and the Church grew to more than one million believers by the end of the first century.
3. By a gradual (not violent) process, Christianity led to the abolition of gladiatorial combat, fostered the liberation of women and children from repressive conditions (cf. Islam), and finally ended slavery (think of Wilberforce and others). Hindu peoples built hospitals for fleas; Christians built hospitals for the sick and afflicted of humanity.
4. Even in the darkest hours, the Bible and Christians kept civilization alive, as in the medieval period. Literacy was preserved in the monasteries and convents.[12]
5. Millions around the world have been converted and their lives changed through missionaries faithful to the gospel of Christ. Rousseau's romantic idea of peaceful paganism is belied by the practice of human sacrifice in the Aztec and Inca religions and by the fear in animism. The Church has taken root in every culture on earth and is unequaled in its universality. Darwin himself said he did not want to visit a land where missionaries had not been first.
6. The Church and the gospel have championed monogamous marriage, decency, and moral purity. They challenged the licentiousness of the classical world and of heathenism.[13] Christianity has been the most potent moral force in the West.
7. Not always consciously, the followers of Christ have promoted democracy and human rights, holding that each individual is made in the image of God and because Christ died for the spiritual emancipation of every individual. The covenantal and federal nature of the Church itself has become a model for Western democracy. Missionary enterprise thus lead to the call for political freedom.

8. The Bible has influenced the great music, art, and literature of the Western world and through contextualization of images found in diverse cultures[14] is considered to have engendered aboriginal expressions of the truth of the gospel.
9. The message of Christ and his cross have been the epitome of self-giving love throughout the world. Bishop Newbigin testifies,

> I still see the cross of Jesus as the one place in all the history of human culture where there is a final dealing with the ultimate mysteries of sin and forgiveness, of bondage and freedom, of conflict and peace, of death and life.[15]

On the Negative Side

1. From the beginning, the scandal of the Church has been the disloyalty and inconsistency of Christ's own followers, undercutting the credibility of the message. Starting with Judas Iscariot ("Everyone in Jerusalem heard about this" [Acts 1:19], the bad news carries faster than the good news), the greatest liability of the Church has been among those of us who professed her truth.
2. Adherents are unable to get along (as when Paul and Barnabas parted) and become a community of love and forbearance. Nietzsche sneered, "Show me that you have been redeemed and then I will believe your redeemer."
3. The deep rootedness of our pride and arrogance fails to reflect the character of our Lord. Young Gandhi was repelled by a racist South Africa when he was seriously giving consideration to the claims of Christ. In the wake of the "Year of the Evangelical," Bible believers became heady and overconfident and downright obnoxious in the United States.
4. The Church has a pronounced tendency to major in minors, to Pharisaically "strain at moths and swallow camels," to fail to "distinguish the things that differ," i.e., the menace of mistaken magnitudes, as when the synod of the Russian Church debated the length of candles while the Marxist revolution swept over their country in 1917. We must all plead guilty.
5. An idolatrous fixation on the status quo moves us much too slowly

in the direction we should take, as with the abolition of slavery. Some believers still argue the Civil War, and we often lag one generation behind on issues.

6. A perilous tolerance for syncretism from the very beginning allowed pagan elements into our belief and behavior patterns. This capitulation in our modern "sensate culture" has created a tendency toward materialism and secularism, seen in the "europeanization" of the North American church, as commitment wanes and attendance drops. Our greed and devotion to capitalism have brought us to flagrant consumerism.

7. While it is true that, like soap, the gospel needs to be continuously applied to defilement, and while it is fair to ask where we would be were it not for the gospel, we who are the Church have been unresponsive to many aspects of the gospel and have allowed bigotry and meanness to be too prevalent among us. That the persecuted become the persecutors is manifest in history, but why must it be so? There is no way to whitewash injustice: Calvin in regard to Servetus, Luther in regard to the Jews, the Puritans in regard to Roger Williams. Exceptions? We have written dark and disgraceful annals in our own time.

8. The indulgence of false doctrine has, from the beginning, diluted or distorted the pure gospel of Christ. An adulterated message has robbed masses of their right to hear the gospel of the grace of God in its simplicity and power. Extreme Calvinism was disinclined to let William Carey go to the heathen in India. Baptismal regeneration gave millions a false hope and became a refuge of lies. God have mercy upon us.[16]

Notwithstanding these deficiencies and debacles, the church of Jesus Christ is now experiencing the greatest gospel harvest in its history. The Church is Christ's!

THE CHURCH AS THE TEMPLE OF GOD

God's household, which is the church of the living God, the pillar and foundation of the truth.

—1 Timothy 3:15

We are . . . God's building. . . . No one can lay any foundation other than the one already laid, which is Jesus Christ. . . . Don't you know that you yourselves are God's temple and that God's Spirit lives in you? If anyone destroys God's temple, God will destroy him; for God's temple is sacred, and you are that temple.

—1 Corinthians 3:9, 11, 16–17

As you come to him, the living Stone—rejected by men but chosen by God and precious to him—you also, like living stones, are being built into a spiritual house to be a holy priesthood, offering spiritual sacrifices acceptable to God through Jesus Christ.

—1 Peter 2:4–5

An unholy church! It is of no use to the world and of no esteem among men. Oh, it is an abomination, hell's laughter, heaven's abhorrence. And the larger the church, the more influential, the worse nuisance does it become when it becomes unholy. The worst evils which have ever come upon the world have been brought upon her by an unholy church.

—Charles Haddon Spurgeon

Life in God is lived in the context of the believing community. Consider John Wesley's words: "Sir, you wish to serve God and go to heaven? Remember you cannot serve him alone. You must therefore find companions or make them; the Bible knows nothing of solitary religion." We need each other as do the interdependent parts of the body (1 Cor. 12:14ff.). Each believer has a unique place and function in the body. At odds with a gospel held in private is the clear teaching of the New Testament about, as John Stott calls it, "God's new society."[17]

The purpose of the church is to function as God's temple in the world, a temple, by definition, being that point in space and time where God meets humankind. In the Old Testament, the tabernacle and temple were physical structures to which people came. Jesus was that temple in his earthly ministry (John 1:14, 18; 2:19). In this church age, God has portable temples, with each believer being a point in space and time where other people may encounter the living God (1 Cor. 6:19–20). Collectively, then, the church is "God's building," "a dwelling in which God lives by his Spirit" (Eph. 2:22). Here, as believer-priests, we offer spiritual sacrifices (1 Peter 2:5);

we render service to God (2 Tim. 4:6); and offer our worship as a praise offering to God (Heb. 13:15–16).[18] Understandably, there will be no temple in the New Jerusalem, because God and the Lamb are its temple (Rev. 21:19).

As seen in Acts 2:42–47, the proper functioning of the people of God as his temple requires four activities performed when the members come together as a community.

1. "They Devoted Themselves to the Apostles' Teaching"

The early Christians submitted themselves to instruction, determining that their own teaching and preaching would reflect "the sound doctrine" that they had received. A body of propositional truth both then and now can be identified as "the apostolic tradition" in terms of which false teaching could be adjudged. "The faith" or the kerygma is developed in the teachings of Jesus (John 7:16–17; 18:19) and concretized in the message about Christ—who he is and what he has come to do.[19] The doctrine of Jesus, then, is the essence of the Church.[20] Truth is not a circle that includes all error. Instead, it is an identifiable body of truth.

2. "They Devoted Themselves to Fellowship"

The healthy church enjoys communion shared at a deep level, and *koinonia,* or fellowship. Found nineteen times in the New Testament, "fellowship" refers to a partnership (Luke 5:10) or a profound participation.

In plane geometry, we learned that "things equal to the same thing are equal to each other." Thus, notwithstanding our many differences, because Christ is in each Christian we are in that sense equal. The word *fellowship* is used of the closest human relationships, of a marriage contract in the days of Augustus. This is more than "chomping jaws and the hip-by-haunch proximity of nice people in a church basement, who would like each other whether any of them were Christians or not."[21] How satisfying is the sharing of the things of Christ among the people of God. "Then those who feared the Lord talked with each other" (Mal. 3:16a). Small-group experience is important for Christians, as is the accountability provided through close association with a group of believers.

3. "They Devoted Themselves to the Breaking of Bread"

They had large-group experience and small-group experience, but an essential component of their gatherings was remembrance of the Lord Jesus in the communion service. The atoning work is to be celebrated among the people of God until Christ returns. The single loaf (as his body) broken, distributed, and eaten links us together, as does the cup of the crushed fruit of the vine (as his blood) (1 Cor. 10:15–17). Are we hungry for the Supper? The practice of communion emphasizes our partaking together of the elements that speak of Christ. "He who sacrifices thank offerings honors me" (Ps 50:23). We evangelicals need a deepening appreciation and participation in sacrament or ordinance.[22]

Shortly before Christmas Evans went home to be with the Lord, he said to those about his bed, "I am leaving you. I have labored in the sanctuary for fifty-three years, and this is my comfort, that I have never labored without blood in the basin." Lord, may it be so today.

4. "They Devoted Themselves to Prayer"

Sharing with prayer partners and entering into united prayer and intercession have been an essential part of worship from the earliest history of the Christian church. Nothing is ever the same after we have prayed about it. The longer I live the more of a mystic I become about prayer. There is much I do not grasp about prayer, but if we do not enjoy fullness of blessings and overcomings it is because we do not ask for them (James 4:2). Jesus needed to pray, and the apostle Paul depended on the intercessory prayers of God's people. On the one hand, we see a drastic decline of prayer meetings in the churches of our day, and on the other hand, we see the renewal of some vital prayer movements within and across denominational lines. Lord, revive your church.

> Prayer is the soul's sincere desire,
> Uttered or unexpressed;
> The motion of a hidden fire
> That trembles in the breast.
>
> Prayer is the simplest form of speech
> That infant lips can try;

Prayer, the sublimest strains that reach
The Majesty on high.

Prayer is the contrite sinner's voice,
Returning from his ways;
While angels in their songs rejoice
And cry, "Behold, he prays!"

Prayer is the Christian's vital breath,
The Christian's native air,
His watchward at the gates of death;
He enters heaven with prayer.

O Thou, by whom we come to God,
The Life, the Truth, the Way;
The path of prayer Thyself hast trod:
Lord, teach us how to pray.
—James Montgomery (1818)

Devotions performed together exemplify the inner life of the church at its best. Out of this spiritual vitality and dynamic come an overflow, an outreach, the fulfillment of a mission.

THE CHURCH AS A FORCE IN THE FIELD

The one who sowed the good seed is the Son of Man. The field is the world.
—Matthew 13:37–38

As the Father has sent me, I am sending you.
—John 20:21

The harvest is plentiful but the workers are few. Ask the Lord of the harvest, therefore, to send out workers into his harvest field.
—Matthew 9:37–38

But you will receive power when the Holy Spirit comes on you; and you will be my witnesses in Jerusalem, and in all Judea and Samaria, and to the ends of the earth.
—Acts 1:8

The church exists by mission as fire exists by burning.

—Emil Brunner

The worshiping and fellowshiping church is under divine marching orders. The Gospels and the Acts present elements of the Great Commission, all of which in context thrust the church into the world for evangelization and disciple-making. Evangelization focuses on bringing nonbelievers to an initial commitment to Christ through repentance and faith, without which there is no such thing as the Christian life. Disciple-making is the process of preparing "God's people for works of service, so that the body of Christ may be built up until we all reach unity in the faith and in the knowledge of the Son of God and become mature, attaining to the whole measure of the fullness of Christ" (Eph. 4:12–13).

It is a shame that the Old Covenant people of God lost much of their missionary vision, as we see illustrated in the experience of Jonah, who grieved because God did not destroy his people's natural enemy, the Assyrians, in Nineveh. Misguided patriotism and unabashed nationalism eclipsed Jonah's desire and passion to reach the nations (cf. Jonah 4). Similarly, the church has often allowed the Great Commission to slip into insignificance.[23] The "feel-good theology" and "country club Christianity" of our time do little to build enthusiasm for evangelism, and the pluralism of broad ecumenism often discourages evangelistic effort: "Why, everyone is all right!" What a betrayal of the gospel.

Six times in Acts, the believers are called "the people of the way." Our purpose is made clear in the thirty-five words of Acts 1:8. We are to proclaim the good and the beautiful. We are to testify of what Christ has done for us. R. Newton Flew speaks of Christians as "the people of the interval," meaning we have a limited time in which to do the work of Christ, for indeed the Church is that fellowship through which Christ works in the world by the Spirit. T. W. Manson said,

> The ministry of Jesus is the standard and pattern of the church's task, but more than that, the church's task is the continuation of the ministry of Jesus.[24]

Pre-Evangelism

In many cases, the effectiveness of our testimony is a function of a relationship with an unbeliever that has been built over time in which, as Christ's ambassadors, we are visual commendations of our Lord, living a reconciled life (2 Cor. 5:18–20). Paul insists that we believers are on display and that "we have been made a spectacle to the whole universe" (a theater, from the Greek *theatron,* 1 Cor. 4:9). So our "good works" are to be seen (Matt. 5:16). We are "to shine like stars" (Phil. 2:15) in "a crooked and depraved generation."

A little boy watched the minister build a porch next door. When asked why he appeared so interested, the child replied, "I wanted to see what preachers say when they hit their thumb with a hammer!" We are under surveillance, closely watched. And our behavior is part of the mix prepared by the Holy Spirit to make a positive impression on hearts.

Jesus spoke of his followers as being "brought to full unity to let the world know that you sent me" (John 17:23). The unity of which he spoke is not organizational and structural but a highly visible spiritual unity in the Savior.[25]

Evangelism

No one ever passes from death to life through the good example of another—not even Christ's example saves. Salvation is effected by the turning of a sinner from sin to Christ as the sin-bearer, and then it is Christ who justifies and regenerates through the Spirit (Acts 16:31; Rom. 10:9–10). At some point, then, the gospel must first be verbalized as must one's response (Rom. 10:13–15). The truth of Christ, expressed in sentences and propositions, must register a positive impact on the one receiving the message. This may happen when he or she reads a gospel tract or other literature; in a worship service by sensing that God is truly among these people (1 Cor. 14:24–25); in a great evangelistic crusade; through an Evangelism Explosion presentation; in a small group setting, Bible camp, Youth for Christ rally, or elsewhere. Leaders in Christian gatherings of all kinds need to be seeker sensitive, careful not to indulge in implicit universalism, that is, speak or pray in such a manner as to imply that everyone present is a Christian.

Certain services (by virtue of the text of Scripture expounded) or special efforts in the church will be, and always have been, seeker focused or seeker centered. Believers, of course, cannot subsist on evangelistic preaching; they need Bible teaching. History shows that successful seeker-focused ministries are transitional; that is, as the percentage of converted persons increases, there is greater demand for more participation in worship and more opening of the Scriptures in exposition for the flock of God. The fact is, a movement of God is occurring around our world in the ingathering of the lost, whether in Latin America, sub-Sahara black Africa, the rim of the Pacific, or the former eastern-bloc countries in Europe. *Jesus still saves.* Keep reading conversion stories of people coming to Christ from around the world.

Post-Evangelism

After huge evangelistic crusades wherein large numbers of people answer the call, preservation of spiritual gains has been lost because of weakness in follow-up. The contemporary, more holistic emphasis on disciple-making—focusing on post-decision baptism, instruction, integration, and being built up in the faith—has had positive results. Thus, building up new Christians is a top priority in an age of evangelism. [26]

THE CHURCH HAS A GLORIOUS FUTURE

Now we see but a poor reflection as in a mirror; then we shall see face to face. Now I know in part; then I shall know fully, even as I am fully known.
—1 Corinthians 13:12

But our citizenship is in heaven. And we eagerly await a Savior from there, the Lord Jesus Christ, who, by the power that enables him to bring every-thing under his control, will transform our lowly bodies so that they will be like his glorious body.
—Philippians 3:20–21

What we will be has not yet been made known. But we know that when he appears, we shall be like him, for we shall see him as he is.
—1 John 3:2

"So, Watson," continued Holmes with a chuckle, "is it not amusing how it sometimes happens that to know the past, one must first know the future?"
—Arthur Conan Doyle

The imperfections of the church and all whom it comprises is a heavy burden. In this we only mirror the general human predicament. In his book, *Shantung Compound,* Langdon Gilkey describes life in a Japanese prison camp in China during World War II. Space was very limited for the nine to eleven individuals housed in each ten-by-eleven-foot room. Most of these prisoners were Christian missionaries, Christian businessmen and their families, teachers, and British government officials. In every situation, these "good, educated, and enlightened people," who had come to China to tell others about Jesus, or who were products of the effort to bring the gospel to China, "could not and did not implement that faith in living as a social group in an institutional arrangement." When the American Red Cross sent fifteen hundred packs of food to the camp, the Japanese suggested that the Americans receive one-and-a-half packs per person, and that other prisoners receive one pack each. The majority of Americans insisted that they receive seven-and-a-half packs each. The Japanese had to step in and adjudicate the deteriorating situation of acute selfishness.[27]

Such moral and ethical failings haunt the church. Generally speaking, the North American church and the European church are in the blahs. We are captive to our popular culture and being strangled with materialism and the sense of entitlement that characterizes our age. No one can say for certain what the Lord will or will not do, but should our Lord tarry, would it not be marvelous if the Lord visited his church with one more sweeping, powerful revival? At the very end of Judah's decline, too late to change the ultimate configuration of her history, God did come and mightily move among his people in the days of King Josiah, after the Word was recovered and the people of God repented (cf. 2 Chron. 34:14ff.). In fact, the Passover observance at that time was more powerful than at any time since the days of Samuel.[28]

Is God done with the Church? No more than with his ancient people, Israel. The Lord has vouchsafed to his people a glorious future. He has committed himself to present this church, whom he loves and for whom he shed his blood, as "a radiant church, without stain or wrinkle or any other blemish, but holy and blameless" (Eph. 5:27). He will welcome her to the marriage supper of the Lamb, and we can almost hear the clicking of the silverware (Rev. 19:6–9). The guarantee of the outcome is his faithfulness and his stability as that rock upon which the church is built (Matt. 16:18).[29]

Everything in a tall building depends on the foundation. My favorite

Chicago skyscraper is the majestic John Hancock Center, towering 1,127 feet over Michigan Avenue. This imposing structure consists of 400 million tons of steel, concrete, and glass. When the wind howls in from Lake Michigan, the water in the sinks of the John Hancock Center swishes back and forth. How does anybody ever dare go up to the top of this building? Lying 200 feet below the surface of Michigan Avenue, below the sandy loam and hardpan clay, is Niagaran bedrock. The John Hancock Center has 200 gigantic steel and concrete caissons, which extend down and anchor into the bedrock. Now there's a foundation! In the church, Christ Jesus is our solid foundation (1 Cor. 3:11).

No one can speak of the future with certainty, but there is no question that Christians are the people of the future. We are the sons and the daughters of the Resurrection. We are the Easter people of God. We are the people who, before the time, are tasting of the glory to come; the Lord's Supper is the "antipasto" of heaven.[30] We are ambassadors, who will be called home before the outbreak of the final hostilities (Rev. 3:10). Glory be to God.

THE CHALLENGE TO THE CHURCH

Examine each of the five statements that comprise the Great Commission. They are found in Matthew 28:16–20; Mark 16:15–18; Luke 24:45–48; John 20:21–23; Acts 1:8. Identify the common threads running through all five of these statements. Identify also the church's unique task in each of the statements. To demonstrate each of the statements in action, supply anecdotes, specific incidents, or stories from (1) the Bible itself (particularly from Acts and the Epistles), (2) church history, and (3) what you have observed of the contemporary scene in your own local church or churches. Remember David Livingstone's words about the Great Commission: "Always bear in mind that these are the words of a Gentleman."

14

THE STRATEGY OF PROVIDENCE

The Passionate Mover

I know, O Lord, that a man's life is not his own; it is not for man to direct his steps.
—Jeremiah 10:23

And my God will meet all your needs according to his glorious riches in Christ Jesus.
—Philippians 4:19

And we know that in all things God works for the good of those who love him, who have been called according to his purpose.
—Romans 8:28

God's works of providence are his most holy, wise and powerful, preserving and governing all his creatures and all their actions.
—Westminster Shorter Catechism

Christians believe in a God who is great enough to create this unfathomably vast universe, yet personal enough to care for each of us.
—George Marsden

The doctrine of divine providence—not mentioned as such is Scripture—has been called "the homeliest of all the Christian doctrines."[1] Many systematic theologies do not even contain a chapter on this doctrine, but like the doctrine of the Holy Trinity (also not mentioned as such in Scripture), it plays a central role in the lives of Christians. The doctrine of providence asserts, in the context of mystery and the unfathomable, that God does know, care, and provide for his own. God is committed to our well-being in time and in eternity. Only to a limited degree can we think his thoughts after him (Isa. 55:9; Rom. 11:33–36), but as Job proved, we can and must trust him.

As a young man, Robert Dick Wilson, the eminent Old Testament scholar of a past generation, spent much time in prayer while planning his life's work: the first fifteen years to study the biblical languages and their cognates; the next fifteen years to apply this learning to the interpretation of the biblical text; the last fifteen years to put into writing the fruit of his scholarship—and Wilson's scenario did, in fact, ensue. Skeptics would attribute events in the life of Wilson to chance, but too many coincidences, large and small, occur in the lives of Christians to attribute them all to happenstance. In grappling with the questions raised when considering the providence of God, suffice it to say that even in the small matters, the Lord wants us to trust him.

At a key point in my own life and ministry, I had the opportunity to move from a fulfilling pastorate into a position at the seminary. The opportunity was tantalizing, but the timing in regard to the situation at my church was inopportune. I dismissed the seminary position as a closed door. Someone else was hired. Two years later, our congregation voted at its annual business meeting to take stock, to rest in the arms of God, and to spend the next five years in study and contemplation of its situation. The very next morning, I received a call from the seminary in question asking me if anything had changed in my situation and if there were any chance I might reconsider. Coincidence?

On another occasion, in the midst of a howling "once-in-a-century blizzard," getting out of Chicago appeared impossible. My brother and his wife were supposed to meet us at O'Hare, from where we were to all head to a warm climate for a little R and R. Then my brother called us the night before and told us that their flight to O'Hare had been canceled. The next morning, as the severe weather continued, our plane was still scheduled to leave—about the only flight to get out that day. Just before we boarded, who should come sauntering along but my brother and his wife, ready to accompany us.

A few years ago, violating all good sense, I drove into the teeth of a storm to fulfill a speaking engagement. Instead, I found myself stranded in a small town in northern Indiana. There were no motels or restaurants in the town, and it was getting colder and later. Everyone's windows were dark. Earlier, I had noticed a sign that said simply "Maxson's Merry Manor." Not knowing what merriment I might find, I gunned my car back through the drifts to what turned out to be a nursing home. There I was given a hot meal and refuge from the storm. I slept in a recliner in the office and even had an opportunity to witness to the residents at breakfast and at devotions. God does know and God does care. (The event at which I had been scheduled to speak had, by the way, been canceled.)

When considering the hand of God working in our lives, innumerable questions nag at us. As will be seen below, the Bible teaches about God and our daily lives—God and the minutia, so to speak. If we truly believe that God started it all in the beginning but is now essentially on sabbatical we follow the thinking of deists. As Christians, however, we believe in a living and active God.

THE CONDITION OF HUMANKIND WITHOUT GOD

The fool says in his heart, "There is no God."

—Psalm 14:1

. . . without hope and without God in the world.

—Ephesians 2:12

What good is it for a man to gain the whole world, yet forfeit his soul?

—Mark 8:36

I know not the answer to the question "whither."

—Friedrich Nietzsche

For centuries, the biblical world view was basic to the culture of Western civilization. Apart from sorties by renaissance humanism, with its tendency to enthrone the self rather than God, the veracity of Scripture and the relevance of God's providence were axiomatic. Indeed, the German philosopher Leibniz (1646–1716) rationalized that the superiority of Western beliefs and its resultant culture were the best of all possible worlds. Taking the argument of creation as the design of a Supreme Being to an extreme, the *Bridgewater Treatises* in England argued that the virtuous nature and character of God are everywhere to be seen in nature.

But it can be argued that nature does not always reach out with loving arms. Voltaire in France (1694–1778) demurred, particularly in the wake of the great Lisbon earthquake and tidal wave, which destroyed two-thirds of the city and left more than 60,000 dead. Actually a deist, Voltaire wrote *Candide* (1757) to mock the notion that a loving God superintends creation. He saw only carnage, violence, and death. Enlightenment rationalism—which dominated the West from the fall of the Bastille in 1789 until the fall of the Berlin Wall in 1989—and romanticism—its more feeling counterpart—mounted a vigorous and scathing challenge against the biblical world view and any idea of a loving heavenly Father and a divinely provided way of salvation. Humankind declared its independence from God. For several centuries the prevailing cultural current has held that "it is just not viable intellectually to believe what is said in the Bible."

The more recent challenge to a the biblical doctrine of providence has been postmodernism, the radical relativism of our time, which argues that there is no truth at all. If Enlightenment thinkers denied the suprahistorical, the postmodernists deny even the historical. With roots in Nietzsche and Heidegger, postmodernists and literary deconstructionists deny the fixedness of any text, fleeing from all authority, including the authority of an author. From the perspective of postmodernism, there is no such thing as objective truth. According to this view, history itself is eliminated, making the historian into one who views the past in whatever ways pleases him or her and who records his or her perceptions in what is in reality a novel. There is no metanarrative, no connectedness.[2] The reader becomes the author.

Having scrapped even Enlightenment mainstays such as truth, justice, reason, morality, and reality,[3] for postmodernism all that remains is nihilism, that is, the destruction of the self itself. Himmelfarb says of postmodernism and of the new post-postmodernism taking over in France, that it is a thinly veiled invitation to intellectual suicide.[4]

Where has the assertion of human autonomy brought modern humankind? Even Charles Darwin recognized the plight of humankind without God:

> A man who has no assured and no present belief in the existence of a personal God or a future existence with retribution and rewards, can have for his rule of life, as far as I can see, only to follow those

impulses and instincts which are strongest or which seem to him the best ones.[5]

If indeed evolution is "an unsupervised, impersonal, unpredictable, and natural process," as a popular high school textbook maintains, "without either plan or purpose," then the outcome, as articulated by evolutionist G. G. Simpson, is not surprising:

> Man is the result of a purposeless and materialist process that did not have him in mind. He was not planned—he is a state of matter, a form of life, a sort of animal and a species of the Order of Primates, akin nearly or remotely to all of life and indeed to all that is material.[6]

This line of thinking resulted in bestializing humankind, ergo the Holocaust and modern aborturaries. Situation ethics has lead to moral chaos. Narcotized by material prosperity, many in the West have left the church or turned off their headsets in the church, where precious little application of biblical truth is permitted. Many thoughtful persons are pessimistic about life and the future, human prospects appearing dim. Many have yielded to cynicism and bitterness. Nonetheless, biblical Christianity has survived the death of God, the death of man, and the death of meaning in history.

The gospel of Christ still brings masses of humankind to saving faith. At the turn of the millennium, reports out of China indicate that young people are swarming into the churches. In America, a professor from the University of Nebraska writes of what is happening to Generation X:

> I recently began attending church again for the first time since childhood. I'm part of a trend—many so-called Gen-Xers are finding their way back to organized religion. Our generation is looking for ways to be countercultural in a secular society; raised on the shaky ground of relativism, we seek the firmer footing of moral absolutes. We want a mystical experience without having to ingest synthetic chemicals.[7]

But searching and open individuals are, of course, sitting ducks for New Age vagaries including the contemporary fad relative to angels (cf. Col. 2:18), the lure of Eastern religions, or other aberrations. Yet the Nebraska professor lays out the challenge to us:

More than my unshakable belief in an all-loving God or anxiety over where I'll be spending eternity, it's this longing that gets me out each Sunday morning to walk the 10 blocks to my church and that draws me to writers who speak a language of the spirit in our secular age.[8]

To all who are weary of the pessimism in the great think-tanks of the Western world, feeling a kind of cosmic loneliness in the vastitudes and infinity of our universe, there is, with all of its problems, the biblical doctrine of providence. In the Word of God there is no respite from hard thinking or from the necessity of human responsibility. But there is also a bulwark of confidence in ultimate meaning and ultimate outcomes, which comes from the character and nature of our God and his promises to us. An alternative exists to the endemic *angst* (despair) that afflicts humankind around the world.

Biblical Portrayals of Divine Providence

O Lord, you have searched me and you know me. You know when I sit and when I rise; you perceive my thoughts from afar. You discern my going out and my lying down; you are familiar with all my ways.
—Psalm 139:1–3

For you created my inmost being; you knit me together in my mother's womb. . . . My frame was not hidden from you when I was made in the secret place. . . . Your eyes saw my unformed body. All the days ordained for me were written in your book before one of them came to be.
—Psalm 139:13–16

Providence is a general action of God, by which he is present with his creatures, sustaining and preserving them, as long as he wishes them to be preserved, and preserves the order of his work appointed by himself, not by any fatal necessity, but as a most free agent; so that, for the sake of men, he controls all things, and moderates, changes, and hinders many things with respect to second causes.
—Chemnitz in Heinrich Schmid's
*Doctrinal Theology of the
Evangelical Lutheran Church*

In our time, disappointment and disillusionment with human life and its prospects have given rise to many neurotic and psychotic symptoms—drug and alcohol addiction, high divorce and suicide rates, and a widening sense of futility and depression.[9] The philosopher Arthur Schopenhauer (1788–1860) sat disheveled in a city park agonizing over the meaninglessness of life. A city policeman confronted him: "Who are you and where are you going?" Schopenhauer's troubled reply was, "Oh, if I only knew!" This is not like unlike Buddhists who moan, "Birth is sorrowful; life is sorrowful; death is sorrowful. Which are more—my sufferings or the waters in the seven seas?" So the bleakness and the restiveness are present not only in the West.

In stark contrast stands the biblical world view, encased in narratives from Genesis to Revelation, which reveals a solicitous and caring God. In the midst of impending judgment, for instance, God tells Noah to build an ark for himself, his family, and the animals so they would be spared in the deluge that was to come. God's provision for Noah is not only an early paradigm for God's salvation, it also demonstrates his providential care for his creatures caught in the calamities that are inevitable in a world in revolt against God.

Likewise, the call of Abram out of Ur of the Chaldees shows how God—although Abram, under the influence of his father, delayed full obedience—ultimately brought Abram into the land of promise. Abram's disobedience, his experience of revelation, and his triumphs are shown in relation to God's eternal purpose, and lend to Abram's life a significance that reaches down to the present. The story of how Abraham's servant found a wife for his master's son is a testimony to "the Lord, the God of my master Abraham, who has led me on the right road" (Gen. 24:48). Without denying the unique context for individuals in Scripture, it can be argued that the Bible reveals that our lives, too, can relate to the metanarrative of God's providential care.[10]

The Joseph cycle in Genesis likewise shows the vicissitudes that young Joseph endured as he was hated and sold into slavery by his brothers, betrayed by Potiphar's wife, and forgotten in the Egyptian prison. For eleven years he experienced hardship, but his confession was, "The Lord was with Joseph" (Gen. 39:2, 6 times). He saw that his adversities and his course were not "a sport of fate, but a plan of God" (James Stewart). "It was not you who sent me here, but God" (45:8) he said to his sheepish brothers. "You intended to harm me, but God intended it for good" (50:20). Contrast Joseph's spiritual optimism with the pessimism of so many people today.

The beautiful book of Ruth is a literary gem as well as a profound illustration of God's providential leading and care. It starts with a famine sent by God, but shows us how the steadfast Ruth was brought to the right place at the right time. Amid the tragedy and sorrow of life (in no way hidden by the author), God is at work incorporating the life of this humble Moabite woman into his great redemptive plan and purpose in Christ. In chapter 2 particularly, marvel at how the wealthy bachelor is drawn to young Ruth. He shares his lunch with her and assures her of good gleaning in his field. Thus the forebear of the Messiah is brought into the lineage of King David—Ruth's great grandson—and her name is forever enshrined in God's book (Matt. 1:5).

In a similar way, the exquisite book of Esther chronicles how a valiant young woman in a Persian harem is used of God to preserve and protect his exiled people. After Esther serves dinner to the emperor, he is unable to sleep (Est. 6:1), so he calls for a scroll to read from the royal archives. But it was a very special scroll that relates the valor of Esther's cousin, Mordecai. God is at work in small things to effect large purposes; great doors swing on small hinges.

But in Scripture God's providence is also demonstrated through the spectacular. Daniel's three compatriots refused to fall down and worship the great image on the plain of Dura. They did not doubt that their God could rescue them from the fiery kiln. But at the same time, they recognized that it has not always been in God's plan to spare his own or to render them immune from great trouble or even death. They state, "He will rescue us from your hand, O King. But even if he does not, we want you to know, O King, that we will not serve your gods or worship the image of gold you have set up" (Dan. 3:17b–18).

At times, God's providence appears to bring hardship. In the book of Habakkuk, the anguished prophet wrestles with what seems to be God's indifference to prayer (1:2), but even more God's use of the wicked Babylonians to judge his own people, the Jews. This seems contrary to the prophet's doctrine of the purity of God (v. 13) and he is frankly horrified by the incongruity of the situation. He makes recourse to his prayer tower and waits on God (2:1). God reassures him as to his justice and the prophet is moved to an extraordinary outburst of praise and worship (3:16–19). God is at work among the nations, as well as among individuals (cf. also Daniel 10 at this point).

The New Testament likewise abounds in examples of divine providence at work. The apostle Paul had a burning desire to preach the gospel in Rome (Rom. 1:8–16), but he submitted his ambition and determination to the will of God. His ultimate path was unexpected—via capture and imprisonment in Palestine and then transport as a prisoner to Rome (Acts 27). Ultimately, Paul had a blessed ministry there, but the framework for God's will was quite different from what Paul had imagined. We are reminded of Borden of Yale '09 and his commitment: *"The will of God—nothing more, nothing less, and nothing else!"*

Doctrine is not, in the final analysis, built on narrative or anecdotes. Yet, in Scripture, we view a rich tapestry of truth about God's providence. Again and again we see the Lord at work in situations major and minor. The section below probes the explicit promises given to believers about God's presence and provision for his own. We can all have our own narratives, like that of the Christian worker who had been repeatedly rebuffed by a hardened skeptic. One day, the skeptic said, "There are only two instances in Scripture where the word 'girl' is used. Name one of these and I will promise to come to church and listen to the gospel." It just so happened (one of those inexplicable "coincidences") that in his morning devotions, the Christian worker had been reading in Joel 3. He had noted the word *girl* in verse 3 and, checking his concordance, found that *girl* occurred only there and in Zechariah 8:5. When the worker gave his answer, the unbeliever was understandably nonplussed. He did go to church and was converted. Should we be surprised?

THE PROMISES OF GOD

For the eyes of the LORD *range throughout the earth to strengthen those whose hearts are fully committed to him.*
—2 Chronicles 16:9

The LORD *is good, a refuge in times of trouble. He cares for those who trust in him.*
—Nahum 1:7

From one man he made every nation of men, that they should inhabit the whole earth; and he determined the times set for them and the exact places where they should live. God did this so that men would seek him and perhaps reach out for him and find him, though he is not far from each one of us.
—Acts 17:26–27,
Paul's sermon in Athens

He [the Lord Jesus] is before all things, and in him all things hold together.
—Colossians 1:17

The doctrine of providence tells us that the world and our lives are not ruled by chance or by fate, but by God, who lays bare his purposes of providence in the incarnation of his son.
—T. H. L. Parker

The popular Greek and Roman gods were but naughty human beings projected on a cosmic screen, seeking their own selfish ends. The more sophisticated deities of great thinkers like Plato and Aristotle were impersonal—be it Plato's "idea of the good," or Aristotle's "unmoved mover." Aristotle's prime mover is "eternal, unchangeable, immovable, wholly independent, separated from all else, thought and thought alone."[11] Lucretius, the Greek atomist, insisted,

What an error to believe that the world was created for us by a divine will! Everything happens in nature without the intervention of the gods.

Muslims believe that life is governed by *kismet,* an impersonal force that shapes events in the universe without reference to individual needs or ends. Omar Khayam saw life as a game of chance:

'Tis all a chequer-board of nights and days
Where Destiny with men for pieces play.

Many would identify with Alexander Pope's view that human life is "a mighty maze without a plan."

In sharp contrast to these popular and often prevailing perspectives, the Bible's world view consists of precepts that convey an entirely different conviction about deity. Jacob confessed to Joseph that God had been "my Shepherd all my life to this day" (48:15). In blessing Joseph, he described the moral ascendancy of his son as due to an obvious cause: "Because of the hand of the Mighty One of Jacob, because of the Shepherd, the Rock of Israel, because of your father's God who helps you, because of the Almighty who blesses you" (49:24–25). Jacob, Joseph, and others in the Bible experience God in their daily lives and know him.

The nation of Israel was a special treasure to the Lord (*segullah,* a word that made the rabbis roll their eyes, cf. Ex. 19:5; Deut. 14:2; 26:18; Ps.135:4; and the New Testament counterpart in Titus 2:14; 1 Peter 2:9). Terms of affection and endearment abound in describing Israel's relationship to God. She is married to God (trace the relationship in the book of Hosea); she is "the apple of his eye" (Zech. 2:8). Although in her infidelity Israel is put away (Jer. 3:8), she is loved by the Lord and he says to her,

> *I have loved you with an everlasting love;*
> *I have drawn you with loving-kindness.*
> *I will build you up again*
> *and you will be rebuilt, O Virgin Israel. . .*
> *"He who scattered Israel will gather them*
> *and will watch over his flock like a shepherd."*
> —Jeremiah 31:3–4, 10

God's commitment to his ancient people is thus understood by many to be a binding and sacrosanct covenant that precludes God, by the terms of his commitment, from ever permanently rejecting his people (Rom. 11:1a). They will yet not only return to their land, but repent there and be saved in great numbers (vv. 26–27).

Thus God is the caretaker of his people. The shepherd metaphor is tender, the very picture of caretaking. Read and rejoice in Psalm 23 and its New Testament complement in which Jesus the Good Shepherd knows his sheep by name and leads them forth, going before them (John 10:4). Even though Old Testament images strongly invoke the shepherd metaphor (cf. Ezek. 34), the Jewish scholar Claude Montefiore maintains that no prophet or rabbi in Israel ever talked about the Divine Shepherd going out into the wilderness to seek a lost sheep, "the picture of God as not merely receiving those who turn to Him, but as taking the initiative in seeking those who have not turned to him."[12]

Jesus as the incarnate God is certainly the seeking shepherd who goes out after the one lost sheep (Matt. 18:12–14). He lays down his life for the sheep (John 10:11), and he is the seeking Savior (Luke 19:10; 1 Tim. 1:15).

The Psalter is replete with reflections of the Lord's intention for his own—to protect them and preserve them. Psalm 32:8 says, "I will instruct you and teach you in the way that you should go; I will counsel you and watch over you." And again, "The Lord delights in the way of the man whose steps he has made firm; though he stumble, he will not fall, for the Lord upholds him with his hand" (37:23–24). Having survived a crisis of confidence triggered by the prosperity of the wicked, the psalmist's doubts seem resolved as reflected in a quiet and private awareness, as experienced in "the sanctuary of God":

> *Yet I am always with you;*
> *you hold me by my right hand.*
> *You guide me with your counsel,*
> *and afterward you will take me into glory.*
> —Psalm 73:23–24

Most strikingly, the providential care and mercy of God extend broadly to every creature:

> *The eyes of all look to you,*
> *and you give them their food at the proper time.*
> *You open your hand*
> *and satisfy the desires of every living thing.*
> —Psalm 145:15–16

The Lord Jesus, in his Sermon on the Mount, asserts similarly that God "causes his sun to rise on the evil and the good, and sends rain on the righteous and the unrighteous" (Matt. 5:45). Yet Jesus teaches that God is committed to his own and that they should not fret over physical nourishment or clothing. The Father is cognizant of all of our needs, and Jesus promises, "Seek first his kingdom and his righteousness and all these things will be given to you" (6:33). We are assured that we are of more value than the sparrows, who are under divine observation, and that the number of our hairs is recorded (10:29–30).

The gracious Holy Spirit—the comforter, the counselor—is sent to stand alongside of the believer and "to be with us forever" (John 14:16). Our Lord has bequeathed us his peace (v. 27), lest we be troubled or afraid. Scripture is studded with promises of succor and support. Consider Proverbs 16:3, 9: "Commit to the LORD whatever you do, and your plans will succeed. . . . In his heart a man plans his course, but the LORD determines his steps." Joseph Parker talks of providence as "God working out his plan and all our little schemes and aims are drawn into it as the whirlpool sucks all streams and currents into its mighty and terrible sweep."[13] God's providence extends to vast circumstances as in Proverbs 21:1: "The king's heart is in the hand of the Lord; he directs it like a watercourse wherever he pleases"; or in Revelation 17:17: "For God has put it into their hearts to accomplish his purpose by agreeing to give the beast their power to rule, until God's words are fulfilled."

Yet individual believers are not presumptuous in supposing that God is vitally interested and involved in the minute matters in our lives.

> Near, so very near to God,
> Nearer I cannot be;
> For in the person in his Son,
> I am as near as he.

C. I. Scofield demonstrated childlike faith that God gives his children the desires of their hearts. In advancing years, he began to ask God for a car. He testified, "God heard my prayers and gave me a car." A minister friend said that he would do the same, since it would help him do his visitation and other duties so much better. Dr. Scofield, with a twinkle in his eye, said, "Well, if you think it could help you like that, by all means ask God for it. I didn't ask God for a car to help my ministry. I told God that I had worked pretty hard all my life and that I was getting on in years, and I wanted an automobile as a toy, a plaything, something in which to rest and enjoy myself. And God gave it to me."[14] Praise to our God.

EVIL AND THE DOCTRINE OF PROVIDENCE

Though he slay me, yet will I hope in him.

—Job 13:15

But he knows the way that I take; when he has tested me, I will come forth as gold.

—Job 23:10

So then, those who suffer according to God's will should commit themselves to their faithful Creator and continue to do good.

—1 Peter 4:19

Providence is that continuous agency of God by which he makes all events of the physical and moral universe fulfill the original design with which he created it.

—Augustus Hopkins Strong

The existence of evil in a universe created by a good God challenges, as do many realities about God, the finite mind. A deterministic world view or theology finds the existence of evil particularly troubling—if God decrees everything that exists, then God is responsible for blasphemy and adultery and the damnation of the lost. Such a conclusion is, of course, contrary to both Scripture and to God's will. But if a sovereign and all-powerful God has given free moral agency to humans, and we can make choices contrary to his will, a moral universe still exists but a universe in which there is pain and deprivation and disaster because of our human revolt against God.[15]

In such a fallen world, disease and accident and death occur to people of all ages. And Christians are not exempt from "the slings and arrows of outrageous fortune." Human mortality runs at 100 percent, and unless Christ comes for his church, we will all die waiting for him. Some difficulties that Christians experience are a matter of divine chastening (cf. Heb. 12:4–11), but the book of Job and John 9 make it clear that, while all human woes are ultimately traceable to sin, a given vicissitude does not necessarily correlate to wrongdoing.

In his volume titled *Christianity and History,* Herbert Butterfield quotes Richard Baxter on an aspect of the Great Plague:

> At first so few of the religiouser were taken away [i.e., in the Great Plague] that [according to the mode of too many such] they began to be puffed up and boast of the great differences which God did make. But quickly after that they all fell alike.[16]

Professor Butterfield then concludes,

> Providence is not a thing to be presumed upon; and indeed the Christian knows that it gives him no guarantee against martyrdom for the faith. What it does guarantee so exultantly in the New Testament is a mission in the world and the kind of triumph out of apparent defeat—the kind of good that can be wrested out of evil.[17]

So suffering may well be part of the perfect permissive will of God for each of us. God has promised to work in all of our circumstances for our good and for his glory (which two features are always in tandem, not in conflict). Suffering produces character (Rom. 5:3–5), and we are to rejoice in times of trial (James 1:2). God does not decree the death of a baby, or a fatal accident, or terminal disease, but God has promised never to fail us or forsake us in times of trials or in times that test our faith (1 Peter 1:3–7). Because God has promised to work in all of these tragedies for his own glory, many, like Robert Murray McCheyne, have come to Christ in the throes of the death of a loved one (in his case, his brother).

We do not often think of suffering as a gift, but Scripture sees it as an opportunity to glorify God (Phil. 1:29–30; cf. John 9:3). The book of Job is an example of physical and mental and spiritual anguish visited upon an upright servant of God. Job experienced grief and illness in which he was pressed to the absolute limit, but he found solace in the greatness of God, who determined the arena of spiritual conflict and who permitted Satan to go only so far as God designated. As Paul's imprisonment was used of God to give him an opportunity to write, so Amy Carmichael's years of confinement allowed for a different kind of fruit in her life.[18] In another story of trial, Mrs. Isabel Fleece tells of the death of her son in an automobile accident. In this great sorrow the Lord made his comfort real to her and her entire family.[19] In a similar testimony, Dr. John Feinberg, my colleague at Trinity Evangelical Divinity School, wrote about the trial that has beset his family in the serious, debilitating illness of his wife.[20] With great candor, he grapples with the question of unfairness, yet bears witness to the truth of Scripture:

> While the affliction is not good, it can serve as an occasion for God to bring some good out of what is evil.

This goodness includes the promotion of holiness in us.[21] The testimony of Feinberg's wife, Pat, makes his book even more a source of insight and comfort. In the final analysis, there are questions for which we shall not find answers in this life, "but then we shall know fully" (1 Cor. 13:12b). Thanks be to God for the sufficiency of his grace (2 Cor. 12:9).

> Sometimes on the mount where the sun shines so bright,
> God leads His dear children along;

Sometimes in the valley, in darkest of night,
God leads his dear children along.

Some thro' the waters, some thro' the flood,
Some thro' the fire, but all thro' the blood;
Some thro' great sorrow, but God gives a song,
In the night season and all the day long.
—G. A. Young

GOD GUIDES AND PROVIDES

Trust in the Lord with all your heart
  and lean not on your own understanding;
in all your ways acknowledge him,
  and he will make your paths straight.
      —Proverbs 3:5–6

Offer your bodies as living sacrifices. . . . Do not conform any longer to the
pattern of this world, but be transformed by the renewing of your mind. Then
you will be able to test and approve what God's will is—his good, pleasing
and perfect will.
                    —Romans 12:1–2

For this reason, since the day we heard about you, we have not stopped pray-
ing for you and asking God to fill you with the knowledge of his will through
all spiritual wisdom and understanding.
                    —Colossians 1:9

[Speaking of Abraham offering Isaac] he shows himself to be utterly devoted to God by taking refuge in Divine Providence, "God
will provide himself a lamb." This example is proposed for our
imitation. Whenever the Lord gives a command. . .means fail, we
are destitute of counsel, all avenues seem closed. In such straits, the
only remedy against despondency is, to leave the event to God, in
order that he may open a way for us where there is none.
                    —John Calvin,
                    Genesis, 568

How, then, do we bring our individual lives under God's superintend-
ing providence? In seeking the answer we may experience what the Puritans called "painful anxieties" and what Dorothy Sayers spoke of as
"questioning providence." Traditionally, our teaching has been that God's
plan for our lives includes our vocations and our preparations for them, the
choice of our life partners, our placement in life, and that if we miss God's
very best for us, there is a second best or a third best.

Some in the "wisdom view," however, argue that the traditional approach places too much weight on inner prompting, and that the Christian's
quest should be to do the wisest thing in all areas of life.[22] The "wisdom
view" might well be termed "new deism," because it posits that God does
not necessarily provide special guidance at crucial points in our lives. This
view depreciates the ministry of the Holy Spirit in the life of the believer
and disregards instances of specific guidance found in Scripture (cf. 1 Kings
17:3–4; Acts 8, etc.).[23] The "wisdom view" further posits that if in each
decision we are to do the wisest thing, is that not tantamount to doing "the
will of God"? Stuart Cook rejoins that if "reasonableness" becomes the
standard for action, God's will becomes limited to our human standard for
the wise course. Is what is acceptable to believers always the will of God? If
we can have faith that the will of God is the function of intelligence and
mental acuity alone, are those who are weaker in faith really following the
will of God?[24]

Rather would we claim with the psalmist that "this God is our God
forever and ever; he will be our guide even to the end" (Ps. 48:14). The
believer needs to be saturated with the Scripture through the Spirit;
the believer needs to be before the Lord in constant prayer, "praying in the
Spirit" (Jude 20); the believer needs to seek good counsel from wise coun-
selors (Prov. 11:14; 15:22; 24:6); the believer needs to consider circumstances related to the situation. Often in a major decision, it is prudent to
make a careful list of the pros and the cons then weight them and weigh
them before the Lord. Even as David inquired of the Lord again and again,
so I am convinced that God will make his way clear. Circumstances alone
must not determine action, for as Oswald Chambers said, if we knock at
any door long enough, the devil will open it.

There is, however, a subjective factor in ascertaining the will of God.
God may, in conjunction with the Word, use conscience (Acts 24:16; 2 Cor.
1:12; 5:11), or the direct nudging of the Holy Spirit (Acts 8:19; 16:6–7), or
a disclosure of his will (Eph. 1:17; Phil. 3:15). To guard us from abuse and

misuse of any of these more subjective factors, believers need to live by faith, being sensitive to the peace of God (Phil. 4:7) and our joy in the Holy Spirit.[25]

And thus daily we are motivated to seek God's perfect will, leaning on his promises to guide us and provide for us. Of exigencies and upsets, we will say with Bishop Taylor Smith, who often on his trips would face delay or change, these are all "just part of the plan." Trusting God's promises is the personal and practical aspect of the doctrine of divine providence. Our prayer constantly needs to be

> Guide me, O Thou great Jehovah,
> Pilgrim thru this barren land;
> I am weak, but Thou art mighty—
> Hold me with Thy pow'rful hand:
> Bread of Heaven, Bread of Heaven,
> Feed me till I want no more,
> Feed me till I want no more.
>
> Open now the crystal fountain
> Whence the healing stream doth flow;
> Let the fire and cloudy pillar
> Lead me all my journey thru:
> Strong Deliv'rer, strong Deliv'rer,
> Be Thou still my strength and shield,
> Be Thou still my strength and shield.
> —William Williams
> from the Welsh

Praise God for His Providence

St. Augustine calls us to take refuge in God's wonderful providence—what he terms "the beauty of the ages"—and this we need to do in an age that says "there is no truth." We can be confident, as was Abraham, that "God will provide himself a lamb."[26] For a personal spiritual stimulus

1. Find three hymns, three gospel songs, and three praise choruses that speak of God's guidance and provision for his own children. Examine them biblically and theologically.

2. Write a poem or hymn lyric, or paint or draw a picture celebrating God's providence in your own life, or in the hearts and lives of those you know, or in God's people over the ages.

3. In a brief essay identify circumstances of God's making and choosing that are not coincidental, but fulfillments of his promises to you and to his people.

THE ESCHATOLOGICAL WEDGE

The Presence of the Future

For in this hope we were saved.

—Romans 8:24

We wait for the blessed hope—the glorious appearing of our great God and Savior, Jesus Christ.

—Titus 2:13

Theology is eschatology.

—Jürgen Moltmann

What oxygen is to the lungs, such is hope to the meaning of life.

—Emil Brunner

I do not think that in the last forty years I have lived one conscious hour that was not influenced by the thought of our Lord's return.

—Lord Shaftesbury,
the great social reformer

Biblical eschatology, or the doctrine of the last things, is neither incidental nor peripheral in Scripture. Among many others George Ladd has analyzed from both Testaments contrast between and the tension inherent in this age and the-age-to-come.[1] The collapse of the tension into the realized eschatology of C. H. Dodd or N. T. Wright, which severely discounts any future elements in the equation, renders the Christian life weak and flabby. Contrasting with the Graeco-Roman cyclical view of history is the biblical linear view, in which history begins as set forth in Genesis with the creation of all things in the beginning; has its decisive midpoint, with the death, burial and resurrection of Christ; and then goes on to the climax of time-space history (the telos)—the return of Jesus Christ. As set forth in 1 Thessalonians 1:9–10, Christianity has a past tense ("you turned to God from idols"), a present tense ("to serve the living and true God"), and future tense ("and to wait up for his Son from heaven").

One verse in every four in the New Testament relates to the second advent of our Lord. Building on the foundation of Old Testament eschatology, the Christian church has always cherished in her proclamation and creeds the expectation that Jesus would return. Our Lord himself often spoke of the end of the age (Matt. 24–25; Mark 13; Luke 21), and the apostle Paul taught prophetic truth in his itinerant ministry (cf. 2 Thess. 2:5). That God knows the end from the beginning and reveals some of these secrets in Holy Writ becomes for Isaiah one of the great evidences for the veracity of God's words (Isa. 46:10ff.; 48:3–6).

With the modern denial of the supernatural in Scripture, predictive prophecy is, of course, invalid. Dean Inge snorted that "the notion of the Second Coming is not now compatible with sanity." The *Atlantic Monthly* described those who hold to the literal second coming of Christ as "the lunatic fringe in American religious life." But recall the warning from the apostle Peter that in the time of the end scoffers would say, "Where is the promise of his coming?" (2 Peter 3:4).

Although Professor Garry Wills of Northwestern underscores the centrality of the Second Coming in American religious life, at the dawn of the third millennium, many respond negatively, if at all, to what the Bible presents as the living hope of the church.[2] In a millennial symposium in the magazine *First Things,* a panel of seventeen conservative thinkers ruminated about "What Can We Reasonably Hope For?" Apart from one criticism of "pop apocalyptic," there wasn't a single reference to the second coming of Christ. Public television's *Frontline* episode on the apocalyptic implied that only nuts and kooks paid any attention to a literal return of Christ. Before he died, A. W. Tozer prophetically lamented what he called "the decline of apocalyptic expectation in the evangelical church."[3]

That many preachers and teachers are strangely silent about what constitutes the Christian hope is especially unfortunate in a time of significant "hope deficit" in our culture as a whole. Many thoughtful people who are deeply troubled and harbor a sense of hopelessness about the human prospect are very open to what the Bible says about the events surrounding the end times. The early believers shocked their generation because they exuded such hopefulness. They were realists (as Christians must be), but they were optimistic realists, because of what the Bible discloses about the end time. Those Christians, often persecuted and frequently from the dregs of society, would greet each other on the streets with the warm salutation, *Maranatha!* which means, "The Lord is coming!"

THE RETURN OF JESUS CHRIST: STIMULATION FOR THE CHRISTIAN LIFE

For the essence of prophecy is to give a clear witness for Jesus.
—Revelation 19:10 NLT

This same Jesus, who has been taken away from you into heaven, will come back in the same way you have seen him go into heaven.
—Acts 1:11,
the angel at the Ascension

You also must be ready, because the Son of Man will come at an hour when you do not expect him.
—Luke 12:40

For the Lord himself will come down from heaven, with a loud command, with the voice of the archangel and with the trumpet call of God. . . . Encourage each other with these words.
—1 Thessalonians 4:16–18

Behold, I am coming soon! . . . "Yes, I am coming soon." Amen. Come, Lord Jesus.
—Revelation 22:7, 20

Even those who are hostile to specific statements about the future times concede that "the early Christians lived in a state of eschatological expectancy."[4] They were heirs to the kingdom expectations of the Old Testament prophets, but even more they took Jesus seriously when he told them not to say, "My Master is taking a long time in coming" (Luke 12:45). Jesus said it in many ways, but always with the thrust that his coming was imminent: "Watch, because you do not know the day or the hour" (Matt. 25:13). The early church held to the imminent return of the Savior, and "imminent" meant impending, threatening to occur immediately. The return was a constant expectation to the followers of Jesus (John 21:22–23), Paul believed he would be alive when Christ returned (1 Thess. 4:17; Phil. 4:5). Thus we find Christ's return mentioned in Hebrews 10:37; James 5:7–9; 1 Peter 4:7; 1 John 2:18; Revelation 22:20.

Not long ago, my wife and I were visiting one of our sons, whose older daughter was eager for her first day of first grade. On the big day, the bus was due at 8:30 A.M. When she awakened, she wanted to go out at 7:00 A.M. to watch for her bus. Her dad told her that it was much too early, but she kept asking if it were time yet for the bus. Finally, at about 8:15, the child was almost hyperventilating with eagerness, so we all went out to stand on the driveway to wait for the bus. "Oh, Daddy," she wailed. "I'm afraid I have missed the bus." She was almost inconsolable until she saw the bus coming, and then, with a whoop of joy, she boarded and was off. Do we have such enthusiasm for our Lord's return? Or have we been spiritually strangled by our affluence and so affected by our culture that the return of the Lord seems vague and distant?

Such indifference did not exist in the early church. And one can understand their expectancy. In some passages, Jesus speaks in such a way that some might suppose his immediate coming in glory: "You will not have gone through the cities of Israel before the Son of Man comes" (Matt. 10:23). In other passages, too, in the Olivet Discourse Christ's use of the second person has been interpreted as a commitment that he would return to his immediate hearers (cf. Matt. 24:15). This understanding of the words of Jesus—"I tell you the truth, this generation will not pass away until all these things have happened" (v. 34)—makes him out to be a deceiver or deceived and hardly a reliable or adequate teacher or savior. Indeed, Albert Schweitzer asserted that the *"parousia* delay" meant that Jesus was plain wrong and probably unbalanced.[5] C. H. Dodd embraced the conviction in his "realized eschatology" that all of the predictions of Jesus have been fulfilled—but in a spiritual sense in which, for instance, there is no future judgment but an ongoing process of judgment in history. The doubts and conflict arising from the apparent inconsistency led Bertrand Russell to jettison his faith altogether; Jesus was a false prophet.[6]

The return of Christ for his church, however, was and is imminent. Jesus gave no timetable for that signless event (cf. Acts 1:7). It is not likely that our Lord connected his coming with a first-century generation or a future generation that would see the founding of the nation of Israel (as per Hal Lindsay). Rather, *ta genea* (generation) means—as in the NIV footnote on Matthew 24:34 and as in Henry Alford[7]—"race or people," which is to say, the Jewish race or family of people will not pass away until all of these prophecies are fulfilled.

What is more, Bertrand Russell and Albert Schweitzer ignored the common biblical phenomenon known as "prophetic perspective" or "prophetic telescoping." In the prophetic view, as the Transfiguration adumbrates the much later coming of Christ in glory (Matt, 17:1ff.), so too does the itineration of the Twelve in Matthew 10 speak not only of their efforts but of their efforts as a foreshadow of the much later efforts of the Jewish remnant in the tribulation at the end of the age. Prophetic perspective is common, too, in the Old Testament, as when the locust plague in the lifetime of the prophet Joel foreshadows the epoch of judgment in the days when the Day of the Lord sees a great outpouring of divine wrath. The destruction of Jerusalem in A.D. 70 does not fulfill the mass of prophetic revelation, but is a foreshadow of what will transpire in the end. Thus, there's no need to abandon imminence and deny future end-time events.

It is the opinion of R. C. Sproul that there are two Second Comings *(parousia)*—one in A.D. 70 and another at the end of the age.[8] I would affirm, on the other hand that a Second Coming will likely be in two phases, but the first phase will be the signless rapture of the church (Rev. 3:10; 1 Thess. 4:13–18) and the second a many-signed coming in glory and power with tens of thousands of the saints and angels (Zech. 14:3–7; Rev. 19:11–21). Only thus is the doctrine of imminence sustained in all of its practical power and pertinence.[9]

From the meeting in the air, the people of the Church will move to heaven and there occupy the rooms prepared for us in the Father's house (John 14:1ff.). If our move is back to the earth to set up the kingdom on earth and rule with Christ, what is the Savior's purpose in mentioning the rooms he was to make ready for us? Any position taken on the sequence of these end-time events described in Scripture is inferential, but imminence is an important inference. He is coming for us, and it seems more likely that he will take us with him back to heaven. Our attitude of readiness, patience, and witness makes us homesick for heaven. "Jesus is coming to earth again. What if it were today?"

The Judgment: The Exoneration of Righteousness

Will not the Judge of all the earth do right?
—Abraham in Genesis 18:25

*For God will bring every deed into judgment, including every hidden thing,
whether it is good or evil.*
—Ecclesiastes 12:14

*He [the Holy Spirit] will convict the world of guilt in regard to sin and
righteousness and judgment. . .because the prince of this world now stands
condemned.*
—John 16:8–11

Paul discoursed on righteousness, self-control and the judgment to come.
—Acts 24:25

*But because of your stubbornness and your unrepentant heart, you are stor-
ing up wrath against yourself for the day of God's wrath, when his righteous
judgment will be revealed. God "will give to each person according to what
he has done."*
—Romans 2:5–6

While ongoing judgment of God upon wickedness is continually in process (Rom. 1:18ff.), a final judgment (Mal. 3:5) is necessary to uphold the
moral foundations of the universe. Its delay emboldens some to unrestrained
evil (Eccl. 8:11), but all will ultimately face justice. The thought of standing before a judge in any tribunal is daunting. I remember my first week as
a student at Stanford University. As a hayseed from the Midwest, I was
awestruck by all that I saw, and in my distraction coasted through an inter-
section, a little faster than the prescribed speed limit. I was arrested and
given a ticket. Not realizing I could pay my fine by mail, I went to the
courtroom. It was to be my first and (I am thankful to say) last such appearance. I felt chastened to be among the accused. When my name was called,
I stood before the judge, my knees shaking, my hands clammy, my head
aching. The judge intoned, "Guilty or not guilty?" With a tremulous voice
I responded, "Guilty, your honor." He dropped the gavel and ordered me
to pay a $15 fine. I didn't enjoy the experience of being held accountable

in a court of law. I was literally ill with guilt and shame. What will it be like for the unsaved to stand in the assizes of the Holy God and give account? Scripture says, "So then, each of us will give an account of himself to God" (Rom. 14:12).

Scripture assumes that we are morally accountable and responsible free agents who can make decisions. Deterministic systems that deny real free choice are ethically dangerous, even if adherents take refuge in paradox: It would be unjust to be condemned for doing something I can't help doing. If indeed we do not exercise freedom in making decisions, then it is true that those decisions are not really moral decisions. Such belief, however, renders humankind devoid of ethics in any meaningful sense. No, we are accountable and responsible. We can decide whether to commit adultery or remain faithful to a spouse, and even unredeemed persons of great depravity can decide whether or not they will take life. If we remove human accountability, we have stripped away human dignity.

Also effectively banishing judgment from evangelical church life, along with a literal heaven or hell, are beliefs that stress the love of God over the righteousness of God. James T. Martin, commenting on yet another attack on eschatology, has shown that, with the triumph of subjectivity in theology and the assertion of autonomy over the moral authority of God, the doctrine of last things came into disrepute "as not fitting into the mould of mathematically exact ideas."[10] The doctrine of providence was then seen as an obstacle to progress. Theology as a whole became noneschatological, rejecting any notion of an eschatological judgment. And with the excision of judgment, forensic justification as herein expounded is also rejected.

Schleiermacher, the father of liberalism, would not countenance any thought of Last Judgment, and, as James T. Martin well observes, "this explains also [Schleiermacher's] failure to interpret rightly the doctrine of justification."[11] Martin further argues that because "eschatology and the cross have to do with the solution of the problem of sin," if Christ is not Judge, then neither can he be Savior. "It is because of the certainty of the Last Judgment that in the process of reconciliation we can see the hand of the Judge, and that the judgment at the cross receives its degree of finality."[12]

Judgment is God's ability to differentiate right from wrong and take appropriate action as the result.[13] Both the Old Testament and the New Testament make clear that there exist a present judgment and a future and ultimate judgment. Because "judgment begins with the family of God" (1 Peter 4:17), Paul strikes a critical chord in saying, "If we judged ourselves, we should not come under judgment" (1 Cor. 11:31). Yet every believer in Christ will stand before the "judgment seat of Christ," the *bema,* "to receive what is due him for the things done while in the body, whether good or bad" (2 Cor. 5:10).

This judgment is not to determine whether or not we are saved. The eschatological judgment for the believer has already been rendered. The final verdict is in (cf. Rom. 8:1), and we are justified! Rather, at the final judgment, believers will be judged on the quality of what we have done for our Lord. Is it wood, hay, or straw; or is it gold, silver, and costly stones? Under his fiery gaze, that which is worthless or improperly motivated will be destroyed (1 Cor. 3:12–15).[14] How ashamed and embarrassed we will be if we have labored for our own aggrandizement (cf. 2 Peter 1:11). Thankfully, God will wipe away all tears.

The final judgment is the time for the rewards of which the New Testament speaks extensively. Some say that they do not work for a reward, but we must be careful that we are not trying to be more holy than the Lord. Lewis Sperry Chafer offers a good word to us:

> The doctrine of rewards is the necessary counterpart of the doctrine of salvation by grace. Since God does not, and cannot, reckon the believer's merit or works to the account of his salvation, it is required that the believer's good works shall be divinely acknowledged. The saved one owes nothing to God in payment for salvation, which is bestowed as a gift; but he does owe God a life of undivided devotion, and for this life of devotion, there is promised a reward in heaven.[15]

The judgment of the believer's works as described is simply an extension of the biblical principle that we are all accountable.

Clearly, the idea of a general judgment of all at the end precludes the holding of a series of judgments at the end of space-time history. Besides the believer's judgment at the "judgment seat of Christ," there will be the judgment of the living nations when Christ returns in power and glory to set up his kingdom and to rule (cf. Matt. 25:31–46). The judgment of the fallen angels (Jude 6) is likewise obviously quite different from the judgment of the wicked dead at the end of the millennium (Rev. 20:11–15).

Some modern thinkers challenge the whole idea of retributive punishment and justice. Remember that the Greeks had no idea whatever of an eschatological judgment, although the idea of some accountability can be found in many cultures.[16] Such a day of accounting is necessary for a Hitler or a Stalin, and for all who have chosen their own way rather than God's way. The nature of our holy God requires it, and the bodily resurrection of Christ guarantees it (Acts 17:31). Even Reinhold Niebuhr speaks of the necessity of a final judgment:

> . . . The necessity . . . of a *final* judgment upon good and evil. The idea of a "last" judgment expresses Christianity's refutation of all conceptions of history, according to which it is its own redeemer and is able by its process of growth and development, to emancipate man from the guilt and sin of his existence, and to free him from judgment.[17]

As there are degrees of reward, so will there be degrees of punishment ("many strokes, fewer strokes"), depending on one's light. Heaven and hell are real places for the destiny of all human beings, and each is of endless duration (Matt. 25:46). There is no painkiller in hell. And eternal isolation, as well as separation from God forever, is unimaginable. But God sends no one to hell; he accommodates those who do not want him in their lives. He will not break down the door of the human will and coerce anyone into trusting or loving him. He knocks. He calls. He pleads. But there comes a day when it is too late to respond (2 Cor. 6:2). Our efforts to win people to Christ are motivated in part by our awareness of the awful reality of saying "no" to Jesus. "Since, then, we know what it is to fear the Lord, we try to persuade men" (5:11). It is sad that when Paul discoursed on themes including "the judgment to come," the Roman governor Felix was "afraid." He trembled and said, "That's enough for now! You may leave. When I find it convenient, I will send for you" (Acts 24:25; cf. John 16:8–11). So many today temper and trivialize what Scripture clearly teaches about our present as well as our ultimate moral accountability and responsibility to Almighty God. To what degree has that attitude been influenced by the mood of eschatological indifference and/or denial?

THE RESURRECTION: THE RESTORATION OF HEAVY LOSSES

If a man dies, will he live again?

—Job 14:14

But your dead will live; their bodies will rise. You who dwell in the dust, wake up and shout for joy. Your dew is like the dew of the morning; the earth will give birth to her dead.

—Isaiah 26:19

For a time is coming when all who are in their graves will hear his voice and come out—those who have done good will rise to live, and those who have done evil will rise to be condemned.

—John 5:28–29

I want . . . to attain to the resurrection from the dead.

—Philippians 3:10–11

I believe . . . in the resurrection of the body.

—The Apostles' Creed

Because of Christ's bodily resurrection, believers in Christ shall also be raised bodily from the dead. Jesus said, "Because I live, you shall live also" (John 14:19b). Christians are part of what the Scripture calls "the first resurrection" (Rev. 20:5), *first* indicating that there is not simply one great resurrection morning: "Blessed are those who have part in the first resurrection" (v. 6). And our participation is possible because of our union with Christ and his own victory over sin and death on Easter (1 Peter 1:3). The order and sequence in the Resurrection are clear: "Christ, the firstfruits; then, when he comes, those who belong to him" (1 Cor. 15:23).

Thus the accent in the New Testament falls on the resurrection of the body, but we should not be reluctant to assert the immortality of the nonmaterial part of human beings as well. Many in ancient civilizations spoke of the immortality of the soul, and even Wordsworth, the "romantic," spoke about "intimations of immortality." The nonmaterial aspect of human existence does not cease for either believer or unbeliever. Unbiblical teachings on soul-sleep or annihilation of the wicked dead do not square with what Scripture clearly represents as the existence of human conscientiousness in the intermediate state (Luke 16:19–31). Believers can expect joy in paradise (cf. Phil. 1:20–26; Ps. 16:11), but that unbelievers languish in torment in Hades (2 Peter 2:9) builds on the Old Testament impression that *sheol* is for the ungodly the acme of unpleasantness (Ps. 19:7; 116:3; Isa. 14:9–17; Ezek. 32:21).

Unlike the ancient Greeks, who tended to disparage the body and referred to it as "the prison-house of the soul," both the Hebrews and Christians affirmed a different creed: the human body is a creative masterpiece of God and bears the marks of our spiritual disaster, but will be redeemed and glorified as was Christ's body. Death is seen in Scripture as an intruder, an interloper, an enemy (1 Cor. 15:26). Physical death is the sacrament or sign of our estrangement in sin from God.

Thus "man is destined to die once, and after that to face judgment" (Heb. 9:27). Human beings can never become accustomed to the specter of death. Death is unnatural, contrary to what God intended for humankind. Jesus wept at the grave of Lazarus while knowing that he would shortly be raised up from the dead. Jesus wept because he saw the havoc and pain wrought by death (John 11:33, 35).[18] As a pastor, I have officiated at hundreds of funerals. Although believers do not mourn as those without hope (1 Thess. 4:13), we feel keenly with the entire race the ravages wrought by death: the amazing human body suddenly cut down in its prime by accident or disease; a baby wrenched from the arms of its parents; a fetus, with full human potential, denied to its parents.

When an aged person becomes reduced and shriveled by the passing years, we are reminded that ours is "the body of death" (Rom. 7:24), and we sometimes feel betrayed by "our lowly body" or "the body of our humiliation" (AV). But our bodies will be transformed and "made like his glorious body" (Phil. 3:20–21). Our likeness to Christ in the age to come will not only be moral and spiritual, but physical as well (1 John 3:2). All of the frailties and liabilities of our mortality will be laid aside. Ours will be "the glorious freedom of the children of God" (Rom. 8:21). Does to be like him mean that we will all be about thirty-three years of age in the Resurrection? The possibility seems more desirable to me with every passing year.

In our present bodies we "inwardly groan" (Rom. 8:23), because of the limitations of our strength and endurance. Even the most vigorous human specimens are struck down when body temperature is elevated by a few degrees. But we shall obtain new bodies no longer subject to death or debility, and this wonderful *metamorphosis* will take place when "the dead in Christ. . .rise first. After that, we who are still alive. . .will be caught up with them in the clouds" (1 Thess. 4:16–17). This reconstitution of our mortal likeness (for we shall be recognizable) into new immortal bodies (1 Cor. 15:42–44) will be accomplished "in a flash, in the twinkling of an eye, at the last trumpet" (v. 52). We shall "bear the likeness of the man from heaven" (v. 49).

Almost all religions evince some belief in an afterlife. That some type of existence continues after death is virtually instinctive in human nature. But what is that afterlife to be like? What is its nature? Only Jesus Christ, who "tasted death for every man" (Heb. 2:9) and who "destroy[ed] him who holds the power of death—that is, the devil—and will free those who all their lives were held in slavery by their fear of death" (vv. 14–15), is in any position to directly address these questions. What a nexus of blessing and hope accrues for those who know Christ. He stands over history and proclaims, "I am the Living One; I was dead, and behold I am alive for ever and ever! And I hold the keys of death and Hades!" (Rev. 1:17–18). When my dear and aged father died, I stood by his bedside during his last moments of consciousness. Then he was gone—the man I respected and revered. But I know where he is. He is not in limbo. He is in paradise beholding the Savior. He is awaiting the resurrection, as are my mother and all my loved ones "we've loved long since lost awhile." We shall be together around our Savior's throne. Such is the hope "which does not disappoint us" (Rom. 5:5), for ours is "an inheritance that can never perish, spoil or fade—kept in heaven for us" (1 Peter 1:4). Glory to God.

> I have a future all sublime.
> Beyond the realm of space and time.
> Where my dear Savior I shall see
> And with him evermore will be.
> —Nils Frykman

The Salvation of the Jews

And I will pour out on the house of David and the inhabitants of Jerusalem a spirit of grace and supplication. They will look on me, the one they have pierced, and mourn for him as one mourns for an only child, and grieve bitterly for him as one grieves for a firstborn son. . . . On that day a fountain will be opened to the house of David and the inhabitants of Jerusalem, to cleanse them from sin and impurity.

> —Zechariah 12:10; 13:1

You will not see me again until you say, "Blessed is he who comes in the name of the Lord."

> —Matthew 23:39

Oh, the depth of the riches of the wisdom and
knowledge of God!
How unsearchable his judgments,
and his paths beyond tracing out!
"Who has known the mind of the Lord?
Or who has been his counselor?
"Who has ever given to God,
that God should repay him?"
For from him and through him and to him are all things.
To him be the glory forever! Amen.
— Romans 11:33–36

In the climax of his exposition on the nation of Israel and its destiny, the apostle Paul tells of Israel at the end of the age, which occasions an eruption of glorious praise and worship. The Jewish people are elected to something very special in the plan and purpose of God. They are a sign of God to the nations; they are the key to human history and Bible prophecy.[19]

Among all the nations of the earth God sovereignly chose Israel as the nation through whom he would give his Word and send his son. In so doing, he linked himself in covenant with them in bonds that even their rejection of him could not break. God promised the land to Abraham and his heirs "as an everlasting possession" (Gen. 17:8), and his covenant with them is "an everlasting covenant" (v. 7). Certainly Israel's permanent occupation of the land and prosperity in the land were conditional upon her obedience (Deut. 28). And her eviction from the land for failure to uphold her end of the bargain bears testimony to God's veracity in regard to the covenant provisions. But we cannot take Israel's judgment literally and historically and then spiritualize the promises. The question is, Does everlasting mean everlasting to God? Ours, too, is a promised "everlasting covenant" with God (Heb. 13:20); God has promised us "everlasting life" (John 3:16). Can we believe God or is the covenant promise subject to change?

Some have argued that, in the fulfillment of prophecy, the church takes the place of Israel. This is the so-called replacement theory, or the supercession of the church over Israel. This view has occasioned no little mischief. I believe that God gave to the prophets a vision of an ultimate and final return of God's ancient covenant people from their worldwide dispersion. Isaiah 11:11 speaks of how the Lord for "a second time" would reclaim the scattered Jews even "from the islands of the sea" and bring them back to the land. Jeremiah indicates that there will be a return of the Jews to the promised land on a scale that will totally eclipse the exodus from Egypt in the days of Moses:

> *"However the days are coming," declares the LORD, "when men will no longer say, 'As surely as the LORD lives, who brought the Israelites up out of Egypt,' but they will say, 'As surely as the LORD lives, who brought the Israelites up out of the land of the north and out of all the countries where he had banished them.' For I will restore them to the land I gave their forefathers."*

> —Jeremiah 16:14–15

In a similar prophesy of a reunited Israel, the great vision given to Ezekiel in the valley of dry bones shows the scattered skeletal remains coming together (37:1–14). This coming together is not a vision that refers to the church but to Israel as becoming "life from the dead" (Rom. 11:15). The prophet Amos describes a return to the land and a prosperity in the land that would never be interrupted (Amos 9:14–15). It might be argued that this prophecy refers to the return from the Babylonian and Persian exile, as described in the books of Ezra and Nehemiah. But no one could credibly argue that that return from exile exceeded the Exodus. For one thing, it was not permanent. Further, the prophecies of return are reiterated *after* the return from the seventy years in Babylon and Persia (cf. Zech. 10:9–12).[20]

To see the church as the fulfillment of the promises to Israel is to lose the natural meaning of the Old Testament text and to endanger any kind of a responsible hermeneutic, to say nothing of undercutting the church's own confidence in the character of God. What is more, as a key study concludes, "Israel is not applied to the Church in the New Testament or the Apostolic Fathers until Justin Martyr in A.D. 160."[21]

Zechariah and Ezekiel speak of a spiritual rebirth for Israel of a most impressive kind, which we search in vain to find anywhere in the Old Testament and which by its nature must take place after Christ's death on the cross (Zech. 12:10). Jesus himself spoke of "the renewal of all things," in which the twelve tribes of Israel would be judged (Matt. 19:28), and of the time when he would be welcomed again by Jerusalem and her people (23:39). Peter, in Acts 3:21, preaches about "the time coming for God to restore everything, as he promised long ago through his holy prophets."

The most stunning argument for Israel's restoration is Paul's exposition regarding a time when the natural branches that had been lopped off because of unbelief would be—after "the full number of the Gentiles had come in"—grafted in again. "All Israel will be saved" (Rom. 11:23–26).[22] Taking "all Israel" to mean "Israel as a whole," James Denney, in the *Expositor's Greek Testament,* quotes E. H. Gifford: All Israel "foretells a conversion of the Jews so universal that the separation into 'an elect remnant' and 'the rest who were hardened' shall disappear."[23]

Through the centuries of Jewish dispersion and suffering, many Christians—including Joachim of Fiore; many of the Puritans, like John Owen and Increase Mather; the continental Pietists, like Spener and Francke—have understood the prophetic word regarding Israel's redemption to refer to the nation and not the church. What we have seen in our time, with the establishment of the state of Israel in 1948 and the massive return of Jews to Palestine, is what many Christians now departed had longed to see. Has indeed the fig tree blossomed? "When these things begin to take place, stand up and lift up your heads, because your redemption is drawing near" (Luke 21:28).

THE MILLENNIUM: SALVATION IN THE CREATED ORDER

Your kingdom come, your will be done on earth as it is in heaven.
—Matthew 6:10

Then the end will come, when he hands the kingdom over to God the Father after he has destroyed all dominion, authority and power. For he must reign until he has put all his enemies under his feet. The last enemy to be destroyed is death.
—1 Corinthians 15:24–26

For the earth will be filled with the knowledge of the glory of the LORD, as the waters cover the sea.
—Habakkuk 2:14

He seized the dragon, that ancient serpent, who is the devil, or Satan, and bound him for a thousand years. He threw him into the Abyss, and locked and sealed it over him, to keep him from deceiving the nations any more until the thousand years were ended. After that, he must be set free for a short time. . . . Blessed and holy are those who have part in the first resurrection. The second death has no power over them, but they will be priests of God and of Christ and will reign with him for a thousand years.

—Revelation 20:2–3, 6

Even as the human body experiences corruption because of human sin, so the physical universe and Earth's ecospheres have been adversely affected by and implicated in the human dilemma. The apostle Paul tells us in Romans 8:19–22,

The creation waits in eager expectation for the sons of God to be revealed. For the creation was subjected to frustration, not by its own choice, but by the will of the one who subjected it, in hope that the creation itself will be liberated from its bondage to decay. . . . The whole creation has been groaning as in the pains of childbirth right up to the present time.

"Nature red with tooth and claw" is not the way God created it, but is a reflection of the cruelty inherent in the natural order as the consequence of sin. The millennial reign of Christ, however, will fulfill the longing of the centuries that God's kingdom will come in its fullness and power, and then God's will shall be done on earth as it is heaven (Matt. 6:10).

Only a Greek aversion to matter and the physical order will reject out of hand all of creation coming into harmony. God will display his glory in the time-space order before the eternities roll, and "God is all in all" (1 Cor. 15:28). The structures of human power and defiance will be shattered by the Smiting Stone, which fills the whole earth. This prophecy in Daniel 2 shows us how "the God of heaven will set up a kingdom that will never be destroyed . . . It will crush all those kingdoms and bring them to an end, but it will itself endure forever" (v. 44). Until Augustine, the early church expected a thousand year "kingdom age," in which the great prophecies of the Old Testament and the implications of the New Testament would find a literal fulfillment in the final movement of history. Indeed, the kingdom will be restored to Israel (Acts 1:6) when Christ comes in power and glory "with all of his holy ones" (Zech. 14:3–5) and stands on the Mount of Olives. Some have attempted to spiritualize this victory, but it is clearly stated that "the Lord will be king over the whole earth. On that day, there will be one Lord, and his name the only name" (v. 9). This prophecy refers to Revelation 19 when the rider on the white horse, called "faithful and true," comes forth from heaven with his vast army and defeats all of his enemies (vv. 11–21). Then, indeed, "He will rule them with an iron scepter" (v. 15). For one thousand years he will rule in justice and equity and we will reign with him (20:6).

Jerusalem will be the religious center of the earth and

> *the law will go out from Zion, the word of the LORD from Jerusalem. He will judge between the nations and will settle disputes for many peoples. They will beat their swords into plowshares and their spears into pruning hooks. Nation will not take up sword against nation, nor will they train for war anymore.*
>
> —Isaiah 2:3–4

The millennial temple will function and flourish (Ezek. 40–48), and the millennium kingdom, as Rene Paché states it, "will not be heaven, but rather a theocracy, an authoritative reign of God upon earth. It will therefore be useful that Israel in a holy and spiritual fashion be at the head of the people to submit them to the Lord."[24]

Not only will the justice system be morally and ethically flawless, but such will be the prosperity of the era that no one will lack, as is intimated by the prophet: "Everyone will sit under his own vine and under his own fig tree, and no one will make them afraid, for the Lord Almighty has spoken" (Mic. 4:4). Infant mortality will be eradicated, and death at one hundred years of age will be considered premature. Indeed, the whole of creation will live in harmony and peace very much as the Quaker artist Edward Hicks depicted in his more than sixty paintings of "The Peaceable Kingdom":

> *The wolf will live with the lamb, the leopard will lie down with the goat, the calf and the lion and the yearling together; and a little child will lead them. The cow will feed with the bear, their young will lie down together, and the lion will eat straw like the ox. The infant will play near the hole of the cobra, and the young child put his hand into the viper's nest. They will neither harm nor destroy on all my holy mountain, for the earth will be full of the knowledge of the LORD as the waters cover the sea.*
>
> —Isaiah 11:6–9

That the millennial reign of Christ is not the final state is indicated by the presence of sin and death, and by Satan being loosed a little time, unregenerate mortals conspiring with him against God (Rev. 20:7–10). The human capitulation to Satan will conclusively demonstrate to all of the created intelligences in the universe the truth of God's contention from the beginning: Apart from a radical change in human nature, the real problem of humankind will remain unaddressed.[25]

But the great longings for a utopia on earth will at last be realized. Plato dreamed of it, as did Sir Thomas More and Alfred Lord Tennyson. Karl Marx, in his severely flawed analysis of the human condition, sought it. Jesus as king will rule it! John, the seer of the Apocalypse, sees it happen: "The Kingdom of this world has become the kingdom of our Lord and of his Christ and he will reign forever and ever" (Rev. 11:15).

> Jesus shall reign where'er the sun
> Does his successive journeys run;
> His kingdom spread from shore to shore,
> Till moons shall wax and wane no more.
>
> To Him shall endless prayer be made,
> And endless praises crown His head;
> His name, like sweet perfume,
> Shall rise with every morning sacrifice.
>
> People and realms of every tongue
> Dwell on His love with sweetest song,
> And infant voices shall proclaim
> Their early blessings on His Name.
>
> Let every creature rise, and bring
> His grateful honors to our King;
> Angels descend with songs again,
> And earth repeat the loud Amen!
>   —Isaac Watts, 1719

The Hallowed Hope

We can't live without hope. Hope is more than Kierkegaard's "passion for the possible," it is, as Lewis Smedes says, "a passion for the promises."[26] Luther said, "Live as if Christ died this morning, rose this afternoon, and is coming back tonight." But he also said, "Even if you knew Christ were coming tomorrow, plant your apple tree today." But how do we connect two seemingly contradictory duties?

Write down some imaginary dialogues in which you explain "a reason for the hope you have" (1 Peter 3:15) to the following individuals: an atheist; a homeless person; a highly educated person; a little child on the death of a Christian grandparent; your New Age neighbor; a cult victim; a developmentally disabled adult; an unbelieving friend who has had a severe accident or sustained a heavy loss. Find some hymns and songs of hope and memorize one of them. The newer music has very little that is eschatological.

NOTES

INTRODUCTION

1. Mark Buchanan, "We're All Syncretists Now—Not Religious, Just Spiritual" *Books and Culture,* January–February 2000, 10.
2. T. W. Manson, *The Sayings of Jesus* (London: SCM, 1949) as quoted by Ralph Martin, *Theology, News and Notes,* December 1999, 11.

CHAPTER I: THE BIBLE: CONDUIT OF TRUTH

1. Aurelius Augustine, *On Christian Doctrine,* vol. 18 (Chicago: Great Books, 1952), chaps. 36–37. His views on Scripture are clear in his "Letter to Jerome" (vol. 28, p. 3): "It seems to me that most disastrous consequences must follow upon our believing that anything false is found in the sacred books; that is to say, that the men by whom the Scriptures have been given to us, and committed to writing, did put down in these books anything false."
2. The thesis of my *The Company of the Creative: A Christian Reader's Guide to Great Literature and Its Themes* (Grand Rapids: Kregel, 1999). Cf. for instance on Herman Melville, 10.1.3 (250 allusions to Scripture in *Moby Dick;* 100 in *Billy Budd*); also Ernest Hemingway, 10.2.8.
3. Christopher Hill, *The English Bible and the Seventeenth-Century Revolution* (London: Penguin, 1993). "The Bible was central to all arts, sciences and literature" (31). "It was everywhere in the lives of men, women and children" (38ff.). Another example is Barbara Tuchman, *Bible and Sword: England and Palestine from the Bronze Age to Balfour* (New York: New York University Press, 1956).
4. J. Sidlow Baxter, *The Strategic Grasp of the Bible* (Grand Rapids: Zondervan, 1968), 24.
5. Casper Wistar Hodge, quoted in *The Banner of Truth,* February 1996, cover quotation.
6. John Baillie, *Baptism and Conversion* (New York: Scribner's, 1963), 84ff.

7. William Barclay, *Train Up a Child: Educational Ideals in the Ancient World* (Philadelphia: Westminster, 1959), 12f.

8. Robert Handy, "Some Patterns in American Spirituality," in *The Study of Spirituality,* ed. Cheslyn Jones, Geoffrey Wainwright, Edward Yarnold (New York: Oxford, 1986), 479.

9. Robert Murray McCheyne's *Calendar for Daily Readings* can be obtained from The Banner of Truth Trust, P.O. Box 621, Carlisle, PA 17013.

10. J. A. Bengel in L. Gaussen, *The Inspiration of the Holy Scriptures* (Chicago, Moody, 1949), 193f. The chapter on Jesus and Scripture (89ff.) is especially insightful.

11. J. I. Packer, *A Quest for Godliness: The Puritan Vision of the Christian Life* (Wheaton: Crossway, 1990), 227.

12. Roy B. Zuck, "Application in Biblical Hermeneutics and Exposition," in *Walvoord: A Tribute* (Chicago: Moody, 1982), 15ff.; also Jack Kuhatschck, *Taking the Guesswork Out of Applying the Bible* (Downers Grove: InterVarsity, 1990).

13. Wilbur M. Smith, *The Word of God and the Life of Holiness* (Grand Rapids: Zondervan, 1957). A collection of five messages delivered at Keswick in England in 1957. J. B. Phillips who so effectively paraphrased the New Testament described his sense of the power and vitality of the New Testament even though he was not predisposed to view it as verbally inspired: "Again and again as I carried out my translation I felt like an electrician who was rewiring an ancient house without being able to 'turn the mains off'" (*Letters to Young Churches* [New York: Macmillan, 1948], xii).

14. Avery Dulles, *The Assurance of Things Hoped For: A Theology of Christian Faith* (New York: Oxford, 1994), 70, 79, 84. Dulles quotes Carl F. H. Henry: "God's Revelation is rational and objectively true." Rationality is to be distinguished from rationalism.

15. Carl F. H. Henry's work, *God, Revelation and Authority* (Waco: Word, 1976–83), in six volumes is the classic statement of the high view of Holy Scripture. On higher criticism, cf. C. S. Lewis, "Faulting the Critics," *Christianity Today,* 9 June 1967, 7ff.; Merrill C. Tenney, "The Limits of Biblical Criticism," *Christianity Today,* 21 November 1960, 5ff.; W. Stanford Reid, "Christian Faith and Biblical Criticism," *Christianity Today,* 26 May 1972, 11ff. Also Gerhard Maier, *The End of the Historical-Critical Method* (St. Louis: Concordia, 1977). He advocates what he calls the "historical-biblical" approach.

16. Cf. Kevin J. Vanhoozer, *Is There a Meaning in this Text?* (Grand Rapids: Zondervan, 1998).

17. Wolfhart Pannenberg, "How to Think About Secularism," *First Things,* June–July 1996, 27.

18. Dan Blazer, *Freud vs. God: How Psychiatry Lost Its Soul and Christianity Lost Its Mind* (Downers Grove: InterVarsity, 1998), 152.
19. A typical expression of this kind of sentiment: "Narrow canons of proof, evidence, logical consistency, and clarity of expression have to go. To insist on them imposes a drag upon progress. Indeed strict canons of objectivity and evidence in academic publishing today would be comparable to the American economy's returning to the gold standard; the effect would be the immediate collapse of the system." Gerald Graff in Robert Hughes, *Culture of Complaint* (New York: Oxford University, 1993), 77. Cf. Jeffery L. Sheler, *Is the Bible True?* (San Fancisco: Harper/Zondervan, 2000). A very useful affirmation.
20. Robert Benne, "Cambridge Evangelicals," *Christian Century,* 27 October 1993, 1036ff.
21. Kathleen Norris, *Amazing Grace: A Vocabulary of Faith* (New York: Riverhead Books, 1998), 280. I do not always agree with Norris but her views are often refreshing. Cf. also the meditation on the engagement of the mind by Cornelius Plantinga Jr., "Pray the Lord My Mind to Keep," *Christianity Today,* 10 August 1998, 50ff.
22. In some respects the chief battle for evangelicals today is not over the reliability and trustworthiness of the Bible so much as it is for the sufficiency of Scripture; that is, is Scripture interchangeable with *Tales of Dracula* in framing messages for youth? Should the biblical text be psychologized for preaching? Can something else less than or other than Scripture be a substitute for Scripture itself?

CHAPTER 2: THE HOLY TRINITY: ABSOLUTE PERFECTION

1. J. R. Illingworth, *Personality: Human and Divine* (London: Macmillan, 1913). Consists of the Bampton Lectures for 1894.
2. Nathan R. Wood, *The Secret of the Universe* (Boston: Warwick, 1936).
3. Aurelius Augustine, *The Trinity* (Washington: Catholic University of America Press, 1963).
4. John Calvin, *Institutes of the Christian Religion,* vol. 1 (Grand Rapids: Eerdmans, 1953), 108ff.
5. The Hebrew word *yachid* is the word for absolute mathematical unity whereas *echad* speaks of a compound unity, meaning several or many in one, such as Adam and Eve were one flesh *(bosor echod)* or "one cluster of grapes" *(eschol echod).* Deuteronomy 6:4 is composite unity.
6. Herman Bavinck, *The Doctrine of God* (Grand Rapids: Eerdmans, 1951), 255. Warfield says that "the mystery of the Trinity underlies the Old Testament revelation, and here and there almost comes into view" (cf. B. B. Warfield,

Biblical and Theological Studies [Philadelphia: Presbyterian and Reformed, 1968], 30f.). Some fine studies of the names of God include works by Herbert F. Stevenson, *Titles of the Triune God* (Westwood, N.J.: Revell, 1956); and Nathan J. Stone, *Names of God in the Old Testament* (Chicago: Moody, 1944).

7. Standard studies of particular worth are J. R. Illingworth, *The Doctrine of the Trinity Apologetically Considered* (London: Macmillan, 1909); and Harold O. J. Brown, *Heresies: The Image of Christ in the Mirror of Heresy and Orthodoxy from the Apostles to the Present* (Grand Rapids: Baker, 1984). The latter study continues to be relevant in our times. The piece de resistance in the field is H. E. W. Turner, *The Pattern of Christian Truth* (London: Mowbray, 1954), which describes the Church's efforts to keep doctrine unsullied and pure.

8. Incisive critique of Barth's position is found in Leonard Hodgson, *The Doctrine of the Trinity* (New York: Scribner, 1944), 229. These are the Croall Lectures 1942–43. His view is renewed in his "Trinitarian Theology: The Glory of the Eternal Trinity," *Christianity Today,* 25 May 1962, 4f.

9. Peter Toon, *Our Triune God: A Biblical Portrayal of the Trinity* (Wheaton: Bridgepoint, 1996), 21f., 24. For a range of eighteen authors, from radical to conservative on this subject, cf. Alvin F. Kimel Jr., ed., *Speaking the Christian God: The Holy Trinity and the Challenge of Feminism* (Grand Rapids: Eerdmans, 1993). A good balance is provided by Donald Bloesh, *Is the Bible Sexist?* (Wheaton: Crossway, 1982). An excellent argument is provided by D. A. Carson, *The Inclusive Language Debate: A Plea for Realism* (Grand Rapids: Baker, 1998).

10. Edward Henry Bickersteth, *The Rock of Ages or Scripture Testimony to the One Eternal Godhead of the Father, the Son, and of the Holy Ghost* (New York: The Bible Scholar, n.d.). A fine older compendium of the truth. Also Alister E. McGrath, *Understanding the Trinity* (Grand Rapids: Zondervan, 1988). I love McGrath's quotation from St. Patrick:

> I bind unto myself today
> The strong name of the Trinity,
> By invocation of the same,
> The Three in One and One in Three.

11. Kevin J. Vanhoozer, *Is There a Meaning in This Text? The Bible, the Reader, and the Morality of Literary Knowledge* (Grand Rapids: Zondervan, 1998), 199.

12. Ibid., 310.

13. Toon, *Our Triune God,* 42.

14. Jurgen Moltmann, *The Trinity and the Kingdom* (San Francisco: Harper, 1981); and idem, *History and the Triune God: Contributions to Trinitarian Theology* (New York: Crossroad, 1992).

15. Carl F. H. Henry, *God, Revelation and Authority,* vol. 2, *God Who Stands and Stays* (Waco: Word, 1982), 177f.
16. Catherine Mowry LaCugna, "The Practical Trinity," *Christian Century,* 15–22 July 1991, 678ff. Her book is *God for Us: The Trinity and the Christian Life* (San Francisco: Harper, 1992).
17. Robert N. Bellah et al., *Habits of the Heart: Individualism and Commitment in American Life* (New York: Harper, 1985), 130.
18. An anniversary update is by Robert N. Bellah et al., "Individualism and the Crisis of Civic Membership," *Christian Century,* 8 May 1996, 510. Bellah reportedly has made a strong confession of faith in the Lord Jesus Christ.
19. Miroslav Volf, *After Our Likeness: The Church in the Image of the Trinity* (Grand Rapids: Eerdmans, 1998). Written from the perspective of "the free churches."
20. Hodgson, *Doctrine of the Trinity,* 47ff.
21. Cyril C. Richardson, *The Doctrine of the Trinity* (Nashville: Abingdon, 1958), 56.
22. Reinhold Niebuhr, *Leaves from the Notebook of a Tamed Cynic* (San Francisco: Harper, 1929), 55ff.

Chapter 3: The Metaphysical Attributes of God: Ultimate Being

1. A. W. Tozer, *The Knowledge of the Holy: The Attributes of God—Their Meaning in the Christian Life* (New York: Harper, 1961), 20. Veritably a classic.
2. J. B. Phillips, *Your God Is Too Small* (New York: Macmillan, 1955).
3. G. Campbell Morgan, *The Crises of the Christ* (London: Pickering and Inglis, n.d.), 34ff.
4. In his journal describing his ministry among the North American Indians, David Brainerd says, "I never got away from Jesus and Him crucified and I found that when my people were gripped by this great evangelical doctrine of Christ and Him crucified I had no need to give them instructions about morality. I found that one followed as the sure and inevitable fruit of the other" (Philip E. Howard, ed. *The Life and Diary of David Brainerd* [Grand Rapids: Baker, 1989], 179, 249). Dorothy Sayers said in the same vein, "We have been trying for several centuries to uphold a particular standard of ethical values which derives from Christian dogma which is the sole foundation for those values. . . . If we want Christian behavior then we must realize that Christian behavior is rooted in Christian belief" (*Creed or Chaos: Why Christians Must Choose Either Dogma or Disaster* [London: Sophia Institute, rep. 1999], 76).
5. John Warwick Montgomery, *The "Is God Dead?" Controversy* (Grand Rapids: Zondervan, 1966).

6. R. T. France, *The Living God* (London: InterVarsity, 1970), 10.

7. Carl F. H. Henry, *Notes on the Doctrine of God* (Grand Rapids: Zondervan, 1948), 137ff. Arthur O. Lovejoy developed the principle of plenitude in his *The Great Chain of Being.*

8. John Calvin, *The Institutes* (Grand Rapids: Eerdmans), 1.1.38; and B. B. Warfield, *Calvin and Augustine* (Philadelphia: Presbyterian and Reformed, 1956), 35ff.

9. A superb meditation on the unchanging God is in J. I. Packer, *Knowing God* (Downers Grove: InterVarsity, 1973), 68ff.

10. For a most helpful symposium, cf. Ronald H. Nash, ed., *Process Theology* (Grand Rapids: Baker, 1987). Discusses prophecy and process theology (346ff.).

11. Millard J. Erickson, *The Evangelical Left: Encountering Postconservative Evangelical Theology* (Grand Rapids: Baker, 1997).

12. For incisive critiques of Nash, *Process Theology,* cf. Carl F. H. Henry, *God, Revelation, and Authority,* vol. 6 (Waco: Word, 1983), 52ff.; C. Samuel Storms, *The Grandeur of God* (Grand Rapids: Baker, 1984), 173ff.; and Gordon Lewis and Bruce Demarest, *Integrative Theology,* vol. 1 (Grand Rapids: Zondervan, 1987), 210.

13. Lewis and Demarest, *Integrative Theology,* 205.

14. A. W. Tozer, *Knowledge of the Holy,* 50.

15. Oscar Cullmann, *Christ and Time* (New York: Westminster, 1950). We sense "a certain rigidity in the thesis" (Amos Wilder) but he is a response to certain extremes.

16. William Lane Craig, *The Only Wise God: The Compatibility of Divine Foreknowledge and Human Freedom* (Grand Rapids: Baker, 1987), 88.

17. Lewis and Demarest, *Integrative Theology,* 232.

18. David L. Hocking, *The Nature of God in Plain Language* (Waco: Word, 1984), 131.

19. Among those arguing for limited knowledge, cf. H. Roy Elseth, *Does God Know? A Study of the Nature of God* (St. Paul: Calvary United Church, 1977). A serious abridgement of who God is.

20. Lewis and Demarest, *Integrative Theology,* 240.

21. William H. Willimon, "Jesus' Peculiar Truth," *Christianity Today,* 4 March 1996, 21.

22. Karl Barth's denial of natural revelation is a serious deficiency in his theology.

23. Kenneth Hamilton, *Revolt Against Heaven* (Grand Rapids: Eerdmans, 1965).

24. Brother Lawrence, *The Practice of the Presence of God* (New York: Revell, 1895), 20.

25. Ibid., 30.

26. Ian Buruma, "The Pilgrimage from Tiananmen Square," *New York Times,* 11 April 1999, 62ff. This is described as "an odd and drastic change."
27. A. W. Tozer, *Knowledge of the Holy,* 26.

CHAPTER 4: THE MORAL ATTRIBUTES OF GOD: ABSOLUTE GOODNESS

1. Arthur W. Pink, *The Attributes of God* (Swengel, Pa.: Bible Truth Depot, 1962), 52.
2. William Bennett in *National Review,* "The Death of Outrage," 14 September 1998, 15.
3. Ralph C. Wood, "In Defense of Disbelief," *First Things,* October 1998, 31.
4. Ibid., 32. Our Lord Jesus addressed his Father as "Holy Father" in John 17:11 and taught us to pray, "Our Father. . .Hallowed be Thy name" in Matthew 6:9 (NASB).
5. J. I. Packer, *Knowing God* (Downers Grove: InterVarsity, 1973), 144.
6. Wilbur M. Smith, *The Word of God and the Life of Holiness* (Grand Rapids: Zondervan, 1857), 9.
7. Ibid., 15. The word *holy* and its cognates is found 150 times in Leviticus.
8. A. W. Tozer, *The Knowledge of the Holy* (New York: Harper, 1961), 113.
9. Jerry Bridges, *The Pursuit of Holiness* (Colorado Springs: NavPress, 1978, 1996); and R. C. Sproul, *The Holiness of God* (Wheaton: Tyndale, 1985).
10. Arthur W. Pink, *Attributes of God,* 36.
11. Ibid., 36. The Cherubim did not say: "Nice, nice, nice" but "holy, holy, holy."
12. William Burt Pope, *A Higher Catechism of Theology* (New York: Phillips and Hunt, 1884), 83.
13. L. Berkhof, *Systematic Theology* (Grand Rapids: Eerdmans, 1953), 75.
14. Norman H. Snaith, *The Distinctive Ideas of the Old Testament* (Philadelphia: Westminster, 1946), 97–98. Not always reliable but insightful at points.
15. Bruce Demarest and Gordon Lewis, *Integrative Theology,* vol. 1 (Grand Rapids: Zondervan, 1987), 126. An excellent work on justice. See also James 5:1–5 on the cries which reach the Lord.
16. Edward John Carnell, *Christian Commitment: An Apologetic* (New York: Macmillan, 1957). A brilliant apologetic—rare and not referred to enough.
17. R. B. Girdlestone, *Synonyms of the Old Testament* (Grand Rapids: Eerdmans, 1897, 1956), 100f.
18. Leon Morris, *Testaments of Love: A Study of Love in the Bible* (Grand Rapids: Eerdmans, 1981) 17. A rich but comprehensive study.
19. Anders Nygren, *Agape and Eros* (Philadelphia: Westminster, 1938, 1939, 1953).
20. B. B. Warfield, *Biblical and Theological Studies* (reprint, Philadelphia: Presbyterian and Reformed, 1968), 509. From a sermon preached by Warfield.
21. L. Berkhof, *Systematic Theology,* 71.

22. The humanistic case is made by Denis de Rougemont, *Love in the Western World* (Garden City: Doubleday-Anchor, 1940). Explores how the Catharist heresy of the Middle Ages challenged orthodoxy. Martin C. D'Arcy in *The Mind and Heart of Love* (New York: Meridian, 1956) demonstrates how divine love *(agape)* is the source of and balance for human passion *(eros)*.

23. Bernard of Clairvaux, *The Love of God* (Portland: Multnomah, 1983), 185.

CHAPTER 5: THE HUMAN FAMILY: MADE IN HIS IMAGE—BUT MARRED

1. Paul Woodruff and Harry A. Wilmer, ed., *Facing Evil: Light at the Core of Darkness* (LaSalle, Ill.: Open Court, 1988). Bill Moyers's symposium for PBS in the "formidable power of Evil," the dark side.

2. Robert H. Schuller, *Self-Esteem: The New Reformation* (Waco: Word, 1982), 39. Schuller argues that the spirit of Paul like Luther and Calvin is "reactionary." He is no champion of the truth of the gospel but of Paul Tillich who claimed, "Joy is nothing else than the awareness of our being fulfilled in our true being, in our personal center."

3. Erich Sauer, *The King of the Earth: The Nobility of Man According to the Bible and Science* (Grand Rapids: Eerdmans, 1962). A veritable classic.

4. Donald E. Chittick, *The Controversy: Roots of the Creation-Evolution Conflict* (Portland: Multnomah, 1984), 87.

5. Hugh Ross, *Creator and Cosmos: An Astrophysicist Reconciles Science and Scripture* (Colorado Springs: NavPress, 1993); Richard Swinburne, *Is There a God?* (Oxford: Oxford University Press, 1997); Phillip E. Johnson, *Darwin on Trial* (Downers Grove: InterVarsity, 1991); and Michael J. Behe, *Darwin's Black Box: the Biochemical Challenge to Evolution* (New York: Free Press, 1996). For a somewhat critical but nevertheless informative study, cf. Ronald Numbers, *The Creationists* (New York: Knopf, 1992). Another choice work is William A. Dembski, *Intelligent Design: The Bridge Between Science and Theology* (Downers Grove: InterVarsity, 1999).

6. Lesslie Newbigin, *Sin and Salvation* (Philadelphia: Westminster, 1956), 19.

7. C. S. Lewis, *The Problem of Pain* (London: Fontana Books, 1940, 1957), 21ff.

8. For some excellent research on original sin and the history of interpretation, cf. N. P. Williams, *The Ideas of the Fall and Original Sin,* the Bampton Lectures (London: Longman Green, 1927); and H. Shelton Smith, *Changing Conceptions of Original Sin,* the Stone Lectures (New York: Scribner's, 1955). For a cultural commentary of significance, see Digby Anderson, ed., *The Loss of Virtue: Moral Confusion and Social Disorder in Britain and America* (London: Social Affairs Unit, 1992).

9. Edward T. Oakes, "Original Sin: A Disputation," *First Things,* November 1998, 24.

10. Ibid., 24

11. Ernest De Witt Burton, *Galatians,* in the International Critical Commentary (Edinburgh: T and T Clark, 1921, 1951). Burton was not a Christian but, because he took Paul's language for what it said, wrote a fine commentary on Galatians. He conceded that Paul quite evidently believed in a substitutionary atonement; he himself did not so believe.

12. Francis Schaeffer, *How Should We Then Live?* (Old Tappan, N.J.: Revell, 1976), 52; and William R. Cannon, *History of Christianity in the Middle Ages* (Nashville: Abingdon, 1960), 266. "Human nature is not totally corrupted by sin."

13. A. W. Tozer, *Paths to Power* (Harrisburg, Pa.: Christian Publications, n.d.), 29ff. Tozer argues that if God tells us to do something, this means we have the ability to do it.

14. Reinhold Niebuhr, *An Interpretation of Christian Ethics* (New York: Meridian, 1956), 109. Niebuhr shows how human *hubris* tinctures even our highest motivations.

15. C. E. M. Joad, *The Recovery of Belief* (London: Faber and Faber, 1952), 64ff.

16. Emile Cailliet, *The Recovery of Purpose* (New York: Harper, 1959), 125.

17. Reinhold Niebuhr, *The Nature and Destiny of Man* (New York: Scribner's, 1955), 150ff. Niebuhr urges that we take Genesis "seriously but not historically." For an important critique, cf. Carl F. H. Henry, *The Protestant Dilemma* (Grand Rapids: Eerdmans, 1948), 134ff.

18. Paul C. Vitz, *Psychology as Religion: The Cult of Self-Worship* (Grand Rapids: Eerdmans, 1977, 1994). Vitz traces the cult of the self in American culture back to Emerson and Whitman. Cf. also Donald Meyer, *The Positive Thinkers: Religion as Pop Psychology from Mary Baker Eddy to Oral Roberts* (New York: Pantheon, 1965, 1980). Deals with religion as therapy—the cult of reassurance.

19. E. La B. Cherbonnier, *Hardness of Heart: A Contemporary Interpretation of the Doctrine of Sin* (Garden City: Doubleday, 1955). Unsound at points but contains searching insights on sin, as one would expect from a follower of Reinhold Niebuhr.

20. Cornelius Plantinga Jr., "The Sinner and the Fool," *First Things,* October 1994, 24ff. This is from Plantinga's book *Not the Way It's Supposed to Be* (Grand Rapids: Eerdmans, 1995). Sin is such bad judgment; we can't get "beyond good and evil" as Nietzsche had hoped.

21. Henry Fairlie, *The Seven Deadly Sins Today* (Washington: New Republic, 1978); and Anthony Campolo, *Seven Deadly Sins* (Colorado Springs: Victor, 1987).

CHAPTER 6: JESUS THE GOD-MAN: THE ONLY SAVIOR

1. F. F. Bruce, *The Spreading Flame* (Grand Rapids: Eerdmans, 1958), 335ff. The word *holy* occurs 150 times in Leviticus and 830 times in the Old Testament.

2. A scholarly and deep study of the "Names," cf. Oscar Cullmann, *The Christology of the New Testament* (Philadelphia: Westminster, 1959). He sees Jesus as the powerful Messiah-King and Savior.

3. W. H. Griffith Thomas, *Christianity is Christ: The Foundation of our Faith* (Chicago: Moody, 1965).

4. John G. Stackhouse Jr., "The Jesus I'd Prefer to Know," *Christianity Today,* 7 December 1998, 69.

5. P. T. Forsyth, *The Person and Place of Jesus Christ* (Grand Rapids: Eerdmans, n.d.). His greatest!

6. John Dominic Crossan, *Jesus: A Revolutionary* (San Francisco: Harper, 1994). Crossan, a leading Roman Catholic scholar who has been part of the Jesus Seminar, "a group of scholars who have met to determine the authenticity of the sayings of Jesus in the Gospels." Cf. Bruce Buursma, "Searching for Jesus: Can This Man Change What Christians Believe?" *Chicago Tribune,* 17 July 1994, 8ff.

7. Peter Stuhlmacher, *Jesus of Nazareth: Christ of Faith* (Peabody, Mass.: Hendrickson, 1988); and Jurgen Moltmann, *Jesus Christ for Today's World* (Minneapolis: Fortress, 1994). Moltmann, who subscribes to "the theology of hope," vacillates on the Resurrection but is clear on many things: "The crucified Christ is the Christ for me!" he insists (3). Stuhlmacher of Tubingen is quite conservative and engaging.

8. David H. Wallace, "This Is the Christ We Preach," *Christianity Today,* 22 July 1966, 5.

9. Arno Clemens Gaebelein, *The Christ We Know* (Chicago: Moody, 1927), 7. This volume was written to rebut Bruce Barton's agnostic and unconvincing *The Man Nobody Knows* (Indianopolis: Bobbs-Merrill, 1925).

10. Alfred Edersheim, *The Life and Times of Jesus the Messiah,* vol. 1 (Grand Rapids: Eerdmans, 1953), 1ff.

11. David L. Cooper, *Messiah: His First Coming Scheduled* (Los Angeles: Biblical Research Society, 1939, 1967). Invaluable. See also E. W. Hengstenberg, *The Christology of the Old Testament,* 4 vols. (1872; reprint, Grand Rapids: Kregel, 1956). The most exhaustive study we have.

12. Wilbur M. Smith, *The Supernaturalness of Jesus* (Boston: W. A. Wilde, 1940), 74ff.

13. William Barclay, *Jesus as They Saw Him* (Grand Rapids: Eerdmans, 1962), 40.

14. Leon Morris, *The Story of the Christ Child* (Grand Rapids: Eerdmans, 1960).

Morris treats this subject beautifully. See also Doremus Hayes, *The Most Beautiful Book Ever Written* (New York: Methodist, 1913), 130f.

15. J. Gresham Machen, *The Virgin Birth of Christ* (New York: Harper, 1930).

16. Ibid., 397. Thorough and thoughtful. Machen was one of the first evangelicals to obtain a mainline publisher.

17. Martin Luther's sermon "On the Nativity" in Roland H. Bainton, *Here I Stand* (New York: Mentor, 1950, 1977), 276. Luther observes, "I am amazed that the little one did not freeze."

18. Henry Bettenson, ed., *Documents of the Christian Church* (London: Oxford, 1943), 73.

19. Murray J. Harris, *Jesus as God: The New Testament Use of Theos in Reference to Jesus* (Grand Rapids: Baker, 1992).

20. Geerhardus Vos, *The Self-Disclosure of Jesus* (Grand Rapids: Eerdmans, 1954). Note also B. B. Warfield, *The Lord of Glory* (Grand Rapids: Zondervan, n.d.). Learning from the designations of Jesus.

21. I am roughly following Gaebelein's development of this point (*The Christ We Know*, 8ff.).

22. B. B. Warfield, *The Person and Work of Christ* (Philadelphia: Presbyterian and Reformed, 1950), 114ff.

23. Harold O. J. Brown, *Heresies* (Grand Rapids: Baker, 1984); and J. N. D. Kelley, *Early Christian Doctrines,* rev. (San Francisco: Harper/Collins, 1960, 1978), 96.

24. A. B. Bruce, *The Humiliation of Christ* (Edinburgh: T & T Clark, 1905). A classic study of kenosis.

25. David L. Larsen, *Telling the Old, Old Story* (Wheaton: Crossway, 1995), 143ff.

26. G. Campbell Morgan, *The Teaching of Jesus* (New York: Revell, 1913).

27. William Barclay, *The Mind of Jesus* (New York: Harper, 1960), 120. The work is more well done than his commentaries.

28. N. T. Wright, "God's Way of Acting," *Christian Century,* 16 December 1998, 1215ff.; also helpful here is C. S. Lewis, *Miracles: A Preliminary Study* (New York: Association Press, 1958).

29. Samuel Cartledge, *Jesus of Fact and Faith* (Grand Rapids: Eerdmans, 1968).

30. H. P. Liddon, *The Divinity of Our Lord* (London: Rivington, 1885).

31. John H. Paterson, *The Greatness of Christ,* The Bampton Lectures for 1866 (Westwood, N.J.: Revell, 1962).

32. H. C. Hewlett, *The Glories of Our Lord* (Chicago: Moody, n.d.); and Jacob G. Bellet, *The Moral Glory of the Lord Jesus Christ* (London: G. Morrish, n.d.).

33. Everett F. Harrison, *A Short Life of Christ* (Grand Rapids: Eerdmans, 1968). I strongly recommended this a sensitive treatment.

34. Vincent Taylor, *The Names of Jesus* (London: Macmillan, 1954); also Leon Morris, *The Lord from Heaven* (Grand Rapids: Eerdmans, 1958).

35. Oswald Chambers, *Bringing Sons unto Glory* (London: Simpkin Marshall, 1941); and idem, *The Psychology of Redemption* (London: Simpkin Marshall, n.d.). These are studies in the life of our Lord.

36. G. Campbell Morgan, *The Crises of the Christ* (London: Pickering and Inglis, n.d.). Magnificent and timeless.

37. G. Campbell Morgan, *The Great Physician* (London: Marshall, Morgan and Scott, 1937). A series of fifty studies on the method that Jesus used with individuals.

38. W. E. Sangster, *He Is Able* (London: Wyvern Books/Epworth Press, 1936).

39. Choice conversion stories are to be found in Harold Begbie, *Twice-Born Men: A Clinic in Regeneration* (New York: Revell, 1909); and Hugh T. Kerr and John M. Mulder, eds., *Conversions* (Grand Rapids: Eerdmans, 1981).

40. Robert E. Coleman, *Songs of Heaven* (Old Tappan, N.J.: Revell, 1980). A 1998 reprint of this work is entitled *Singing with the Angels* (Old Tappan, New Jersey: Revell, 1998).

41. Ronald H. Nash, *Is Jesus the Only Savior?* (Grand Rapids: Zondervan, 1994).

42. Paul Galloway, "Theologians Opening Heaven's Gate a Bit Wider," *Chicago Tribune,* 28 January 1996, 1.

43. A study of our custodianship of the Name and its power, cf. Watchman Nee, *Sit, Walk, Stand* (London: Witness and Testimony, 1957), 45ff.

CHAPTER 7: THE HEALING CROSS: OUR BLEEDING GOD

1. William Mitchell Ramsay, "The Cross. . .Central Fact in History," *Moody Monthly,* March 1959, 23ff.

2. John R. W. Stott, *The Cross of Christ* (Downers Grove: InterVarsity, 1986).

3. *The New Yorker,* 17 April 1995, magazine cover.

4. "A controverted conference," reporting on Re-Imaging, *Christian Century,* 16 February 1994, 160.

5. Leo D. Lefebure, "Victims, Violence and the Sacred: The Thought of Rene Girard," *Christian Century,* 11 December 1996, 1226ff. Philip Yancey seems too positive about Girard, an enemy of the cross, in his *Christianity Today* article, "Why I Can Feel Your Pain," 8 February 1999.

6. Rebecca Denova, review of *The Birth of Christianity: Discovering What Happened in the Years Immediately After the Execution of Jesus,* by John Dominic Crossan, *Christian Century,* 6–13 January 1999, 22. Crossan considers Jesus as a first-century Gandhi or M. L. King. A Roman Catholic scholar who did take the cross seriously and reverently was the late Raymond E. Brown whose *The Death of the Messiah* (New York: Doubleday, 1994) runs to 1,608 pages.

7. David L. Larsen, *The Company of the Creative: A Christian Reader's Guide to*

Great Literature and Its Themes (Grand Rapids: Kregel, 1999). A subtext throughout, but with typical emphasis on Melville and Hemmingway (10.1.3, 10.2.8, with special reference in the latter to *The Old Man and the Sea*).

8. Michael Walsh, "Minimalist Magic," *Time,* 23 August 1993, 68f.

9. Clive Davis, "Yanks Discover Stanley Spencer, Britain's Most Interesting Artist," *Insight,* 1 December 1997, 36f. He transposes New Testament subjects to the streets of his native Cookham in Berkshire.

10. Leon Morris, *The Apostolic Preaching of the Cross* (Grand Rapids: Eerdmans, 1955). One of several studies by Morris of Australia.

11. H. A. Ironside, *Lectures on the Levitical Offerings* (Neptune, N.J.: Loizeaux, 1929, 1951). The "grandfather" of these studies is J. H. Kurtz, *Sacrificial Worship in the Old Testament* (Edinburgh: T and T Clarke, 1863).

12. Leon Morris, *The Atonement: Its Meaning and Significance* (Downers Grove: InterVarsity, 1983). Choice!

13. Devotionally rich is Andrew Bonar, *Leviticus* (Edinburgh: Banner of Truth, 1846); in the Expositor's Bible series, cf. S. H. Kellogg, *The Book of Leviticus* (London: Hodder and Stoughton, n.d.).

14. On the tabernacle in the wilderness, cf. James Strong, *The Tabernacle of Israel in the Desert* (Grand Rapids: Baker, 1952); I. M. Haldemann, *The Tabernacle, Priesthood, and Offerings* (New York: Revell, 1925); W. G. Moorhead, *The Tabernacle* (Grand Rapids: Kregel, 1957); Charles W. Slemming, *Made According to Pattern* (Chicago: Moody, 1938, 1956); A. B. Simpson, *Christ in the Tabernacle* (New York: Christian Alliance Publishing, 1896); and Louis T. Talbot, *Christ in the Tabernacle* (Los Angeles: Church of the Open Door, 1942).

15. On the actual events themselves, cf. Leon Morris, *The Story of the Cross* (Grand Rapids: Eerdmans, 1957); Jim Bishop, *The Day Christ Died* (New York: Pocket Books, 1957); and Max Lucado, *Six Hours One Friday* (Portland: Multnomah, 1989). On the physical suffering, cf. Pierre Barbet, *A Doctor at Calvary* (Garden City: Image, 1963); and C. Truman Davies, "The Crucifixion of Jesus: The Passion of Christ from a Medical Point of View," *Arizona Medicine,* March 1965, 183ff.

16. Dallas Willard, *The Divine Conspiracy* (San Francisco: Harper, 1998), 403. Very disappointing is the assault on forensic justification, the collapse of eschatology, and the minimization of the cross in this work.

17. George Smeaton, *The Doctrine of the Atonement as Taught by Christ Himself* (Grand Rapids: Zondervan, 1871, 1953), 128. Cf. also, R. W. Dale, *The Atonement* (London: Congregational Union, 1897).

18. Ibid., 279. Another key work, Thomas J. Crawford, *The Doctrine of Holy Scripture Respecting the Atonement* (Grand Rapids: Baker, 1871, 1954). He argues that "God's love is not the consequence but the cause of God's willingness to save sinners" (159).

19. James Oliver Buswell Jr., *A Systematic Theology of the Christian Religion,* vol. 2 (Grand Rapids: Zondervan, 1962), 126ff. Sheds light on "We behold His glory."

20. Vincent Taylor, *Jesus and His Sacrifice* (London: Macmillan, 1951), 104–105.

21. Some works on the seven statements are Russell Bradley Jones, *Gold from Golgotha* (Chicago: Moody, 1945); Lehman Strauss, *The Day God Died* (Grand Rapids: Zondervan, 1965); and Richard Allen Bodey, ed., *The Voice from the Cross* (Grand Rapids: Baker, 1990). The greatest preaching on the cross is by F. W. Krummacher, *The Suffering Saviour: Meditations on the Last Days of Christ* (Chicago: Moody, 1952); F. W. Tholuck, *Light from the Cross* (Chicago: Moody, 1952); W. M. Clow, *The Day of the Cross* (London: Hodder and Stoughton, 1909); idem, *The Cross in Christian Experience* (London: Hodder and Stoughton, 1908); and the great trilogy by K. Schilder, *Christ in His Suffering, Christ on Trial,* and *Christ Crucified* (Grand Rapids: Eerdmans, 1940, 1944).

22. Gerhard Forde, "On Being a Theologian of the Cross," *Christian Century,* 22 October 1997, 947f., from Gerhard Forde's, *On Being a Theologian of the Cross* (Grand Rapids: Eerdmans, 1997).

23. Charles L. Feinberg, "The Scapegoat of Leviticus 16," *Bibliotheca Sacra,* October 1958, 320ff.

24. Colin Chapman, *Christianity on Trial* (Wheaton: Tyndale, 1974), 484ff.

25. James Denney, *The Death of Christ* (London: Tyndale, 1951), 103.

26. George Smeaton, *The Apostles' Doctrine of the Atonement* (Grand Rapids: Zondervan, 1870, 1957), 457. Another important study, H. E. W. Turner, *The Patristic Doctrine of Redemption* (London: Mobray, 1952). It is quite clear that Tertullian introduced *satisfactio.*

27. Thomas Jenkins, *The Character of God: Recovering the Lost Literary Power of American Protestantism* (New York: Oxford, 1997). Convoluted at points but piercing. We have come to see what H. Richard Niebuhr warned us about in often-quoted words: "a God without wrath who brings humans without sin into a kingdom without judgment by a Christ without a cross."

28. Ethelbert Stauffer, *New Testament Theology* (New York: Macmillan, 1955), 145.

29. Roger R. Nicole, "C. H. Dodd and the Doctrine of Propitiation," *Westminster Theological Journal* 17, no. 2 (1955): 117ff. So substantive. Stott picks up the research here (*The Cross of Christ,* 171ff.).

30. A. A. Hodge, *The Atonement* (Grand Rapids: Eerdmans, 1867, 1953), 243.

31. John Bunyan, *The Pilgrim's Progress* (Edinburgh, Banner of Truth, 1977), 36.

32. Robert E. Coleman, *Written in Blood* (Old Tappan, N.J.: Revell, 1972). Beautiful!

33. Lesslie Newbigin, *Unfinished Agenda: An Autobiography* (Grand Rapids: Eerdmans, 1985), 11, 254. Newbigin is convinced of "the centrality and objectivity of the atonement accomplished on Calvary" (30). While Barth is confusing and C. H. Dodd liberal, James Denney offers this response to the question, "What is the meaning of the death of Jesus?" His answer was:

> Bearing shame and scoffing rude,
> In my place condemned He stood;
> Sealed my pardon with His blood:
> Hallelujah! what a Savior!
> —P. P. Bliss

CHAPTER 8: THE VACANT TOMB: THE GROUNDBREAKING

1. R. W. Dale, *The Atonement* (London: Congregational Union, 1897). Magnificent! A pastor-theologian.
2. D. W. Lambert, "The Scholar and the Evangelist: R. W. Dale and D. L. Moody," *Life of Faith,* 15 February 1975, 3. Dale became a counselor for the Moody-Sanky meetings and was convinced.
3. Leon Morris, *The Wages of Sin* (London: Tyndale, 1955), 12.
4. Ibid., 28.
5. Oscar Cullmann, *Immortality of the Soul or Resurrection of the Dead?* (New York: Macmillan, 1958).
6. Morris, *Wages of Sin,* 20.
7. Ibid., 21
8. Loraine Boettner, *Immortality* (Philadelphia: Presbyterian and Reformed, 1956), 59.
9. S. D. F. Salmond, *The Christian Doctrine of Immortality* (Edinburgh: T and T Clark, 1895), 252.
10. Carl Armerding, "Asleep in the Dust," *Bibliotheca Sacra,* April 1964 (he argues for spiritual interpretation); and John F. Walvoord, "The Resurrection of Israel," *Bibliotheca Sacra,* January 1967 (he argues for the physical resurrection).
11. Rene Paché, *The Future Life* (Chicago: Moody, 1962). A rich repository.
12. G. B. Caird, *The Language and Imagery of the Bible* (Philadelphia: Westminster, 1980), 217.
13. George Ladd quoted in Donald T. Rowlingson, "Interpreting the Resurrection," *Christian Century,* 10 April 1963, 459.
14. Steve Rabey, "Liberals Pooh-Pooh Jesus' Resurrection," *Christianity Today,* 24 April 1955, 45.
15. William H. Willimon, "Jesus' Peculiar Truth: Modern Apologists for

objective truth are making a tactical error," *Christianity Today,* 4 March 1996, 21f.

16. Wilbur M. Smith, *Therefore Stand* (Boston: W. A. Wilde, 1945). Also see John Wenham, *Easter Enigma: Are the Resurrection Accounts in Conflict?* (Grand Rapids: Zondervan, 1984).

17. Pinchas Lapide, *The Resurrection of Jesus: A Jewish Perspective* (Minneapolis: Augsburg, 1983).

18. Merrill C. Tenney, *The Reality of the Resurrection* (New York: Harper and Row, 1963), 8. This is the strongest single volume we possess on the resurrection of Christ. Some important collections of effective preaching on the resurrection are Wilbur M. Smith, ed., *Great Sermons on the Resurrection* (Natick, Mass.: W. A. Wilde, 1964); Warren W. Wiersbe, comp., *Classic Sermons on the Resurrection of Christ* (Grand Rapids: Kregel, 1991); Curtis Hutson, ed., *Great Preaching on the Resurrection* (Murfreesboro, Tenn.: Sword of the Lord, 1984); and Marcus Loane, *Our Risen Lord* (Grand Rapids: Zondervan, 1965). The latter is a series of messages on John 21.

19. James Orr, *The Resurrection of Jesus* (New York: Jennings and Graham, 1909), 277.

20. C. E. B. Cranfield, *Epistle to the Romans,* vol. 1 (Edinburgh: T and T Clark, 1975), 252.

21. Tenney, *Reality of the Resurrection,* 178. Donald Grey Barnhouse's Keswick messages on our identification with Christ are in Herbert F. Stevenson, ed., *The Ministry of Keswick,* vol. 2 (London: Marshall, Morgan and Scott, 1964), 153–209.

22. Reviews in the *Chicago Tribune,* the *National Review, Time* magazine, and *Insight* magazine and others helped shape my impressions and observations about "the Force."

23. Daniel P. Fuller, *Easter Faith and History* (Grand Rapids: Eerdmans, 1965), 259.

24. Michael Horton, *In the Face of God: The Dangers and the Delights of Spiritual Intimacy* (Waco: Word, 1997).

25. From Richard John Neuhaus, "In the Public Square," *First Things,* October 1998, 95.

26. H. Wayne House and Richard Abanes, *The Less-Traveled Road and the Bible* (Camp Hill, Pa.: Horizon Books, 1995), 59. Peck sees the Bible as a book of myths—an admixture of the true and the false.

27. Richard Bewes, "An Unstoppable Force," *Decision* magazine, March 1995, 6ff.

28. Tenney, *Reality of the Resurrection,* 78.

29. Jacques Ellul, *The Humiliation of the Word* (Grand Rapids: Eerdmans, 1985), 251.

30. Murray J. Harris, *Raised Immortal: Resurrection and Immortality in the New Testament* (Grand Rapids: Eerdmans, 1983). If Harris is right, how do the "appearances" differ from a Christophany? Neither does he address our resurrection bodies.

31. Eldon W. Koch, "The Power of the Resurrection," *Christian Heritage,* April 1977, 9.

32. Eugene H. Peterson, *Subversive Spirituality* (Grand Rapids: Eerdmans, 1997), 242.

CHAPTER 9: THE ASCENSION: THE NEGLECTED DOCTRINE

1. Arthur C. Clarke, "Outer Space: What Is Out There?" *Reader's Digest,* February 1959, 123ff.

2. Wilbur M. Smith, *The Biblical Doctrine of Heaven* (Chicago: Moody, 1968), 27ff. A unique study.

3. Everett F. Harrison, *A Short Life of Christ* (Grand Rapids: Eerdmans, 1968), 252ff.

4. Peter Toon, "Historical Perspectives on the Doctrine of Christ's Ascension," *Bibliotheca Sacra,* October–December 1983, 293. A series of four, being the Griffith Thomas Lectures at Dallas Seminary.

5. John F. Walvoord, "The Present Universal Lordship of Christ," *Bibliotheca Sacra,* April 1964, 100.

6. Ibid., 102. Part of a series by Dr. Walvoord on "The Present Work of Christ."

7. Toon, "Historical Perspectives on the Doctrine of Christ's Ascension," 291.

8. Ibid., 292.

9. G. Campbell Morgan, *The Crises of the Christ* (London: Pickering and Inglis, 1903), 282.

10. Ibid., 292.

11. Toon, "Historical Perspectives on the Doctrine of Christ's Ascension," 298.

12. Peter Toon, *Bibliotheca Sacra,* January–March 1984, 17.

13. Ibid., 17.

14. B. F. Westcott, *The Revelation of the Risen Christ* (London: Macmillan, 1902), 180.

15. J. Oswald Sanders, "What Christ Is Doing Right Now," *Eternity,* August 1958, 10ff.; Egerton C. Long, "What Is Christ Doing for Us Now?" *Moody Monthly,* March 1959, 18ff.; and Bruce M. Metzger, "The Meaning of Christ's Ascension," *Christianity Today,* 27 May 1966, 3f.

16. Toon, *Bibliotheca Sacra,* January–March 1984, 23–24.

17. H. B. Swete, *The Ascended Christ* (London: Macmillan, 1913), 71.

18. Walvoord, "The Present Universal Lordship of Christ," July 1964, 197.

19. John Buchanan, "Identity Check," *The Christian Century,* 30 June–7 July

1999, 667, in response to "The Gospel of Jesus Christ: An Evangelical Celebration" presented in *Christianity Today,* 14 June 1999, claims that "Bible
scholars are not convinced that the biblical writers who referred to Christ as
a sacrifice 'for us' were necessarily thinking of Christ's death as the payment
of a penalty to God. . . . Theologically, the substitutionary penal theory has
long been unsatisfying for logical reasons." There are many "Bible scholars"
who think otherwise.

20. Toon, *Bibliotheca Sacra,* January–March 1984, 22.
21. Ibid., 25. Another excellent study, William Milligan, *The Ascension and Heav-
    enly Priesthood of our Lord* (London: Macmillan, 1894).
22. John F. Walvoord, *Bibliotheca Sacra,* October 1965, 244.
23. Morgan, *Crises of the Christ,* 298.
24. John F. Walvoord, *Bibliotheca Sacra,* July, October, 1964, 195–208, 291–302.
25. Swete, *The Ascended Christ,* 120.
26. Robert E. Coleman, *Singing with the Angels* (Grand Rapids: Revell, 1980,
    1998).

CHAPTER 10: THE LIFE-GIVING SPIRIT: THE DIVINE BARRISTER

1. Marcus Dods quoted in Charles L. Feinberg, *God Remembers: A Study of
   Zechariah* (Wheaton: Van Kampen, 1950), 72.
2. Carl F. H. Henry, *God, Revelation and Authority,* vol. 5 (Waco: Word, 184ff.);
   John F. Walvoord, *The Holy Spirit: A Comprehensive Study of the Person and
   Work of the Holy Spirit* (Grand Rapids: Zondervan, 1954, 1991) 254; and
   Jurgen Moltmann, *The Spirit of Life: A Universal Affirmation* (Minneapolis:
   Fortress, 1992), 13.
3. Emily Griesinger, "A Hermeneutic of Faith," *Books and Culture,* July–August
   1999, 38.
4. L. Berkhof, *Systematic Theology* (Grand Rapids: Eerdmans, 1941, 1953), 434.
5. Roy B. Zuck, *The Holy Spirit in Your Teaching* (Wheaton: Scripture Press, 1963).
6. Bernard Ramm, *The Witness of the Spirit: An Essay on the Contemporary Relevance of the Internal Witness of the Holy Spirit* (Grand Rapids: Eerdmans, 1959).
   Written before Ramm went Barthian.
7. David L. Larsen, *The Evangelism Mandate: Recovering the Centrality of Gospel
   Preaching* (Wheaton: Crossway, 1992), 22ff.
8. George Smeaton, *The Doctrine of the Holy Spirit* (reprint, Edinburgh: Banner
   of Truth, 1958).
9. A. W. Tozer, *Ten Sermons on the Ministry of the Holy Spirit* (Harrisburg: Christian Publications, 1958), 128.
10. John Owen, *The Holy Spirit: His Gifts and Power* (reprint, Grand Rapids:
    Kregel, 1954), 135.

11. B. B. Warfield, *Biblical and Theological Studies* (reprint, Philadelphia: Presbyterian and Reformed, 1968), 402ff.

12. B. B. Warfield, *Perfectionism* (reprint, Philadelphia: Presbyterian and Reformed, 1967), 177. Good critique of Oberlin Theology but disappointing on Keswick Theology and Charles G. Trumbull of *The Sunday School Times,* although incongruously he seemed sympathetic toward James H. McConkey.

13. Owen, *The Holy Spirit,* 136.

14. Ibid., 141.

15. Timothy L. Smith, *Whitefield and Wesley on the New Birth* (Grand Rapids: Francis Asbury/Zondervan, 1986).

16. Samuel Chadwick, *The Way to Pentecost* (London: Hodder and Stoughton, 1921), 32f.

17. J. I. Packer, "The Witness of the Spirit in Puritan Thought," in *A Quest for Godliness: The Puritan Vision of the Christian Life* (Wheaton: Crossway, 1990). N.B. chap. 11. This is why "persuasion" is such a prominent motif in Acts and the Epistles, viz. follow the word *peitho* in the New Testament.

18. Samuel Ridout, *The Person and Work of the Holy Spirit* (New York: Loizeaux, 1899, 1954), 50.

19. William Edward Biederwolf, *A Help to the Study of the Holy Spirit* (Chicago: Winonah, 1904), 40.

20. Good survey studies are W. H. Griffith Thomas, *The Holy Spirit of God* (reprint, Grand Rapids: Eerdmans, 1955), 9ff.; H. B. Swete, *The Holy Spirit in the New Testament* (Grand Rapids: Baker, 1910, 1964), a serious and scholarly study; A. B. Simpson, *The Holy Spirit or Power from On High: An Unfolding of the Doctrine of the Holy Spirit in the Old and New Testaments,* 2 vols. (Harrisburg: Christian Publications, 1896). Probably Simpson's masterpiece.

21. Walvoord, *The Holy Spirit,* 70ff. An excellent statement on the Spirit in Old Testament times.

22. "An Unknown Christian," *God's Greatest Precious Promise* (London: Marshall, Morgan and Scott, n.d.). I am drawing here on the classic statements in G. Campbell Morgan, *The Acts of the Apostles* (New York: Revell, 1924).

23. John R. W. Stott, *Baptism and Fullness: The Work of the Holy Spirit Today* (Downers Grove: InterVarsity, 1964); Robert C. McQuilkin, *The Baptism of the Spirit: Shall We Seek It?* (Columbia, S.C.: Columbia Bible College, 1935); and Merrill F. Unger, *The Baptizing Work of the Holy Spirit* (Wheaton: Scripture Press, 1953).

24. J. I. Packer, *Keep in Step with the Spirit* (Old Tappan: Revell, 1984), 65–66. Superb vintage Packer with his vendetta, as expected, against the Keswick message.

25. Helpful on the filling of the Spirit: J. Oswald Sanders, *The Holy Spirit of*

Promise: The Mission and Ministry of the Comforter (London: Marshall, Morgan and Scott, 1940); Samuel Ridout, *The Person and Work of the Holy Spirit* (New York: Loizeaux, 1899, 1954); L. Bowing Quick, *The Sevenfold Work of the Holy Spirit* (Harrisburg: Christian Publications, n.d.); and L. L. Legters, *The Simplicity of the Spirit-Filled Life* (Philadelphia: Christian Life Literature Fund, 1930).

26. John F. Walvoord, *The Holy Spirit,* 198; Lewis Sperry Chafer, *He That Is Spiritual* (Findlay, Ohio: Dunham, 1918); and E. F. Kevan, *The Saving Work of the Holy Spirit* (London: Pickering and Inglis, 1953), Keswick readings.

27. James Gilchrist Lawson, *Deeper Experience of Famous Christians* (Anderson: Warner,1911); James H. McConkey, *The Threefold Secret of the Holy Spirit* (Pittsburgh: Silver Publishing, 1897); and R. A. Torrey, "Definitely Endued with Power from On High," in *Why God Used D. L. Moody* (Murfreesboro: Sword of the Lord, n.d.), n.b. chap. 7.

28. S. D. Gordon, *Quiet Talks on Power* (New York: Revell, 1903).

29. F. B. Meyer, *The Christ-Life for the Self-Life* (Chicago: Moody, 1897).

CHAPTER 11: JUSTIFICATION BY FAITH ALONE: THE FINAL ACCEPTANCE

1. G. Campbell Morgan, *The Answers of Jesus to Job* (reprint, Westwood, N.J.: Revell, 1964).

2. Elizabeth Gleick and Andrea Sachs, "The Charms of Fantasy Worlds," *Time* magazine, 20 September 1999, 71.

3. Roger E. Olson, "Theology for the Post-Graham Era," *Christian Century,* 1 September 1999, 816ff.

4. Gabriel Fackre, "Ecumenical Admonitions," *Christian Century,* 1 September 1999, 817ff.

5. N. T. Wright, *The Paul of History and the Apostle of Faith* (Cambridge: Tyndale Bulletin, number 29, 1978); and James Dunn and Suggate, *The Justice of God* (London: Paternoster, 1993), 246.

6. Alistair McGrath, *Justification by Faith: What It Means to Us Today* (Grand Rapids: Zondervan, 1986).

7. Multiple authors, "The Gospel of Jesus Christ: An Evangelical Celebration," *Christianity Today,* 14 June 1999, 9.

8. Miroslav Volf, "Washing Away, Washing Up," *Christian Century,* 1 September 1999, 820.

9. Susan Pendleton Jones, "The Obedient Son," *Christian Century,* 15 September 1999, 849.

10. Ray S. Anderson, *Ministry on the Fireline: A Practical Theology for an Empowered Church* (Downers Grove: InterVarsity, 1993), 66ff., 81.

11. Lewis Sperry Chafer, "For Whom Did Christ Die?" *Bibliotheca Sacra,*

October–December 1980, 310–326. An especially fine treatment in favor of unlimited redemption.

12. James Nance, "His Justifying Cross," *Credenda* 9, no. 5, 20.

13. William H. Smith, *World* magazine, 7 June 1997, 26.

14. David van Biema, "Preach It, Caveman!" *Time*, 19 April 1999, 51.

15. James Buchanan, *The Doctrine of Justification* (reprint, Grand Rapids: Baker, 1955). A heavyweight in the field—the must read book of justification, its history, and doctrinal formulation.

16. Many signatories, "The Gospel of Jesus Christ," 2ff.

17. Ibid., 7.

18. Howard W. Ferrin, "Justification by Faith Alone," *Christian Heritage,* January 1973, 12.

19. Howard W. Ferrin, "Justification by Faith Alone," *Christian Heritage,* April 1973, 23.

20. "Vatican Revises Manual on Earning Forgiveness," *Chicago Tribune,* 18 September 1999, section 1, 11.

21. Donald S. Whitney, *Spiritual Disciplines for the Christian Life* (Colorado Springs: NavPress, 1991).

22. A. W. Tozer, *The Christian's Book of Mystical Verse* (Harrisburg: Christian Publications, 1963).

23. Some choice studies of the "in Christ" texts are J. R. Macduff, *In Christo* (London: Charles J. Thynne, n.d.); A. J. Gordon, *In Christ* (Chicago: Moody, 1872); and E. Stanley Jones, *In Christ* (Nashville: Abingdon, 1961).

24. W. D. Davies, *Paul and Rabbinic Judaism* (London: SPCK, 1970), 88.

25. James S. Stewart, *A Man in Christ: The Vital Elements of St. Paul's Religion* (New York: Harper, 1954).

26. Donald Grey Barnhouse, "Baptized into Christ," in *The Ministry of Keswick,* vol. 2, ed. Herbert F. Stevenson (London: Marshall, Morgan and Scott, 1964), 155–209, being the Bible Readings at the Keswick Convention in England in the summer of 1948. Barnhouse demonstrates how we are incorporated into Christ's election, birth, circumcision, increase, baptism, temptation, ministry, death, burial, resurrection, ascension, and return in glory.

27. Hudson Taylor, *Union and Communion: Thoughts on the Song of Solomon* (Chicago: Moody, n.d.); James Cuthbertson, *An Old Love Letter* (London: Chas. Davy, n.d.); and Watchman Nee, *Song of Songs* (Ft. Washington: Christian Literature Crusade, 1965).

28. Dennis Prager, "When Forgiveness Is a Sin," *Wall Street Journal,* 15 December 1997.

29. Wendell E. Miller, *Forgiveness: The Power and the Puzzles* (Warsaw, Ind.: Clearbrook, 1994). Psychiatry and psychology (the mental health movement)

in our country have strangely neglected the phenomenon of forgiveness, but there is evidence of some new interest. Cf. Gary Thomas, "The Forgiveness Factor," *Christianity Today,* 10 January 2000, 38ff.

CHAPTER 12: SANCTIFICATION BY GRACE: CRISIS AND GROWTH

1. Paul S. Rees, "Holiness," in *Baker's Dictionary of Theology,* ed. Everett F. Harrison (Grand Rapids: Baker, 1960) 269f. For a powerful study of the book of Leviticus with its strong emphasis on the holiness of God and of his people, cf. Andrew Bonar, *Leviticus* (Edinburgh: Banner of Truth, 1846).
2. Dietrich Bonhoeffer, *Ethics* (London: SCM, 1967), 189–90.
3. F. B. Meyer, "The Trinity of Temptation," in *Back to Bethel* (Chicago: Moody, n.d.), 40–52.
4. J. Russell Howden, "A Man's Foes," in *The Ministry of Keswick,* vol. 2, ed. Herbert F. Stevenson (London: Marshall, Morgan and Scott, 1964), 55–110. Being the Bible Readings at Keswick in 1924.
5. C. Dominique van de Stadt, "Messner's Latest First," in *World Press Review,* January 1987, 49.
6. Max Stirner, *The Ego and His Own* (New York: Revisionist Press, 1984).
7. Recommended studies on Satan: Lewis Sperry Chafer, *Satan* (Findlay, Ohio: Dunham, 1919); Frederick A. Tatford, *Satan: The Prince of Darkness* (Grand Rapids: Kregel, n.d.); Mark I. Bubeck, *The Adversary* (Chicago: Moody, 1975); Hal Lindsey, *Satan Is Alive and Well on Planet Earth* (Grand Rapids: Zondervan, 1972); Herbert Lockyer, *Satan: His Person and Power* (Waco: Word, 1980); and Jessie Penn-Lewis with Evan Roberts, *War on the Saints* (reprint, Ft. Washington, Pa.: Christian Literature Crusade, 1968).
8. John Bunyan, *The Holy War* (reprint, Chicago: Moody, 1948). For analysis of Bunyan's work, cf. my *The Company of the Creative: A Christian Reader's Guide to Great Literature and Its Themes* (Grand Rapids: Kregel, 1999), 5.4.
9. David C. Needham, *Birthright* (Portland: Multnomah, 1979). Ably reviewed by Frederic R. Howe, review of *Birthright,* by David C. Needham, *Bibliotheca Sacra,* January–March 1984, 68ff.
10. Howe, review of *Birthright,* 76.
11. Renald E. Showers, *The New Nature* (Neptune, N.J.: Loizeaux, 1986), 17.
12. Ibid., 49. Calvin was right: "God does not justify anyone he does not also sanctify."
13. F. B. Meyer, *Light on Life's Duties* (Chicago: Moody, n.d.), 41f.
14. Antoine de Saint-Exupery, *Wind, Sand, and Stars* (New York: Harcourt, Brace, 1939), 96.
15. Melvin E. Dieter, editor, *Five Views of Sanctification* (Grand Rapids: Zondervan, 1987).

16. W. E. Sangster, *The Path to Perfection* (London: Epworth, 1943); and also George Allen Turner, *The Vision Which Transforms* (Kansas City: Beacon Hill, 1964).

17. Quoted in Dwight Hervey Small, *The High Cost of Holy Living* (Westwood: Revell, 1964), 9. Exceptionally fine sermons on the theme from a Keswick perspective.

18. Ruth Paxson, *Life on the Highest Plane,* 3 vols. (Westwood: Revell, 1928), 1:13ff.

19. David F. Wells, *Losing Our Virtue: Why the Church Must Recover Its Moral Vision* (Grand Rapids: Eerdmans, 1998), 140. Also Digby Anderson, ed., *The Loss of Virtue: Moral Confusion and Social Disorder in Britain and America* (New York: National Review, 1992). For example, studies show that in 1930, 8 percent of girls or women were unmarried when they had their first child; between 1990 to 1994, 41 percent were unmarried when they had their first child. Source: *Insight into the News,* 10 December 1999, 31.

20. Watchman Nee, *The Normal Christian Life* (Ft. Washington, Pa.: Christian Literature Crusade, 1958).

21. J. Gilchrist Lawson, *Deeper Experiences of Famous Christians* (Anderson, Ind.: Warner Press, 1911).

22. Donald Grey Barnhouse, *God's Methods for Holy Living* (Grand Rapids: Eerdmans, 1951); and William Culbertson, *God's Provision for Holy Living* (Chicago: Moody, 1958). Both of these books consist of messages delivered at English Keswick. For the best exposition of the Keswick message, cf. Evan H. Hopkins, *The Law of Liberty in the Spiritual Life* (reprint, Philadelphia: Sunday School Times, 1952).

23. Charles G. Trumbull, *Victory in Christ: Messages on the Victorious Life* (Philadelphia: Sunday School Times, 1959). Includes his famous address on "The Life That Wins." For background on Trumbull and his father and their leadership of the *Times,* cf. my *The Company of the Preachers* (Grand Rapids: Kregel, 1998), 607. See also J. C. Ryle, *Holiness* (reprint, Grand Rapids: Kregel, 1956). Choice!

24. C. I. Scofield, *The New Life in Christ: Messages of Joy and Victory* (Chicago: Moody, 1915); Andrew Murray, *Absolute Surrender* (Chicago: Moody, 1897); and Frances Ridley Havergal, *Kept for the Master's Use* (New York: H. M. Caldwell, 1879). These are wondrously luminous messages.

CHAPTER 13: BELOVED COMMUNITY: THE DIVINE COMMONWEALTH

1. F. J. A. Hort, *The Christian Ecclesia* (London: Macmillan, 1914). The great old classic. A more recent study of the basics is Robert L. Saucey, *The Church in God's Program* (Chicago: Moody, 1972).

2. Cf. David L. Larsen, *Jews, Gentiles, and the Church: A New Perspective on History*

and Prophecy (Grand Rapids: Discovery House). The case is made that God has not rejected his ancient people.

3. J. Robert Nelson, *The Realm of Redemption* (Greenwich, Conn.: Seabury, 1951), 35.

4. John F. Walvoord, "The Nature of the Church," *Bibliotheca Sacra,* October 1959, 296.

5. F. W. Dillistone, *The Structure of the Divine Society* (Philadelphia: Westminster, 1951), 213.

6. Lesslie Newbigin, *The Household of God* (New York: Friendship Press, 1953), 127, 130.

7. Gordon D. Fee, *God's Empowering Presence* (Peabody, Mass.: Hendrickson, 1994), 801.

8. Newbigin, *Household of God,* 146.

9. J. B. Phillips, introduction to *The Young Church in Action* (London: Geoffrey Bles, 1955). About this paraphrase, cf. J. B. Phillips, *The Price of Success* (Wheaton: Shaw, 1984), 157ff.

10. Daniel Jenkins, *The Strangeness of the Church* (Garden City: Doubleday, 1955).

11. Peter O'Brien, "Principalities and Powers," in *Biblical Interpretation and the Church: Text and Context,* ed. D. A. Carson (Exeter: Paternoster, 1984), 110ff. We need to remember that the church is not the kingdom, although they are related. The church is the people of God and the kingdom is the rule of God. The rule of God is expressed within the church (Colossians 1:13, etc.).

12. Thomas Cahill, *How the Irish Saved Civilization* (New York: Doubleday, 1995). Interesting testimony by the great German-Jewish scientist, Albert Einstein: "Only the Church opposed the fight which Hitler was waging against liberty. Till then I had no interest in the Church, but now I feel great admiration and am truly attracted to the Church which had the persistent courage to fight for spiritual truth and moral freedom" (Julius Reiger, *The Silent Church: The Problem of the German Confessional Witness* [London: SCM, 1944]).

13. The Hindu holy books are well known for their eroticism. cf. Earle V. Pierce, *The Church and World Conditions* (New York: Revell, 1943), 49; and Wilbur M. Smith, *The Word of God and the Life of Holiness* (Grand Rapids: Zondervan, 1957), 13ff.

14. David L. Larsen, *The Company of the Creative: A Christian Reader's Guide to Great Literature and Its Themes* (Grand Rapids: Kregel, 1999); and idem, *The Influence of the English Bible upon the English Language and upon English and American Literatures* (New York: American Bible Society, n.d.).

15. Lesslie Newbigin, *Unfinished Agenda: An Autobiography* (New York: Eerdmans, 1985), 254.

16. Pierce, *Church and World Conditions,* 25–93. See especially chapters 3 and 4.

17. John R. W. Stott, *God's New Society: The Message of Ephesians* (Downers Grove: InterVarsity, 1980).

18. Erich Sauer, *From Eternity to Eternity* (Grand Rapids: Eerdmans, 1954), 38.

19. David L. Larsen, *The Company of the Preachers: A History of Biblical Preaching from the Old Testament to the Modern Era* (Grand Rapids: Kregel, 1998), 43.

20. G. Campbell Morgan, *The Birth of the Church: An Exposition of the Second Chapter of Acts* (Old Tappan: Revell, 1968), 160.

21. Theodore Gill, "Memo," *The Pulpit,* May 1959, 3.

22. Beautiful preparatory guides for the Lord's Supper: Matthew Henry, *The Communicant's Companion* (1843; reprint, Joplin, Mo.: College Press, 1969); and Andrew Murray, *The Lord's Supper* (Chicago: Moody, n.d.).

23. David L. Larsen, *The Evangelism Mandate: Recovering the Centrality of Gospel Preaching* (Wheaton: Crossway, 1992), 45–66. We are not interested so much in church work as in the work of the church. William Hendrickson said, "In the Kingdom of God there is no room for drones, only for working bees."

24. T. W. Manson, *Ministry and Priesthood: Christ and Ours* (London: Hodder and Stoughton, 1948), 14.

25. D. Martyn Lloyd-Jones, *The Basis of Christian Unity: An Exposition of John 17 and Ephesians 4* (Grand Rapids: Eerdmans, 1963).

26. David L. Larsen, *Caring for the Flock* (Wheaton: Crossway, 1991). Chapters 1–3 especially.

27. As summarized in Robert C. Worley, *Change in the Church: A Source of Hope* (Philadelphia: Westminster, 1971), 34f.

28. The deeper the darkness, "the brighter the grace of God shone out," as the feast in Hezekiah's time was better than Solomon's (2 Chronicles 30:26), Josiah's better than any since Samuel (2 Chronicles 35:18), and Nehemiah's better than any since Joshua (Neh. 8:17). Cf. W. T. P. Wolston, *The Church: What Is It?* in *The Serious Christian,* vol. 4 (Charlotte, N.C.: Books for Christians, n.d.), 191.

29. "And I tell you, 'you are Peter' [Petros, a stone] 'and on this rock' [Petra, rock ledge, massive rock] 'I will build my church.'" Some argue that since Jesus spoke Aramaic, the wordplay in the Greek may not be possible. In our Greek manuscript the writer does make this play on words. Cf. also G. Campbell Morgan, *Peter and the Church* (New York: Revell, 1938).

30. Geoffrey Wainwright, *Eucharist and Eschatology* (New York: Oxford, 1981), 18ff.

CHAPTER 14: THE STRATEGY OF PROVIDENCE: THE PASSIONATE MOVER

1. Roger Hazleton, *God's Way with Man: Variations on the Theme of Providence*

(Nashville: Abingdon, 1956), 1. This book, not from an evangelical perspective, contains more information than that of Georgia Harkness, *The Providence of God* (Nashville: Abingdon, 1960).

2. Gertrude Himmelfarb, "Postmodernist History," in *On Looking into the Abyss* (New York: Knopf, 1994), 131ff.

3. Ibid., 149. Edgar Sheffield Brightman, the Boston University personalist, adds also a category that includes "surds," persons who because of developmental disabilities do not subscribe to a worldview positing an omnipotent God. Like Rabbi Howard Kushner (*Why Bad Things Happen to Good People* [New York: Avon, 1994]), he holds to a limited or finite god.

4. Ibid., 160.

5. Quoted in Renald E. Showers, *What on Earth Is God Doing? Satan's Conflict with God* (Neptune, N.J.: Loizeaux Brothers, 1973), 96.

6. Ibid., 160

7. Jon Ritz, "Language of the Spirit: Religious Literature Leads to Some Revelations," *Chicago Tribune,* 19 December 1999, sec. 14, p. 3.

8. Ibid.

9. H. Richard Niebuhr, "Theology in a Time of Disillusionment," in *Theology, History, and Culture* (New Haven: Yale University Press, 1996), 102ff.

10. Alexander Carson, *The History of Providence as Explained in the Bible* (reprint, Grand Rapids: Baker, 1977).

11. Wilhelm Windelband, *A History of Philosophy,* vol. 1 (reprint, New York: Harper Torchbooks, 1958), 145.

12. Donald Baillie, *God Was in Christ* (New York: Scribner's, 1948), 63.

13. Gardner C. Taylor, *The Scarlet Thread* (Elgin, Ill.: Progressive Baptist Press, 1981), 29.

14. Charles Gallaudet Trumbull, *The Life Story of C. I. Scofield* (New York: Oxford University Press, 1920), 136. Young, heavy-drinking lawyer C. I. Scofield was converted when a friend pressed the claims of Christ from a well-worn pocket Testament.

15. C. S. Lewis, *The Problem of Pain* (London: Fontana Books, 1940). An excellent treatment of the question, "If God is good and all-powerful, why does he allow his creatures to suffer pain?"

16. Herbert Butterfield, *Christianity and History* (London: Fontana Books, 1949), 147ff.

17. Ibid., 147.

18. Frank Houghton, *Amy Carmichael of Dohnavur* (Ft. Washington, Pa.: Christian Literature Crusade, n.d.). During her last twenty years, she was an invalid. Even though the "Warfare of the Service" was over, she was "climbing unawares."

19. Isabel Fleece, *Not by Accident* (Chicago: Moody, 1964).

20. John S. Feinberg, *Deceived by God? A Journey Through Suffering* (Wheaton: Crossway, 1997).

21. Ibid., 95, 105.

22. Garry Friesen, *Decision-Making and the Will of God: A Biblical Alternative to the Traditional View* (Portland: Multnomah, 1980).

23. Robert P. Evans, review of *Decision-Making and the Will of God: A Biblical Alternative to the Traditional View*, by Garry Friesen, *The Fundamentalist Journal*, October 1983, 43f.

24. Stuart S. Cook, review of three articles on "the wisdom view,"—"Wisdom Along the Way," *Eternity*, April 1986, 19–23; "Paths of Righteousness," *Eternity*, May 1986, 32–37; "True Guidance," *Eternity*, June 1986, 36–39, all by J. I. Packer, *Bibliotheca Sacra*, April–June 1987, 107.

25. These thoughts were expressed in a discussion on this subject with Dr. Wayne Grudem of Trinity Evangelical Divinity School about ten years ago.

26. Sidney Greidanus, *Preaching Christ from the Old Testament: A Contemporary Hermeneutical Method* (Grand Rapids: Eerdmans, 1999), 303.

CHAPTER 15: THE ESCHATOLOGICAL WEDGE: THE PRESENCE OF THE FUTURE

1. George E. Ladd, *The Last Things* (Grand Rapids: Eerdmans, 1978), 106ff.

2. Garry Wills, *Under God: Religion and American Politics* (New York: Simon and Schuster, 1990), 24.

3. A. W. Tozer, "The Decline of Apocalyptic Expectation," *Alliance Witness*, 28 November 1952, 3ff.

4. W. Sibley Towner, "Rapture, Red Heifer, and Other Millennial Misfortunes," *Theology Today*, October 1999, 383. Towner does not believe that Scripture is able to speak predictively.

5. R. C. Sproul, *The Last Days According to Jesus: When Did Jesus Say He Would Return?* (Grand Rapids: Baker, 1998), 21. Sproul has moved to a praeterist position, which sees A.D. 70 as the time of prophetic fulfillment, a view requiring a redating of Revelation to a time prior to 70.

6. Ibid., 12. Sproul will not go so far as the radical praeterist James Russell, who denies any eschatological events after A.D. 70 (167). The Rapture took place unnoticed, Russell argues, in A.D. 70.

7. Henry Alford, *The New Testament for English Readers* (Chicago: Moody, n.d.), 169.

8. R. C. Sproul, *Last Days According to Jesus*, 157. In this book, Sproul remains undecided on major points. It has been argued recently that Jesus could not see beyond A.D. 70, at which time he foresaw the final days.

9. Imminency is effectively argued in John F. MacArthur, *The Second Coming: Signs of Christ's Return and the End of the Age* (Wheaton: Crossway, 1999);

Gerald B. Stanton, "The Doctrine of Imminency: Is It Biblical?" in *The Return: Understanding Christ's Second Coming and the End Times,* ed. Thomas Ice and Timothy J. Demy (Grand Rapids: Kregel, 1999), 107ff.; and in the "Left Behind" novels of Tim LaHaye and Jerry Jenkins.

10. James T. Martin, *The Last Judgment in Protestant Theology from Orthodoxy to Ritschl* (Grand Rapids: Eerdmans, 1963), 116. Cartesian doubt went beyond the doctrine of verbal inspiration. In the art of the medieval church, however, the Last Judgment theme was virtually universal in local churches.

11. Ibid., 149. Schleiermacher rejects any literal fulfillment of Bible prophecy, even prophecies of A.D. 70.

12. Ibid., 188. Kahler says, "Without eschatology, there can be no Christology, no soteriology, no Christian ethics and no theodicy."

13. Leon Morris, *The Biblical Doctrine of Judgment* (Grand Rapids: Eerdmans, 1960), 17.

14. Merrill F. Unger, *Great Neglected Bible Prophecies* (Chicago: Scripture Press, 1955), 99ff.

15. Lewis Sperry Chafer, *Major Bible Themes* quoted in Unger, *Great Neglected Bible Prophecies,* 116. Unger also provides an excellent study of the five crowns of Christian reward, 125ff.

16. The Vikings believed in an afterlife called Nifflheim, where wicked and adulterous men would sit forever on a cake of ice.

17. Reinhold Niebuhr, *Human Nature and Destiny* (New York: Scribner's, 1955), quoted in Morris, *Biblical Doctrine of Judgment,* 66.

18. B. B. Warfield, *The Person and Work of Christ* (reprint, Philadelphia: Presbyterian and Reformed, 1950), 115ff. "It is death that is the object of his wrath, and behind death him who has the power of death."

19. For vastly more detailed treatment of this, see David Larsen, *Jews, Gentiles, and the Church: A New Perspective on History and Prophecy* (Grand Rapids: Discovery House, 1995).

20. Walter C. Kaiser Jr., "The Land of Israel and the Future Return," in *Israel—The Land and the People,* ed. H. Wayne House (Grand Rapids: Kregel, 1998), 209ff.

21. Peter Richardson, *Israel in the Apostolic Church* (Cambridge: Cambridge University Press, 1969), ix.

22. Merrill F. Unger, *Great Neglected Bible Prophecies,* 149.

23. E. H. Gifford quoted in James Denney, *The Expositor's Greek Testament,* vol. 2 (reprint, Grand Rapids: Eerdmans, 1951), 683.

24. Rene Paché, *The Return of Christ* (Chicago: Moody, 1955), 418.

25. Larsen, *Jews, Gentiles, and the Church,* 307ff.

26. Lewis Smedes, "The Trials of an Unauthor," *Theology, News and Notes,* December 1999, 6. Modern frustration is examined in Andrew Delbanco, *The*

Real American Dream: A Meditation on Hope (Cambridge: Harvard University Press, 1999). Concerned profoundly in regard to modern melancholy, Delbanco sees that the contemporary penchant for immediate gratification is only leading to further moral decay. He resists belief in God and consciousness as the answer, yet hesitates.

Eugene Peterson says, "Everything in the New Testament is written under the pressure of the end. Christ is coming back" (*Subversive Spirituality* [Grand Rapids: Eerdmans, 1997], 242).

SCRIPTURE INDEX

Genesis
1:1 .... 25, 132
1:1–25 26
1:26 .... 27, 67
1:26–27 30
1:27 ...... 67, 68
1:28 68
1:31 68
2:7 67
2:15 69
2:17 117
2:18–23 67
2:22–24 15
2:24 27
3 189
3:1 70
3:3 168
3:4 70
3:7 117
3:15 82
3:17–19 67
3:21 100
3:22 ...... 27, 117
4:2ff. 100
5 117
6:3 155
11:7 27
15:6 171
15:7 101
16:6–13 27
17:7 253
17:8 253
18 27
18:14 49
18:25 ..... 55, 246
19 27
22 27
24:48 228
25:8 118

28:13–18 27
28:16 45
39:2 228
39:9 15
45:8 228
48:15 231
49:22f. 15
49:24–25 231
49:33 118
50:20 228

Exodus
3:13–14 40
15:11 52
19:5 232
19:8 73
20:2–26 18
20:5 .... 53, 71
20:6 58
20:18 53
28:3 152
30:29 185
31:3 152
35:31 152

Leviticus
1–7 101
8:10 185
10:1ff. 542
14 92
16:20ff. 181
16:22 181
17:11 101
19:2 ..... 161, 184

Numbers
6:24–26 27
7:1 185
7:89 32

11:25–29 165
11:29 165
13:23 27
16:41–50 101
25:11–13 101
32:23b 80

Deuteronomy
4:14ff. 68
4:15ff. 46
6:4 .... 27, 263n
6:5 64
7:7–9 58
14:2 232
26:18 232
28 253

Joshua
1:7–8 15

1 Samuel
3:1b 32
3:7b 32
3:9b 32
3:21 32
15:29 42
17:26, 36 40

2 Samuel
6:6ff. 54
12:23 118

1 Kings
8:27 45
17:3–4 238

2 Chronicles
7:16 185
16:9 230

30:26 .... 285n
34:14ff. 16, 220
35:18 .... 285n

Nehemiah
8:17 .... 285n

Esther
6:1 229

Job
9:32–33 143
13:15 234
14:14 ..... 118, 249
15:14–16 166
16:19ff. 118
17:10–16 118
19:25–27 118
23:10 ... 45, 88, 234
23:12 15
25:4 166
32:8 151
38–41 46

Psalms
1:2–3 15
2 27
8:4 67
14:1 ..... 25, 224
16:9 119
16:10 119
16:11 250
17:15 119
19 46
19:1ff. 25
19:7 250
22 101
22:16 101
23 232

23:4 47
23:6 119
24 137
32:1–2 180
32:8 232
33:6 49
37:23–24 233
45:6–7 27
48:14 238
50:23 215
51:5 71
60:6 52
62:11b 48
72:1–2 56
72:12–14 56
73:23–24 233
85:10 104
90:17 93
91:1 179
97:10 78
100:3 ...... 41, 67
100:4 148
103:8 62
103:10 62
103:12 181
103:13 59
103:14 45
110 27
110:1 133
110:3 55
115:8 39
116:3 250
119 .... 15, 24
119:11 15
119:30 15
119:40 15
119:45 15
119:52 15
119:68 51
119:97 15
119:105 192
119:113 15
119:129 15
119:140 13
119:143 15
119:173 15
135:4 232
139:1–3 227
139:1–6 43
139:7 45
139:13–16 227
139:23–24 76
145:13 57
145:15–16 233
146:6 57

Proverbs

3:5–6 237

9:10 54
11:14 238
13:15 80
15:22 238
16:3 233
16:9 233
17:15 171
21:1 234
24:6 238
28:13 79
29:18 199
30:4 28

Ecclesiastes

8:11 246
8:11–13 57
12:14 ..... 56, 246

Isaiah

1:9 209
2:3–4 257
6:1 35
6:1ff. 54
6:3 54
6:6ff. 202
6:8 27
6:19 35
7:14 86
9:6 86
9:6–7 134
11:2–4 152
11:6–9 257
11:11 253
14:9–17 250
14:13–14 188
14:13–15 .... 40, 76
26:13 41
26:19 ..... 119, 250
44:3–4 195
44:3–5 146
44:6–8 45
46:10ff. 242
48:3–6 242
48:16 28
50:9 177
52:11 200
53 .... 101, 107, 197
53:2b 95
53:2ff. 16
53:5 101
53:5–6 .... 107, 172
53:6 197
53:10 99
53:11 . 124, 144, 177
55:8–9 31
55:9 223
55:10–11 15
57:15 49

59:15b 56
61:8 56
61:10 .... 166, 177
64:6a 168
64:6 72
65:24 44
66:13 59

Jeremiah

2:13 75
3:8 232
8:22 20
9:24 57
10:23 222
16:14–15 254
17:8 15
17:9 72
20:9 15
23:5–6 180
31:3 58
31:3–4 232
31:10 232
31:34 181

Ezekiel

2:2 14
8 132
10 132
13:22 198
18:1–32 71
18:4 169
18:4b 72
28:25 198
32:21 250
34 232
36:20 209
36:23 198
36:24–32 153
36:26 191
37:1–14 ... 119, 254
37:9 .... 28, 36
39:27 198
40–48 257
44:23 198

Daniel

2 256
2:44 256
3:17b–18 229
6:20 40
7:13–14 91
10 229
11:35 202
12:1 119
12:2–3 119

Hosea

11:8f. 58

13:2 39

Joel

2:28ff. 159
2:28–32 146
3 230

Amos

5:24 55
9:14–15 254

Jonah

3:10 42
4 217
4:2 58

Micah

3:8 149
4:4 257
6:8 .... 56, 161
7:18b 61
7:19 181

Nahum

1:7 230

Habakkuk

1:2 229
1:13 53
2:1 229
2:14 255
3:16–19 229

Zechariah

2:8 232
4:6 150
4:7 150
8:5 230
10:9–12 254
12:10 . 102, 252, 254
13:1 252
13:1ff. 101
14:3–5 256
14:3–7 245
14:9 256

Malachi

1:11 205
3:3 202
3:5 246
3:6 41
3:12 205
3:16a 214

Matthew

1:5 229
1:12 150
1:18 87

1:20–23 86
1:21 . . . . . . 103, 186
3:17 59
4:4 14
4:19 135
5 95
5:6 . . . . 80, 198
5:13 208
5:14 208
5:16 . . 198, 208, 218
5:45 233
6:8 44
6:9 . . . . . . 47, 267n
6:10 . . . . . 255, 256
6:15 182
6:33 233
7:21–23 178
7:29 91
9:37–38 216
10 245
10:23 244
10:29–30 233
11:4–6 91
11:27 90
13:37–38 216
16:15 83
16:18 . 158, 204, 206, 220
16:22 103
16:24 . . . . . 109, 188
17:1ff. 245
17:5 59
17:9 127
18:12–14 232
18:20 146
19:28 254
21:10 83
21:43 206
23:37 . . . . . 59, 157
23:39 . . . . 252, 254
24–25 242
24:15 244
24:34 244
24:36 43
24:37 200
25:13 244
25:31–46 248
25:46 249
26:38 104
26:61–62 122
27:62ff. 103
27:64 122
27:40 122
27:51–53 143
28:7 136
28:11–15 122
28:16–20 221
28:18–20 . . . 90, 129

28:19–20 28
28:20 144

Mark
6:2 91
7:20–21 91
8:36 224
9:24 92
10:32–34 103
10:45 . . 91, 104, 105
13 242
13:32 90
12:36 134
14:27 103
14:62 134
15:29 122
16:15–18 221

Luke
1:26–38 87
1:32–33 134
1:37 . . . . 49, 96
1:74–75 200
2:40 . . . 86, 90, 152
2:46–51 89
2:52 90
4:27 92
5:10 214
5:24 92
7:40 154
9:51 103
11:13 . . . . . 91, 149
12:40 243
12:45 243
13:35 103
15:11–32 . . . . 75, 91
16:19–31 250
17:28–29 200
18:8 209
18:34 103
19:10 . . . . . 91, 232
19:12 134
21 242
21:28 255
22:19 104
22:20 . . . . . 104, 207
22:31 140
22:37 103
22:43 104
22:44 104
23:24 182
23:43 89
24:27 100
24:45 103
24:45–48 221
24:47 112
24:50–51 131
27:63–64 122

John
1:1 88
1:1–5 84
1:9–10 59
1:11–12 159
1:14 . 47, 86, 92, 213
1:16 62
1:17 62
1:18 . 34, 88, 90, 213
1:29 . . . 59, 103, 181
1:36 181
2:1–11 89
2:19 . . . . . 103, 213
2:19–22 122
2:25 89
3:1ff. 153
3:2 91
3:5 . . . . 17, 153
3:12 153
3:13 84
3:14 . . . . . 101, 103
3:16 . 59, 61, 187, 253
3:17 59
3:19 59
3:36 . . . . . . 157, 128
4 89
4:14 194
4:24 46
4:42 59
5:22 129
5:24 . . 128, 155, 157
5:25 128
5:28–29 . . . 128, 250
5:40 . . . . . . 77, 157
6:27 158
6:33 59
6:44 59
6:51 59
6:51–57 103
6:62 . . . . . . 84, 134
7:4 59
7:7 59
7:16–17 214
7:37–39 . . . 163, 194
7:38–39 145
7:46 91
8:12 59
8:23 59
8:26 90
8:28 154
8:28–29 90
8:31–32 151
8:34 74
8:38 90
8:42 90
8:55 90
8:56–58 84
9 234

9:3 236
10:4 . . . . . . 136, 232
10:10 194
10:11 232
10:18 103
10:35 15
10:36 185
11 89
11:25 126
11:33 251
11:35 251
12:23–28 103
12:24–25 126
12:26 136
12:31 190
12:32 59
12:47 59
13:31–32 104
13:34–35 61
14:1ff. 245
14:2 . . . . . . 47, 132
14:2–3 . . . . 135, 137
14:6 96
14:9 91
14:11 177
14:12ff. 140
14:16 . . . . . 164, 233
14:16–17 145
14:17 159
14:19 . . . . . 59, 126
14:19b 250
14:20 . . . . . 124, 177
14:23 92
14:26 . . . . . 34, 145
14:27 233
15:1–7 183
15:3 19
15:4 178
15:5 . . . . 92, 93
15:7 160
15:13 61
15:15 34
15:19 59
15:26 . . 34, 145, 153
15:26–27 160
16:8 59
16:8–11 . . . .75, 155, 199, 246, 249
16:11 59
16:12–13 151
16:13–15 . . 145, 160
16:14 161
16:14–15 34
16:28 . . . . . 132, 159
16:33 205
17 140
17:3 126
17:5 84

17:6 ...... 59, 187
17:9 59
17:11 .... 187, 267n
17:14 ...... 59, 187
17:15 188
17:17 20
17:17b 13
17:18 188
17:19 185
17:20 140
17:21 59
17:23 ...... 59, 218
17:24 133
18:19 214
18:36–37 59
18:37 91
19:30 143
20:7 122
20:9 122
20:17 .... 134, 137
20:21 216
20:21–23 221
20:28 .... 28, 88
21:22 135
21:22–23 244

Acts

1:1 159
1:3 120
1:6 ...... 134, 256
1:7 244
1:8 .... 162, 216,
    217, 221
1:9–10 131
1:11 243
1:19 211
2:4 163
2:23–24 105
2:24–25 119
2:33 ...... 133, 145
2:36 133
2:36–37 75
2:37 ...... 155, 156
2:41 124
2:42–47 214
2:47 205
3:14 57
3:21 254
4:12 96
4:13 93
4:27 57
4:30 57
5:1–11 54
5:3–4 28
5:11 54
5:28 127
6:3 152
7:38 206
7:51ff. 155

7:56 134
7:60 182
8 238
8:19 238
9:11 140
10:39–40 105
10:40–43 129
11:18 157
15:18 43
15:41 206
16:6–7 238
16:31 ..... 156, 218
17:26–27 230
17:31 ...... 57, 116,
    129, 249
19:32 206
19:39 206
19:41 206
20:21 156
20:28 ...... 29, 88
24:16 238
24:25 .... 246, 249
25:19 116
26:14 156
27 230

Romans

1–3 76
1:1–4 192
1:4 129
1:8–16 229
1:16–17 ..... 22, 50
1:17 201
1:18 53
1:18ff. . 39, 169, 246
1:20ff. 25
2:4 157
2:5–6 246
2:14–15 57
2:15 70
2:24 208
3:9–20 .... 72, 168
3:23 76
3:23–26 167
3:25ff. 107
3:25–26 101
3:26 57
3:28 171
4 170
4:5 169
4:25 .. 123, 124, 171,
    178
5 75
5:1 112
5:3–5 236
5:5 .... 60, 252
5:6 .... 60, 107
5:8 .... 58, 106
5:10 .. 107, 123, 140

5:12 .... 69, 117, 167
5:12–21 71
5:17 ...... 168, 173
5:18 172
5:20 62
5:20b 194
6:1 185
6:1ff. 109
6:1–11 136
6:1–23 .... 192, 193
6:3–4 124
6:4 124
6:14 193
6:17 9
6:23 ... 72, 116, 168
7 191
7:4 183
7:6 124
7:7 73
7:12 53
7:12b 76
7:13 74
7:14ff. 186
7:17 78
7:18 .... 66, 188
7:21–23 191
7:24 251
7:24–25 191
8 191
8:1 .... 111, 174, 248
8:4 ...... 73, 186
8:9 ...... 145, 154
8:11 ...... 14, 127
8:13 189
8:13–14 149
8:16 ...... 17, 158
8:17 185
8:18–25 128
8:19–22 256
8:21 251
8:23 251
8:24 241
8:26–27 144
8:28 222
8:29 ... 44, 160, 185
8:33 174
8:33–34 172
8:34 ...... 134, 142
8:35–39 142
8:37 195
10:8 35
10:9–10 ...122, 129,
    218
10:11 129
10:13–15 218
10:17 ...... 17, 157
11 179
11:1a 232
11:15 ..... 119, 254

11:17 ..... 179, 205
11:22 ...... 53, 169
11:23–26 255
11:25–26 209
11:26–27 232
11:33 56
11:33–36 .. 223, 253
12:1–2 237
12:2a 187
12:18–20 182
14:8 77
14:12 247
14:23b 74
16:1 207
16:16 206
16:25–27 205

1 Corinthians

1:9 179
1:18–25 99
1:23–24 111
1:25 50
2:2 112
2:4 153
2:8–10 153
2:9–16 18
2:10 ...... 18, 153
2:13 153
2:13b 19
2:14 72
2:15 153
2:16 153
3:1–3 197
3:9 213
3:11 ...... 213, 221
3:12–15 248
3:16–17 213
4:9 218
5:7 101
6:17 179
6:19 157
6:19–20 .... 47, 213
9:16 112
10:4 101
10:11 208
10:12 187
10:13 ...... 79, 187
10:15–17 215
10:16 146
11:18 112
11:31 248
12 ...... 134, 183
12:11 ..... 124, 160
12:13 . 158, 160, 204
12:14ff. 213
13:4–7 61
13:9 43
13:12 219
13:12b 236

14:24–25 218
15:1–4 124
15:3 101
15:6 120
15:9 192
15:17–18 123
15:20–22 115
15:20–23 128
15:23 250
15:24–26 255
15:25 135
15:26 251
15:28 256
15:32f. 129
15:42–44 .. 128, 251
15:45 143
15:49 251
15:52 251

2 Corinthians

1:9b 127
1:12 238
1:21–22 158
2:14 195
3:14–15 152
3:16 152
3:17–18 160
3:18 ..... 192, 200
4:2 151
4:4 70
4:8 205
4:10 93
5:6–8 143
5:10 248
5:11 ..... 238, 249
5:14 .... 41, 50, 61
5:17 ...... 49, 155
5:18–20 218
5:19 107
5:21 ..... 106, 170
6:2 249
6:16 40
7:1b 188
11:2 183
11:14 78
12:9 236
13:4 50
13:14 ..... 28, 159

Galatians

1:9 66
2:20 ....59, 93, 109,
    159, 189
3:3 186
3:6–9 205
3:13 107
3:13–14 170
3:23–25 73
3:24–25 171

3:26–28 205
3:28 ..... 183, 206
4:4 .... 44, 84
4:4–5 85
4:19 179
5:17 191
5:19–21 188
5:22–23 .... 61, 161,
    183, 203
5:24 186
5:25 161
6:8 188
6:14 ...... 98, 172

Ephesians

1 35
1:3–6 35
1:4 197
1:6 .... 35, 174
1:7 185
1:7–8 181
1:7–12 35
1:12 35
1:13 158
1:13–14 35
1:14 35
1:17 238
1:18 185
1:19–21 127
1:20–22 134
1:22 206
2:1 72
2:1–2 65
2:1–3 187
2:1–4 155
2:4 62
2:6 134
2:8 157
2:8–9 62
2:10 185
2:11–22 183
2:12 224
2:13 174
2:13ff. 47
2:15b–16 205
2:17 112
2:20 206
2:21–22 158
2:22 ..... 204, 213
3:6 205
3:8 ...... 185, 192
3:8–11 .... 61, 205
3:14 205
3:14–21 35
3:16 35
3:17 ..... 35, 157
3:17–19 58
3:20–21 50
4:3 207

4:4–6 206
4:5 160
4:8 145
4:8ff. 143
4:11–16 183
4:12–13 217
4:30 158
4:32 180
5:2 109
5:18 162
5:25 59
5:26 202
5:27 220
5:29 138
5:31–32 183
6:10–18 187

Philippians

1:20–26 250
1:23 143
1:29–30 236
2:5ff. 61, 110
2:6 .... 84, 90
2:9 133
2:10–11 135
2:13 189
2:15 218
3:3 188
3:8–9 .... 172, 177
3:8–10 95
3:10 ..... 125, 128
3:10–11 250
3:12–14 196
3:15 238
3:18ff. 99
3:20–21 128,
    219, 251
4:5 244
4:7 239
4:13 146
4:19 222

Colossians

1:9 237
1:12 186
1:13 .... 155, 284n
1:15 161
1:15–17 84
1:17 231
1:18 .... 134, 209
1:18–19 134
1:19–20 107
1:20 112
1:27 ....93, 126,
    145, 208
2:3 16
2:7 183
2:9 ...... 28, 84
2:13–15 106

2:14 169
2:16–19 183
2:18 226
3:1 124
3:9–10 .... 161, 185
3:10 192
3:13 180
3:16 93
4:12 139

1 Thessalonians

1:9–10 . 40, 155, 242
4:3 55
4:7 ...... 55, 197
4:13 251
4:13–18 ... 145, 159,
    245
4:16–17 251
4:16–18 243
4:17 244
5:23 67
5:23–24 195

2 Thessalonians

2:5 242
2:7 155

1 Timothy

1:15 ...... 83, 232
2:3–4 151
2:5 144
2:5–6 ... 34, 59, 81
3:15 212
4:1–3 209
4:10 40
6:13 91

2 Timothy

1:9–10 115
1:13 9
2:15 20
3 200
3:1 188
3:1ff. 76
3:1–9 209
3:15 19
3:16–17 .... 15, 19
4:3 9
4:3–4 .... 39, 209
4:6 214

Titus

2:1 10
2:13 241
2:14 232
2:14ff. 62
3:3–7 62
3:4–7 ..... 81, 154
3:5–6 192

Hebrews
1:1–3 15
1:2–3 90
1:3 .... 47, 161
1:12 41
2:8 134
2:9 . 88, 95, 134, 252
2:10 136
2:14–15 252
2:14–18 88
2:15 117
2:17 141
2:18 141
3:13 79
4:7 77
4:12 .... 17, 67
4:13 43
4:15 ... 90, 141, 189
5:7 104
5:12 18
5:13–14 18
6:1 200
6:4–5 201
6:5 ...... 128, 208
6:6 201
6:19–20 137
6:20 141
7:25 ... 49, 139, 141
7:26 90
9:12 144
9:14 ... 80, 112, 172
9:22 100
9:24 141
9:26 ... 141, 143, 172
9:27 251
9:28 141
10:5–10 83
10:10 172
10:11–12 143
10:12 144
10:14 ..... 172, 184
10:17 181
10:19 102
10:19–22 47
10:31 54
10:37 244
11:3 68
11:4 100
11:6 69
11:25 79
11:40 184
12:1 78
12:1–2 161
12:1–3 202
12:2 ... 94, 133, 136
12:3 144
12:4–11 235

12:10 184
12:11 60
12:14 184
12:28–29 54
12:29 59
13:8 42
13:12 184
13:15–16 214
13:20 253

James
1:2 236
1:5 152
1:13–15 .... 79, 187
1:17 .... 41, 57
1:18 17
1:21b 17
1:27 56
2:10 76
4:2 215
4:4 187
4:6 62
4:17 74
5:1–5 .... 267n
5:7–9 244

1 Peter
1:2 44
1:3 ...... 127, 250
1:3–7 236
1:4 252
1:6–8 202
1:15–16 .... 55, 161
1:19–20 101
1:23 17
1:24–25 22
2:2–3 17
2:4 136
2:4–5 ..... 183, 213
2:5 213
2:6–7 16
2:8 144
2:9 ...... 198, 232
2:11 190
2:21 ... 92, 109, 136
2:24 107
3:15 ...... 129, 259
3:18 107
3:18–20 143
3:22 134
4:1–6 194
4:7 244
4:17 247
4:19 234
5:8–9 186

2 Peter
1:3 .... 61, 162, 185

1:4 ...... 157, 191
1:11 248
1:16 ...... 47, 120
2:1 59
2:9 250
2:19 79
3:3–7 209
3:4 242
3:9 59
3:11b 203
3:18 ...... 17, 200

1 John
1:1–3 93
1:3–7 179
1:5 ...... 51, 59
1:7 ... 111, 183, 192, 201
1:9 ..... 55, 77, 183
2:1–2 140
2:2 .... 59, 107, 172
2:5–6 160
2:6 ...... 92, 109
2:15 187
2:16 70
2:16–17 187
2:18 244
2:27 163
3:2 ... 128, 202, 219, 251
3:3 202
3:4 76
3:8 189
3:9 192
3:16 ...... 61, 109
3:20 43
3:24 160
4:2–3 88
4:14 88
4:16 58
4:19 59
5:4 186
5:6–12 153
5:13 158
5:17 75
5:19 209
5:19b 70

2 John
7 83
9–11 82

Jude
6 248
20 238

Revelation
1–3 146

1:9–20 96
1:17–18 252
1:18 125
2 209
2:24 153
3 209
3:10 ..... 221, 245
3:16 209
3:20 146
3:21 134
4:1 47
4:8 148
4:11 148
5:6 .... 96, 134
5:9–10 148
5:12 ...... 113, 148
5:13–14 148
6:10 148
7:10 148
7:12 148
11:15 ..... 148, 258
11:17–18 148
12:4 68
12:10–12 148
12:11 190
13:8 100
13:9 84
15:3–4 .... 54, 148
16:7 57
17:17 234
19 256
19:1–2 57
19:1–4 148
19:6 49
19:6–7 148
19:6–9 220
19:7 183
19:10 243
19:11 15
19:11–21 . 210, 245, 257
19:13 15
19:15 257
20:2–3 256
20:5 250
20:6 .. 250, 256, 257
20:7–10 258
20:11–15 248
21:19 214
21:22 47
22:7 243
22:14 202
22:17 183
22:20 .... 243, 244

SUBJECT INDEX

Abel 100
Abelard 105–6
Abraham 49, 118, 171, 198, 205, 228, 237, 239, 246, 253
Achan 79
Adam and Eve 60–61, 69, 71, 81, 100, 117, 178, 189, 263
adoptionism 89
agnosticism 21
Alexander, Archibald 180
Alexander, Cecil F. 102
Alford, Henry 245
Allegro, John 82
Allen, Roland 149
Amos 254
Ananias 139–40
Ananias and Sapphira 54, 79
Anderson, Digby 52
Andrewes, Lancelot 67
Anna 86
Anselm of Canterbury 38, 39, 106–7
Anthony the Hermit 110
antinomianism 196
Apollinarianism 89
Apostles' Creed 20–21, 136
Aquinas. See Thomas Aquinas.
Arianism 29, 89
Aristotle 42, 231
Arius. See Arianism.
Arminius 174
Ascension 131–47
Athanasius 29
Atonement
    application of 108–10, 143–44, 180–82

cross of 74, 84–85, 98–113, 170–73
Day of 53, 181
vicarious 107, 172, 269, 275, 278
views of 105–7
Auberlen, C. H. 116
Augustine 13, 15, 20, 27, 31, 44, 58, 71, 72, 131, 138, 156, 168, 239, 261
Aulen, Gustav 106
authority of Scripture 20–23

Bach, J. S. 113
Bacon, Francis 151
Baillie, Donald 86, 107
Baillie, John 26
Bainton, Roland T. 175
Balthaser, Hans Ur von 71
baptism
    by Spirit 158–60
    of Jesus 103
Barclay, William 18, 91
Barnabas 211
Barnhouse, Donald Grey 281
Barth, Karl 21, 29, 45–46, 73, 87, 152, 266
Bavinck, Herman 27
Baxter, Richard 235
beata culpa 60–61
Beecher, Henry Ward 77
Behe, Michael 68
Bellah, Robert 33
Bellet, J. G. 95
Bengel, J. A. 19
Bennard, George 95, 100
Bennett, William 52
Berger, Peter 58

Berkhof, Louis 55–56, 59, 191
Berkouwer, G. C. 108
Bernard of Clairvaux 63–64, 173, 176
Bewes, Richard 127
Bible. *See* Scripture.
Bickersteth, Edward H. 112
Bliss, P. P. 105
blood of Christ 101
Bloom, Harold 76–77
Bonar, Horatius 114, 201
Bonhoeffer, Dietrich 108, 182, 185
Borden 230
Brainerd, David 265
Brent, Charles 19
Bridges, Matthew 133
Bridgewater Treatises 224
Brightman, Edgar Sheffield 286
Brooks, Phillips 77, 111
Brown, Raymond E. 272
Browning Robert, 188
Bruce, Michael 136
Brunner, Emil 29, 152, 184, 217, 241
Bryars, Gavin 100
Buchanan, James 166, 174
Buddhism 189, 228
Budziszewski, J. 78
Bultmann, Rudolf 45–46, 152
Bunyan, John 67, 72, 111, 182, 190
Burton, Ernest De Witt 269
Bushnell, Horace 77
Butterfield, Herbert 235

Cailliet, Emile 75
Cain 100
Caird, G. B. 121
Calvin, John 15, 27, 40, 69, 144, 212, 237,
    268, 282
Campolo, Anthony 80
Carey, William 212
Carmichael, Amy 236, 286
Carnell, Edward John 40
Carter, Stephen 126
Catharism 268
Chadwick, Samuel 154
Chafer, Lewis Sperry 146, 159, 248
Chalcedon Deliverance 21–22
Chambers, Oswald 96, 176, 202, 238
Charbonnier, E. La B. 77
Charnock, Stephen 55
Chemnitz, Martin 227
Chesterton, G. K. 65

China 220, 226
Chisholm, Thomas 162
Christology 33, 81–97
"Christus victor" view of atonement 106
Chrysostom, John 31, 137
church 204–21
    courage of 284
    discipline 207
    spirituality and 33
Clement, Olivier 115
Clinton, William 188
Coleman, Robert 148
communication, Holy Spirit and 30–32
community, Holy Spirit and 32–34
conversion 17, 154–55, 196
conviction 155–57
coram Deo 45
Cornelius 129
Cowper, William 102
Craig, William Lane 44
creation 25, 42, 59
Crosby, Fanny J. 104
cross, theology of 105. *See also* atonement.
Crossan, John Dominic 84, 99, 270
Cullmann, Oscar 44

Dale, R. W. 116, 275
Daniel 40, 198, 202, 229
D'arcy, Martin 268
Darwin, Charles 210, 225. *See also*
    evolution.
David 118, 171, 229, 238
Davies, W. D. 178
Dawkins, Richard 68
death 115–30
death of God theology 47
deconstructionism 21
deCoulanges 116
Deissmann, Adolph 178
Delbanco, Andrew 288–89
Demarest, Bruce 42, 44, 56
Demas 79
Denney, James 106, 255, 275
depravity, radical 78–79
design of universe 25
determinism 247
Diabolus 190
Dibelius, Martin 111
Dillistone, F. W. 207
Dinesen, Isak 23
disciple-making 216–19

docetism 89
Dodd, C. H. 107, 134, 241, 244
Dods, Marcus 150
"domestication of transcendence" 51
Donne, John 110
Doyle, Arthur Conan 219
Drummond, Henry 178
Duncan, John 136
Dunlop, Merrill 114
Dunn, James 169

Einstein, Albert 284
Eldad and Medad 165
Elijah 119
Eliot, T. S. 208
Ellis Island 166–67
"embryonic goodness" 75
Emerson, Ralph Waldo 22, 76, 168, 269
Enlightenment 21, 22, 225
Enoch 118, 198
Episcopius 13, 104
Erickson, August 114
Erickson, Millard 32, 39
Esau 79
Esther 229
Eutychianism 89–90
evangelism 218–19
Evans, Christmas 215
evolution 67, 68, 75
"experience of God" movement 74
Ezekiel 119, 254

Fackre, Gabriel 169
Fairbairn, Andrew 93–94
Fairlie, Henry 80
Fall 69–80
Fee, Gordon 208
Feinberg, John and Pat 236
Fenelon, François 176
Findley, G. G. 105
Finney, Charles G. 73
Fleece, Isabel 236
flesh 188–89
Flew, R. Newton 217
Forde, Gerhard 105
Forensic justification 169
forgiveness of sin. See atonement.
Forsyth, P. T. 102, 173, 204
Francke, A. 255
Franson, Fredrik 201
Fromm, Erich 77

Frykman, Nils 252
Fuller, Daniel 126

Gandhi 211, 272
generation X 226
Gerstner, John 202
Gifford, E. H. 255
Gilkey, Langdon 79, 220
Girard, René 99, 272
Gnosticism 51, 76
God
    attributes of 38–64
    being of 25–37
    holiness of 52–55, 267, 282
    image of 67–69
    immutability of 41–43
    justice of 55–58
    mercy of 61–63
    omnipotence of 48–50, 286
    omnipresence of 45–48
    omniscience of 43–45
    providence of 222–40
    self-existence of 39–41
    spiritual nature of 46
Goethe, Johann 66
Goforth, Jonathan 162
"golden bridal, the" 71
goodness of God 51–64
Gordon, S. D. 163
Goreh, Ellen Lakshmi 180
Grace, sanctification by. See sanctification.
Graham, Billy 82–83
Gray, James M. 85
Gregory of Nyssa 32, 137
Griffith Thomas, W. H. 145
Grotius, Hugo 106
Gruenler, Royce 42
Guignebert, Charles 121
Guyon, Madam 176

Habakkuk 229
Hall, Elvina M. 107
Hanby, Benjamin R. 87
Handel, G. F. 135
Handy, Robert 19
Hart, Johnny 173
Hartshorne, Charles 42
Hauerwas, Stanley 106
Havergal, Frances Ridley 141
heaven 46–47
Heber, Reginald 30

Hedstrom, C. B. 184–85
Heidegger, M. 225
Helvetic Confession, Second 136
Hendrickson, William 285
Henry, Carl F. H. 21, 262
Herod the Tetrarch 16
Hewitt, E. E. 154
Hewlett, H. C. 95
Hezekiah 285
Hicks, Edward 257
Hill, Rowland 135
Hilton, Walter 60
Himmelfarb, Gertrude 225
Hippolytus 30
Hocking, David 44
Hodge, A. A. 109
Hodge, Casper Wister 16
Hodge, Charles 109, 191
Holy Spirit 145–46, 149–65, 218, 238
   baptism in 124
   conviction of 75
   grace in 72
   holiness in 192, 194
   Scripture and 13, 17
   spirituality and 9
   worship of 34–37
holiness 52–55, 267, 270, 282
Homer 190
Hooker, Morna 123
hope, theology of 270
Hopkins, Gerard Manley 51
Horace 168
Hosea 58
Houghton, Will R. 19
Howard, Clinton 95
Howe, John 55
Hubble's Law 49
Hudson, Ralph E. 111
humanism 21, 60, 72–73, 74, 76–78
Hume, David, 25, 120–21
hypostatic union 89

idolatry 32 46, 51, 79
image of God 67–69
immanence of God 35
immutability of 41–43
imputation 108
Incarnation 46, 83, 131
incurvatus en se 70
individualism 205
Inge, Dean 242

intercession of Christ 139–42, 201
Irenaeus 36, 154
irrationalism 21
Isaac 237
Isaac of Nineveh 83
Isaiah 15, 45, 86, 202
Islam 25, 95, 121, 231
Israel 45, 119, 205, 208–9, 209, 231–32,
   245, 252–55

Jacob 231
James, William 77
Jehovah's Witnesses 29
Jenkins, Daniel 209
Jeremiah 15, 181
Jerome 72, 261
Jesus Christ 14, 81–97
   as Good Shepherd 232
   as Lamb 84, 96, 100–4, 112, 172, 190
   atonement of 74, 84–85, 98–114, 143–
      44, 170–73, 180–82, 274
   incarnation of 92–93
   intercession of 139–42
   mediation of 143–47
   miracles of 91–92
   offices of 90–91
   prayer and 139–42
   procession of 135–38
   resurrection of 74, 115–30, 115–30,
      149, 221, 249–52, 270, 277
   return of 242, 243–45, 289
   teachings of 91
Jesus-only Pentecostals 29
Jesus Seminar 82, 84, 270
Jewel, John 23
Jews, salvation of 252–55
Joachim of Fiore 255
Joad, C. E. M. 73
Job 15, 118, 235, 236
Joel 245
John the apostle 140, 189
John the Baptist 91
Johnson, Philip 68
Johnson, Samuel 66, 71
Jonathan Livingston Seagull 168
Jones, Lewis E. 112
Joseph, husband of Mary 86, 89
Joseph the patriarch 14–15, 89, 198, 228, 231
Joshua 15, 198, 285
Josiah 220, 285
Jowett, John Henry 75

Judas Iscariot 79, 211
judgment 246–49, 288
justice of God 55–58
justification 166–83, 282
Justin Martyr 254

Kabbalism 51
Kant, Immanuel 21, 25, 73
Kantonen, T. A. 120
Keck, Leander 52
Keillor, Garrison 110
Kepler, Johannes 46
Keswick Convention 279, 281
Khayam, Omar 231
Kierkegaard, Søren 258
King, Christ as 90
King, Martin Luther, Jr. 272
Kipling, Rudyard 33
Knox, John 15
koinonia 214
Koran. *See* Qur'an.
Kushner, Howard 286
Kuyper, Abraham 48, 159

LaCugna, Catherine Maury 33
Ladd, George E. 121, 241
Lamb of God, Jesus as 84, 96, 100–4, 112,
    172, 190, 239
Lapide, Pinchas 122
Last Supper 103–4
Law, William 197–98
Lawrence, Brother 47, 201
Lawson, J. Gilchrist 201
Lazarus 89
lecto divino 23
Leibniz, G. W. 224
Lennon, John 188
Lewinsky, Monica 188
Lewis, C. S. 40, 69, 168
Lindsay, Hal 245
Little Engine that Could, The 168
Litton, Edward Arthur 178
Livingstone, David 83, 221
Lord's Supper 146, 215. *See also* sacraments
Lot 79
Love of God 58–61, 105–7
Lovejoy, Arthur O. 266
Lowry, Robert 130
Loyola, Ignatius 176
Lucas, George 125
Lucretius 231

Luedemann, Gerd 121
Lull, Raymond 25
Luther, Martin 15, 16, 42, 70, 81, 88, 129,
    168, 175, 190, 212, 259, 268, 271
Lutheran theology 176
Lyte, Henry F. 41

McCheyne, Robert Murray 19, 236
McGrath, Alister 169
Machen, J. Gresham 87
MacIntosh, Douglas Clyde 26
Mackintosh, H. R. 51
Maclaren, Alexander 122
Mailer, Norman 82
Manson, T. W. 10, 217
"Maranatha" 243
Marcion 34
Marsden, George 222
Marston, Charles 22
Martin, James T. 247
Marx, Karl 258
Marxism 210, 211
Mary 86, 87, 89, 137
materialism 74
Mather, Increase 255
mediatorial role of Christ 143–47
Melito of Sardis 81
mercy of God 61–63
Messiah 82, 84, 86–87, 208, 229
Messner, Reinhold 188
Meyer, F. B. 146–47, 164, 188, 193, 197
Meyer, H. A. W. 98
Micah 181
Michael the archangel 119
Millennium 255–59
Miller, Arthur 175
Milton, John 29, 117
Moffat, James 58
Mohammed. *See* Muhammad.
Moltmann, Jürgen 32–33, 34, 98, 241, 270
Monophysitism 89–90
Montefiore, Claude 232
Montgomery, James 142, 215–16
Moody, D. L. 180
moral government view of
    atonement 44–45, 106
moral influence view of atonement 106
Mordecai 229
More, Sir Thomas 258
Morgan, G. Campbell 13, 96, 137, 146,
    162

Mormons 29–30, 46
Morris, Leon 100, 117
Moses 32, 53, 165, 198
Mote, Edward 174
Mother Earth 51
Moule, H. C. G. 82, 94
Mueller, J. Theodore 144
Muggeridge, Malcolm 88
Muhammad 53
Murray, Andrew 158
myth, Scripture as 21

Nadab and Abihu 54
Nash, Ronald 96
Nee, Watchman 201
Needham, David 191
Nehemiah 285
Neil, William 107
Nestorianism 89
Neuhaus, Richard John 209
New Age 9, 39, 46, 51, 226–27
New Haven Theology 106
Newbigin, Lesslie 70, 114, 208, 211, 275
Newton, Isaac 29
Nicene Creed 20–21, 28–29
Nicodemus 91, 153
Nicole, Roger 19, 107
Niebuhr, Reinhold 35, 70–71, 73, 75, 249, 274
Nietzsche, Friedrich 40, 41, 120, 224, 225, 269
Noah 198, 200, 228
Norris, Kathleen 121–22
Novation 38
numinous 35
Nyssa, Gregory of 137

Oakes, Edward T. 71
Oberlin Theology 279
Old Testament saints 143
Olivet Discourse 244
Olson, Roger 169
omnipotence of God 48–50, 286
omnipresence of God 45–48
omniscience of God 43–45
Orr, James 124
Otto, Rudolph 35
Owen, John 20, 78, 156, 157, 255

Paché, Rene 257
Packer, J. I. 53, 99
Pannenberg, Wolfhart 121

pantheism 42, 46, 51
Parker, Joseph 233–34
Parker, T. H. L. 231
Parmenides 42
Pascal, Blaise 55, 67, 69
Paterson, John 95
Patrick of Ireland 29, 264
Paul 66, 70–71, 94–95, 98, 116, 122–23, 129, 139–40, 152, 153, 156, 159, 170–71, 179, 198, 205, 211, 229–30, 236, 242, 244, 247–48, 268, 269
Peale, Norman Vincent 77
Pearson, John 136
Peck, M. Scott 126
Pelagius 72, 81–82, 168
Pentecost 74, 119, 133, 149–50, 155, 159–60, 163, 206
perichoresis 32
Peter 17, 119, 129, 145, 163, 285
Peterson, Eugene 129, 289
Phillips, J. B. 39, 209, 262
pietism 17
Pink, Arthur W. 52, 55
Plato 44, 53, 231, 258
Pontius Pilate 16, 151
Pope, Alexander 231
Pope, W. B. 55
postmodernism 20–22, 225
Pounds, Jesse Brown 183
Prager, Dennis 182
prayer 139–42, 215–16, 267
pre-evangelism 217–18
Prenter, Regin 149
Priest, Christ as 90, 144
process theology 42–43, 152
prophecy, fulfillment of 241–59, 287
Prophet, Christ as 90–91
providence 222–40
psychology 75, 263, 281
Puritans 20, 55, 158, 212, 255

Qur'an 53

Rahner, Karl 33
Ramm, Bernard 66, 153
Ramsay, William M. 98
Rand, Ayn 82
ransom, atonement as 105–6
redemption 49–50, 108–10
Rees, Paul S. 198
Reformation 15, 21, 90–91, 116, 153, 167, 175

regeneration 157, 191–93
Renan, Joseph 120
"representative" view of atonement 106
Resurrection 74, 115–30, 115–30, 149, 221, 249–52, 270, 277
Richardson, Cyril 34
Ridout, Samuel 158
Ritschl, Albrecht 29
Robinson, J. A. T. 87
Roman Catholic Church 143–44, 175–77
Romero, Oscar 23
Ross, Hugh 68
Rousseau, Jean Jacques 71
Rowling, J. K. 168
Rowlingson, Donald 121
Russell, Bertrand 244, 245
Russell, James 287
Ruth 198, 228–29

Sabellianism 29
sacraments 207
sacrifice 100–1
Saint-Exupery, Antoine de 194
salvation 57–64, 98–114, 218
Samuel 32, 42, 285
sanctification 184–203, 282
Sandell, Lina 147
"Santa Claus theology" 53
Sartre, Jean Paul 82
Satan 69–71, 99, 105, 153, 155, 180, 187, 189–90, 191, 193, 258
satisfaction 104–110
Savonarola, Girolamo 17
Sayers, Dorothy 39, 238, 265
Schlatter, Adolph 84
Schleiermacher, Friedrich 21, 29, 247, 288
Schmid, Heinrich 227
Schonfield, Hugh 121
Schopenhauer, Arthur 228
Schuller, Robert 66, 77
Schweitzer, Albert 83–84, 244, 245
Scofield, C. I. 234, 286
Scripture 13–23, 70, 189, 207, 218–19, 261, 262, 263, 288
Second Coming of Christ 242, 243–45, 289
"selfism" 22, 70, 76–77, 269
Semler, Johannes 39
Seneca 65
Servetus, Michael 212
Seventh Day Adventists 176

sexual purity 15, 77–78, 193, 199
Shaftesbury, Anthony 241
Shakleton, Mary 164
Shedd, William 55
Sheldon, Charles 92
Showers, Renald 191
Simeon 86
Simeon, Charles 114
Simpson, A. B. 50
Simpson, G. G. 226
sin 71, 72–78, 108. *See also* sanctification.
Smart, James 21
Smedes, Lewis 258
Smith, Gypsy 95
Smith, Taylor 239
Smith, Timothy 157
Smith, Wilbur 87
Socinianism. *See* Unitarianism.
Solomon 202, 285
Spafford, Horatio B. 181
Spencer, Stanley 100
Spener, Phillip 255
Sproul, R. C. 245, 286
Spurgeon, Charles Haddon 128, 213
Stackhouse, John 84
Stalin, Josef 71
Stanley, Henry 83
Star Wars 125–26
Stauffer, Ethelbert 107
Stephen 155, 182
Stewart, James 125, 179, 228
Stirner, Max 189
Stott, John R. W. 99, 213
Strauss, David 83–84
Strong, Augustus Hopkins 235
substitutionary atonement. *See* vicarious atonement.
substitutionary penal theory 278
Sweete, H. B. 131, 146
Swinburne, Algernon C. 209
Swinburne, Richard 68
syncretism 211–12

tabernacle 47
Taylor, J. Hudson 114, 164
Taylor, Vincent 104
Temple, William 79
Ten Commandments 14, 198–99
Tenney, Merrill C. 123, 124, 127, 128
Tennyson, Alfred Lord 258
Teresa of Avila 176

Tertullian 34
thief on cross 89
Thielicke, Helmut 108, 170
Thomas à Kempis 167, 176
Thomas Aquinas 72
Thornton, L. S. 116
Tillich, Paul 121, 268
time 43–45
Toon, Peter 144
Toplady, Augustus M. 101
Torrey, R. A. 80
Tozer, A. W. 38, 43, 50, 55, 73, 242
transcendence 35, 48–49, 55, 58
Trent, Council of 175
triadic worship 35
Trinity 25–37
    eternality of 34
    ontological 82
    social 33
Trueblood, Elton 82
Truman, Harry S. 110–11
Trumbull, Charles G. 279
truth 14, 21–22, 46
Turner, Ted 99
Turner, Tina 189

Uncle Tom's Cabin 65
Unitarianism 29, 82, 89
Updike, John 123
utilitarianism 52
Uzziah 54

Van Hooser, Kevin 31
verbal inspiration 262, 288
vicarious atonement 107, 172, 269, 275, 278
Vidal, Gore 82
Vikings 118, 288
Vineyard 193–94
Virgin Birth 83, 86–87
Vitz, Paul C. 269
Volf, Miroslav 33–34
Voltaire, François 225

Waldensians 67
Wallace, David 84
Walvoord, John 145,
Warfield, B. B. 156, 263
Watts, Isaac 110, 258
Wells, David 199
Wesley, Charles 62, 90, 138, 139, 177, 196

Wesley, John 17, 43, 65, 88, 115, 154, 157, 174, 195, 196, 213
Westcott, B. F. 138
Western culture 22–23, 60
Westminster Confession and Catechisms 21, 195, 222
Whitefield, George 78, 157
Whitman, Walt 77, 188, 269
Whittle, Daniel W. 125, 151
Wilberforce, Robert 178
Wilberforce, William 210
Williams, Delores 99
Williams, Roger 212
Williams, William 239
Willimon, William 121
Wills, Garry 242
Wilson, Robert Dick 223
Wilson, Woodrow 14
Winfrey, Ophrah 168–69
Wolfe, Alan 126
Wood, A. Skevington 135
Wood, Nathan 26
Word of God. *See* Scripture.
Wordsworth, William 118
world system 187–88
worship 34–36, 218
Wright, N. T. 92, 241

year of the evangelical 211
Young, G. A. 237

Zechariah and Elizabeth 86, 254
Zerubbabel 150
Zinzendorf, Ludwig, von 174
Zuck, Roy 20
Zwingli, Ulrich 15